Ethnic Studies
in the United States

GARLAND REFERENCE LIBRARY OF SOCIAL SCIENCE
VOLUME 923

ETHNIC STUDIES IN THE UNITED STATES
A GUIDE TO RESEARCH

GRETCHEN M. BATAILLE
MIGUEL A. CARRANZA
LAURIE LISA

GARLAND PUBLISHING, INC.
NEW YORK AND LONDON
1996

Library of Congress Cataloging-in-Publication Data

Bataille, Gretchen M., 1944–
    Ethnic studies in the United States : a guide to research / Gretchen M.
Bataille, Miguel A. Carranza, Laurie Lisa.
        p.   cm. — (Garland reference library of social science ; v. 923)
    Includes bibliographical references.
    ISBN 0-8153-1476-0 (alk. paper)
    1. United States—Ethnic relations—Study and teaching (Higher)—Direc-
tories.   2. United States—Race relations—Study and teaching (Higher)—
Directories.   3. Minorities—Study and teaching (Higher)—United States—
Directories.   4. Publishers and publishing—United States—Directories.
I. Carranza, Miguel.   II. Lisa, Laurie.   III. Title.   IV. Series.
E184.A1B275   1996
305.8'0071'173—dc20   95-44834
                                                                              CIP

Printed on acid-free, 250-year-life paper
Manufactured in the United States of America

Contents

Introduction

Background

Contemporary "culture" in the United States encompasses many different cultures existing and interacting in a complex pattern of harmony and conflict. A review of the history of the United States reveals the interplay among immigrants from every continent and the indigenous peoples who had tenure on the land. European immigrants and their descendants, along with Native Americans, Hispanic Americans, African Americans, and Asian Americans, have all contributed to the contemporary U.S. culture. Together these groups have shaped the past and will have an impact on the future of the United States. Increasingly, educators at all levels are recognizing that an understanding of the multiple perspectives with which American citizens view their world is an essential aspect of education. By recognizing both the historical and the future diversity of the American population and by appreciating differences, teachers, scholars, and students experience a more complete education.

This response to diversity has been labeled multicultural education, culture studies, and ethnic studies. Generally, the label "ethnic studies" has been applied to postsecondary courses and programs that focus on persons of color in the United States; however, the impetus for ethnic studies has been guided by many factors, and any discussion demands attention to curriculum, demographic factors, politics, and history. Ethnic studies are broader than any single discipline, not falling between fields but rather defined as a multidisciplinary area, encompassing relevant knowledge and methodology from the humanities, the sciences, and the social sciences. Anthropologist Clifford Geertz has used the term "blurred genres" to describe the interdisciplinary approach that characterizes much scholarship in the area of ethnic studies or culture studies (3).

Ethnic studies as a viable academic area of enquiry first developed in colleges and universities as a result of the political and social action of the 1950s and 1960s. The 1968 Kerner Commission Report on Civil Disorders clearly stated the growing national problem: "Our nation is moving toward two societies, one black, one white—separate and unequal." Academic programs responded haphazardly to faculty and student demands for relevance in academia, initially focusing on African Americans and on contemporary issues. Black literature courses emphasized contemporary writers; political science courses focused on civil rights legislation, school desegregation, and issues of black political power. For a nation of citizens divided by their colors as well as their opportunities, such emphases were appropriate for the time.

Ethnic studies curricula began to expand at all levels in response to a number of events in the early 1970s. Court-ordered desegregation as well as the Ethnic Heritage Act of 1972 prompted many teacher education programs and state departments of education to require courses in multicultural education for prospective teachers who would be expected to bring this knowledge into elementary and high school classrooms. As a result, courses were designed with a focus on precollege education and frequently taught in a department or college of education. A growing recognition of the diversity in the population resulted in the inclusion of Hispanics, American Indians, and Asian Americans, expanding the scope of ethnic studies beyond an initial focus on African Americans.

Departments outside of education added courses as well. Most often there were courses in African American literature or history, but depending on geographical location, courses in American Indian or Chicano literature, Asian or Jewish history, or Portuguese studies were added to the curriculum. As college and university faculty moved into the area of teaching ethnic studies, they also increased research efforts in the area, often encouraged by federal or institutional grants. A number of interdisciplinary journals— among them the *Journal of Ethnic Studies, Minority Voices, Explorations in Ethnic Studies,* and *MELUS*—responded to the scholarly community. Specialized journals such as the *Western Journal of Black History* and *American Indian Culture and Research Journal* focused on specific groups. In Canada, the *Journal of Canadian Ethnic Studies* was established in 1971.

State and institutional requirements for courses with ethnic content, ethnic studies courses and programs, publications designed to further scholarship in ethnic studies, and campus and community efforts to improve communication among various constituencies have all supported the move toward pluralism. At the same time, criticism from the political right, intensified during the Reagan years, underscored the need for ethnic studies courses and required that attention be given to clear definitions of content and methodology.

Ethnic studies courses have not only been criticized but also have been met with ethnocentrism, backlash, hostility, and even violence. Such responses to difference have no place in institutions of higher learning, and often ethnic studies programs were established as a political antidote to such reactions. Most departments and programs have successfully outlived these original purposes, and although faculty and students are still eager to transform society, most programs have adopted a stronger academic or practical focus to replace earlier political motivations.

These programs have often been the impetus for institutional change and expanded curriculum in other disciplines. For many years the curriculum operated according to an established canon that changed very slowly. Since the 1960s the canon has been changing much more rapidly. Unfortunately, there are scholars who have internalized whatever the canon was at a given point in time and have assumed that it is frozen in that era. The old center of the canon was male-centered, Euro-centered, and exclusionary, marginalizing women and people of color. Ethnic and women's studies scholars have challenged that frozen entity, and these scholars have demanded and instituted programs and courses that challenge the curriculum modeled on outdated assumptions. Increasingly, ethnic materials are moving outside of the separate ethnic studies units and into established and required courses. Full integration of ethnic materials is significant and important; however, as ethnic studies practitioners establish theory and method for the study of a particular body of material, there will remain a need for separate units where students learn new and interdisciplinary approaches to knowledge.

Ethnic studies programs were established to critique the traditional disciplinary approaches and theories that validated European influence and colonization; increasingly, these same programs are supporting scholars who are creating new theoretical constructs that consider community issues and community participation as well as the influence of a different historical reality on people who were subdued, enslaved, or sought refuge in a new country. John Liu has written, "The founders of ethnic studies were concerned with more than merely documenting a people's presence; they were committed as well to changing institutional arrangements which dehumanized people of color" (281). In short, ethnic studies is a process of reconceptualizing American culture, of rethinking the ways peoples and cultures have interacted and have changed one another and their shared society.

Initial approaches to ethnic studies in colleges and universities often emanated from disciplinary bases. Historians were interested in who came to the Americas, who was already here, and what happened in the encounter. Sociologists focused on communities and community institutions such as churches, schools, and clubs. Conflict among groups, intermarriage, and the relationships between urban and rural communities remain focal points for sociological study. Political scientists often focused on exclusion laws, census data, the racism perpetuated by national origin quotas, and political agendas. Literary scholars and journalists remain interested in the ethnic press, theater, and both fiction and nonfiction as a means of understanding the cultural life of ethnic peoples. Teachers and critics in the arts specialize in areas such as ethnomusicology, museum studies, and the influence of traditional arts on contemporary expression.

Initially, dates, names, places, and people were the essence of content; more recently, world view, philosophy, and comparative cultural perspectives are emphasized. Early courses focused on groups in a geographical region—Indians and Chicanos in the Southwest, Jews and Puerto Ricans in New York—but the recognition of a broadly diverse and increasingly mobile society has made such parochialism outdated. Many elementary schools still tend to see ethnic studies as celebratory—Black History Month, Cinco de Mayo in May, or pumpkin pie with the Indians in November; however, such isolated exposure to ethnic experiences distorts history and contemporary reality. Although the purpose of many courses originally was to direct political and social change, that focus was refined during the late seventies and eighties. More recently, an interest in Afrocentricity and an increasing awareness of the economic and social pressures in urban areas and elsewhere are leading to a resurgence of interest in political and social change.

Current Status

Methodology and administrative structure continue to be issues in both teaching and scholarship. Some scholars continue to follow traditional disciplinary modes in response to different subject matter, but such approaches might be characterized as colored studies in "whiteface." Internal administrative structures, such as courses taught in existing departments, interdisciplinary programs, separate departments, or "umbrella" departments such as Berkeley's Ethnic Studies Department, are all legitimate and quite different institutional responses to ethnic studies.

As with any new area of scholarship, terminology has divided scholars in the field. The appropriateness of terms such as person of color, mainstream, cultural pluralism, multicultural, culture studies, disadvantaged groups, acculturation, assimilation, melting pot, feminism, and minority group continues to be debated. African American, black, Hispanic, Latino, Chicano, Native American, American Indian, and hyphenated labels of all sorts continue to confound writers and persons who want to be "politically correct" but are unsure of the "correct" terminology. Labeling continues to be rooted in both tradition and geography, and names of programs and courses often reflect these influences.

A number of issues remain unresolved in the curriculum and scholarship grouped together under the rubric of ethnic studies. In attempting to provide legitimacy to these programs, the debate continues over content and the presence of a common curriculum for ethnic studies, and there are discussions over the "canon" and "political correctness" in professional meetings and journals. Scholars debate the efficacy of using theoretical developments and approaches in disciplinary research as they approach what is generally a cross-disciplinary area. The influence of women's studies, culture studies, immigration studies, and gay studies—all interdisciplinary in focus—has been felt in ethnic studies programs and scholarship. Immigration studies have previously focused on male experiences, but feminist critics are using the female immigrant experience to broaden study in ethnicity. Related to immigrant experiences are the experiences of refugees, generally persons who cannot go back "home" and must adapt to a new environment. As political realities change, the approach in the academy changes as well, changing disciplinary courses as well as ethnic studies programs. It is unlikely that politics and the curriculum will ever be separated, for, as Paul Lauter has argued, "The literary canon is, in short, a means by which culture validates social power" (435).

Competition among groups remains a sensitive political issue within academic institutions and national organizations. The inclusion or exclusion of groups, level of funding, and the scramble to hire the "best" or most visible scholars sometimes have diverted attention from course content and student outcomes.

Devastating to all courses and programs are diminishing funds for education in general, a situation that has adversely affected new programs, particularly when departments with longer tenure see their own funds reduced. As the field of ethnic studies widens to include newly arrived Southeast Asian groups or redefines itself to include groups with European origins, the competition for funds will become more intense.

Perceptions that thirty years of new legislation has eliminated prejudice, discrimination, and bigotry often cause faculty, voters, and legislatures to ask why the programs are needed. Attacks from ethnic scholars such as Richard Rodriguez, Thomas Sowell, and Dinesh D'Souza, although healthy when viewed as honest academic parrying, cause the public to distrust efforts to expand ethnic studies.

CHANGING DEMOGRAPHICS AND INSTITUTIONAL PRIORITIES

Understanding the historical as well as the future role of ethnic studies requires an understanding of America's changing demographics. Not only is the population becoming more diverse, the expectations of who will be educated have changed considerably over the last century. Entering college classes already include close to 50 percent of students of color at many universities, and by the year 2000 no group will be a majority in some states. Arizona, California, New York, Florida, and Texas have large and diverse ethnic populations. The 1990 census data reported nearly thirty million African Americans, over twenty-two million Hispanics, over seven million Asian Americans, and nearly two million Native Americans in the United States. Los Angeles has the largest number of Mexicans of any city outside of Mexico as well as large populations of Koreans, Vietnamese, and Japanese. There are over one million Cubans in the United States, and over half of the nearly three million Puerto Ricans in the United States live in New York and New Jersey.

In spite of the 1908 production of Zangwill's play *The Melting Pot* and assumptions throughout the century of assimilation, and in spite of recent calls for a return to an idealistic view of a homogenous America, the spirit of America remains one of pluralism and diversity. Such a spirit does not make a Lakota woman or a Vietnamese immigrant any less an American than an Irish American whose ancestors fled Ireland to seek a better world. Every American or immigrant who participates in United States society contributes the experiences of an accumulated past. For many, both the recent and distant pasts include discrimination and systematic exclusion. For new immigrants, ties to Mexico, Puerto Rico, or Laos are like tautly stretched rubber bands—a tenuous link to people, to land, and to tradition. By the year 2000, it is estimated that one-third of the United States population will be nonwhite Americans. These numerical realities and the diverse cultural environments will continue to exert pressure on American colleges and universities to respond to the needs of society to embrace difference rather than to assume it will "melt" away.

CONCLUSIONS

The 1960s brought the programs and courses; the 1970s refined them or, at times, lost them through mismanagement, lack of focus, or institutional neglect. The 1980s brought a new kind of pressure—declining funds, holdover negative attitudes toward those programs that faltered or failed because of internal friction, students interested in training rather than education, and general naiveté about the social, political, and literary dimensions of ethnicity. The 1990s are bringing new theoretical approaches, ethnic-specific criticism, challenges to traditional scholarship, and a reassessment of how ethnicity should be approached in the curriculum.

USING THIS DIRECTORY

The NAES office frequently receives calls or correspondence requesting information on ethnic studies programs. Sometimes the caller is a student looking for an appropriate course of study; at other times publishers enquire to determine the level of interest that might exist for a new book, or call seeking potential authors for new publications on ethnic issues. This directory provides information to prospective students, to scholars seeking like-minded colleagues, and to publishers assessing markets or soliciting manuscripts.

According to an earlier study undertaken by the National Association for Ethnic Studies, there were more than eight hundred programs or departments in American colleges and universities that described their focus as ethnic studies. Of these, approximately six hundred are ethnic-specific programs, the majority of which are African American programs or departments. Other ethnic-specific programs include Asian American, Chicano/Latino, American Indian/Native American, and Puerto Rican Studies as well as scattered programs in Jewish Studies, Portuguese Studies, and others. In preparation for this publication, we queried the more than eight hundred programs previously identified in addition to new programs identified through research and announcements. We sent questionnaires to all eight hundred programs on our previous list, requesting updated information. Those entries include only basic information and have not been updated if we did not receive a response to our multiple mailings. In some cases, the programs may no longer exist; in other cases, mail may have been lost on local campuses, or the contact person for some entries may no longer be current. A form is included with this publication for those programs interested in providing updated information for the next edition of this directory.

The term "ethnic" is often used interchangeably with "immigrant" or "foreign," sometimes assuming nationality. Although ethnicity is not limited to persons of color by definition, the popular interpretation presumes this limitation. Recognizing that there are programs in Scandinavian studies, German studies, European studies, and several other regional studies programs, the editors have chosen to focus on those programs with an emphasis on people of color. Thus, we have excluded many programs that focus more on country of origin than on the American experience. There are African American programs with curricula reflecting the diaspora, and such programs have been included. The directory is organized according to the primary focus of the unit and by state and zip code within sections.

DEFINITIONS

For the purposes of this directory, we have adopted the following definitions:

African American	Those programs with a focus on the peoples with origins in any of the black racial groups of Africa and the United States.
Hispanic American	Those programs with a focus on the peoples of Mexican, Puerto Rican, Cuban, Central or South American, or other Spanish culture or origin regardless of race. Chicana/Chicano studies programs are included in this category.
Asian American/ Pacific Island	Those programs with a focus on any of the peoples of the Far East, Southeast Asia, Indian subcontinent, or the Pacific Islands. This includes China, India, Japan, Korea, the Philippines, Samoa, Polynesia, and Melanesia.
Native American/ American Indian	Those programs with a focus on the original peoples of North America. The directory does not include Native studies programs in Canada; however, some U.S. programs include study of Canadian Native peoples.

BIBLIOGRAPHY

Geertz, Clifford. *Local Knowledge: Further Essays in Interpretative Anthropology.* New York: Basic Books, 1983.

The Kerner Report: The 1968 Report of the National Advisory Commission on Civil Disorders. New York: Pantheon, 1988.

Lauter, Paul. "Race and Gender in the Shaping of the American Literary Canon: A Case Study from the Twenties." *Feminist Studies* 9 (Fall 1983): 435–63.

Liu, John M. "Asian American Studies and the Disciplining of Ethnic Studies." In *Frontiers of Asian American Studies,* edited by Gail M. Nomura, Russell Endo, Stephen H. Sumida, and Russell C. Leong, 271–90. Pullman: Washington State University Press, 1989.

Acknowledgments

As with any project of this scope, this 1996 edition of *Ethnic Studies in the United States: A Guide to Research* has been a collaborative effort, one that involved the participation of people, programs, departments, and universities throughout the United States. Our appreciation begins with the help of John Walter and Kate Bolland at the University of Washington for working with Miguel A. Carranza, at the University of Nebraska-Lincoln, to establish the original database of names and universities. To Catherine Udall Turley, the former managing director of the National Association for Ethnic Studies (NAES), we owe a special debt of gratitude. Catherine, who organized databases and supervised the first two directory mailings, is responsible for launching the final format of this manuscript. Ken Lee, at Arizona State University, spent countless hours entering data, and to him we owe a special thanks. Thomas Sanchez, a graduate student at the University of Nebraska, assisted in compiling the list of ethnic studies associations, journals, newsletters, and publishers.

Several colleagues assisted in reviewing the manuscript: Denise Segura and Sucheng Chan at the University of California-Santa Barbara, Alberto Pulido at Arizona State University-West, Duane Champagne at the University of California-Los Angeles, and Otis Scott at California State University-Sacramento. We are indebted to all those who provided their skill and assistance along the way to publication.

We appreciate, once again, the academic and financial support that Arizona State University and the College of Liberal Arts and Sciences willingly continue to give to NAES. Dr. Gary Krahenbuhl, dean of the College of Liberal Arts and Sciences (CLAS), has especially championed the objectives of NAES and its projects, and we are immensely grateful for his energies and commitment. Tammie Chestnut and Roxana Martin, hired through the office of CLAS, have been diligent, punctual, and even cheerful as they helped to polish this *Guide* through its many drafts. The final manuscript owes a great deal to their invaluable service. We also want to express our appreciation to the library staff at Hayden Library at Arizona State University, and particularly to those in the interlibrary loan service whose research skills continue to be competent and cordial. To this same end the University of Nebraska-Lincoln and the College of Arts and Sciences have provided solid support to NAES publication efforts, including this valuable research guide.

Finally, our appreciation and gratitude extend to all of the programs, departments, centers, and institutions that responded to our call for information. The scholars, instructors, and staff members at these institutions have ultimately shaped the final scope and diversity present in this work. To their past and continuing vision we want to applaud their efforts in the field of ethnic studies. And to the faculty, staff, and students who will benefit from this *Guide,* we hope that you find this helpful in your journey toward a more comprehensive education and wish you success in your endeavors.

Gretchen M. Bataille
Miguel A. Carranza
Laurie Lisa

Ethnic Studies
in the United States

African American Studies

ALABAMA

Institution:	Talladega College
Unit:	Black Studies
Contact Person:	Leon P. Spencer
Address:	Talladega, AL 35160

Institution:	**Miles College**
Institution Type:	Private, 4 year
Unit:	African-American Studies Program
Contact Person:	Digambar Mishra, Chair
Address:	Division of Social & Behavior Sciences
	Birmingham, AL 35208
Phone:	(205) 923-2771
Fax:	(205) 923-9292
Unit Offers:	Minor, classes
Degrees Offered:	Minor in African-American Studies
Special Features:	Miles College is an HBCU. It offers an "African-American experience" course for all who matriculate at Miles. It also offers courses such as African-American literature and African-American history for various majors.

Institution:	**Alabama A & M University**
Unit:	Afro-American Studies
Contact Person:	Mary Brown
Address:	Normal, AL 35762

Institution:	**Alabama State University**
Institution Type:	Public, 4 year + graduate
Unit:	The Humanities through the African American Experience
Unit Type:	Course
Contact Person:	Kathy Dunn Jackson, Chair
Address:	Box 295
	Montgomery, AL 36101-0271
Phone:	(205) 263-5165
Unit Offers:	Classes
Faculty:	9
Established:	1982
Special Features:	Humanities 103 is designed to introduce students to college-level study in the humanities and to make the humanities a basic experience in the education of all students entering Alabama State University. The course provides an integrated study of the art, literature, music, and history inherent in the African American culture. A primary purpose of the course is to promote awareness of the many contributions and achievements of African Americans. The course also provides an opportunity for students to tap their own unique skills, talents, and powers through various creative activities. A final purpose of the humanities course is to extend the writing skills emphasized in the freshman composition courses.

Institution:	**University of South Alabama**
Unit:	Black Studies
Contact Person:	Jean McIver
Address:	HUMB 268
	Mobile, AL 36688

ARKANSAS

Institution:	**University of Arkansas-College Heights**
Unit:	Black Studies
Contact Person:	Merrill Pritchett

Address:	College Heights, AR 71655
Institution:	**Southern Arkansas University**
Unit:	Black Studies
Contact Person:	David Sibey
Address:	Box 1369
	Magnolia, AR 71753
Institution:	**Philander Smith College**
Unit:	Black Studies
Contact Person:	Raphael Lewis
Address:	Little Rock, AR 72203
Institution:	**University of Arkansas-Little Rock**
Unit:	Black Studies Program
Contact Person:	Patricia McGraw
Address:	Little Rock, AR 72205
Institution:	**University of Arkansas-Fayetteville**
Institution Type:	Public, 4 year + graduate
Unit:	African American Studies Program
Contact Person:	Nudie Eugene Williams, Chair
Address:	416 Old Main
	Department of History
	Fayetteville, AR 72701
Phone:	(501) 575-3001
Unit Offers:	Combined major, minor
Majors Per Year:	1-2
Minors:	6-12
Established:	1968
Special Features:	Students who wish to gain knowledge and understanding of the history, social organization, current status, and problems of African Americans and of their contributions to the American heritage may elect a combined major in African American Studies, together with a major in anthropology, economics, history, philosophy, political science, psychology, sociology, or social welfare.

ARIZONA

Institution:	**University of Arizona**
Unit:	Black Studies
Address:	Tucson, AZ 85721

CALIFORNIA

Institution:	**University of California-Los Angeles**
Institution Type:	Public, 4 year + graduate
Unit:	Afro-American Studies Program
Unit Type:	Program and Center
Contact Person:	Elizabeth Bean, Curriculum Coordinator and Special Projects Coordinator
Address:	160 Haines Hall
	405 Hilgard Avenue
	Los Angeles, CA 90034
Phone:	(310) 825-3776
Fax:	(310) 206-3421
E-mail:	bean@others.sscnet.ucla.edu
Unit Offers:	Major, classes
Degrees Offered:	B.A., M.A. Afro-American Studies
Majors Per Year:	70
Faculty:	22
Established:	1974
Special Features:	The B.A. program is designed to offer students an opportunity to systematically study origins, experiences, and conditions of people of African descent. The M.A. program in particular is international in scope and focuses on African-origin cultures in the United States, the Caribbean, and Central and South America. This program provides a theoretical base of knowledge, methods of research, and a context for analyzing and interpreting the African diasporic experience.

Institution:	**Loyola Marymount University**
Unit:	Afro-American Studies

Address:	7101 W. 80th Street
	Los Angeles, CA 90045
Institution:	**California State University-Dominguez Hills**
Institution Type:	Public, 4 year + graduate
Unit:	African American Studies
Contact Person:	Joyce Johnson, Director
Address:	1000 E. Victoria Street
	Carson, CA 90747
Unit Offers:	Major, minor
Degrees Offered:	B.A.
Institution:	**California State University-Long Beach**
Unit:	Department of Black Studies
Contact Person:	Maulana Karenga, Chair
Address:	Long Beach, CA 90840
Phone:	(310) 985-4624
Institution:	**Pasadena City College**
Institution Type:	Public, 2 year
Unit:	Social Sciences Department
Unit Type:	Section of Department
Contact Person:	Susie Ling, Assistant Professor
Address:	1570 E. Colorado Boulevard
	Pasadena, CA 91106
Phone:	(818) 585-7248
Unit Offers:	Classes
Degrees Offered:	A.A.
Faculty:	7
Special Features:	This is a community college with a seventy-five percent nonwhite population, offering courses such as Introduction to Ethnic Studies: African American history, sociology, and psychology; Chicano history, sociology, and psychology; and Asian American history, sociology, and psychology.
Institution:	**California State University-Northridge**
Institution Type:	Public, 4 year + graduate
Unit:	Pan-African Studies Department
Contact Person:	Bamidele J. Bracy, Acting Chair

Address:	18111 Nordhoff Street
	Northridge, CA 91330
Phone:	(818) 885-3311
Fax:	(818) 885-3619
Unit Offers:	Major, minor, certificate, classes
Degrees Offered:	B.A. Afro-American Studies, currently in history/ economics/political science, arts/humanities, psychology/sociology/anthropology; proposed degrees in Pan African Studies Generalist, African American Economic Development, African American Community Development
Majors Per Year:	110
Minors:	35
Faculty:	11
Established:	1969

Institution:	**Los Angeles Valley College**
Unit:	Afro-American Studies Program
Contact Person:	Barbara Stoffer, Department Representative
Address:	Van Nuys, CA 91401

Institution:	**The Claremont Colleges**
Unit:	Intercollegiate Department of Black Studies (IDBS)
Contact Person:	Marie Denise Shelton, Chair
Address:	222 Steele Hall
	241 E. 11th Street
	Scripps College
	Claremont, CA 91711-3948
Phone:	(909) 621-8000 x3070
Fax:	(909) 629-8796
E-mail:	jberkley@scripps.claremont.edu
Unit Offers:	Major, classes
Degrees Offered:	B.A.
Majors Per Year:	7
Faculty:	10

Institution:	**Mount San Antonio College**
Unit:	Black Studies
Address:	1100 N. Grand
	Walnut, CA 91798

Institution:	**Southwestern College**
Institution Type:	Public, 2 year
Unit:	African-American Studies
Contact Person:	Stanley James
Address:	900 Otay Lakes Road
	Chula Vista, CA 91910
Phone:	(619) 482-6371
Fax:	(619) 482-6323
Unit Offers:	Major, classes
Degrees Offered:	A.A. African-American Studies

Institution:	**University of California-San Diego**
Unit:	Contemporary Black Arts Program
Contact Person:	Floyd Gaffney
Address:	La Jolla, CA 92037

Institution:	**Mesa College**
Institution Type:	Public, 2 year
Unit:	Black Studies Department
Contact Person:	Starla Lewis, Chair
Address:	7250 Mesa College Drive
	San Diego, CA 92111
Phone:	(619) 627-2753
Unit Offers:	Major, minor, classes
Degrees Offered:	A.A. Black Studies
Faculty:	1 full-time, 9 adjunct
Special Features:	Mesa College Black Studies Department welcomes students of every ethnicity to an interdisciplinary studies curriculum that focuses on experiential connections and cultural differences in an atmosphere of mutual respect. We offer multiple learning experiences through team teaching and practical and field experiences.

Institution:	**San Diego State University**
Institution Type:	Public, 4 year
Unit:	Africana Studies Department
Contact Person:	Norman E. Chambers, Chair
Address:	San Diego, CA 92182
Phone:	(619) 594-6531

Fax:	(619) 594-4998
E-mail:	clove@sciences.sdsu.edu
Unit Offers:	Major, minor, classes
Degrees Offered:	B.A. Africana Studies, with areas of specialization including history, political science, humanities, sociology, and psychology
Majors Per Year:	28
Minors:	37
Faculty:	5

Institution:	**California State University-San Bernardino**
Unit:	Black Studies
Contact Person:	Brij Khare
Address:	San Bernardino, CA 92407

Institution:	**Riverside City College**
Unit:	Black Studies
Address:	4800 Magnolia Avenue
	Riverside, CA 92506

Institution:	**University of California-Riverside**
Unit:	Afro-American Studies
Contact Person:	Jacquelyn Haywood
Address:	Watkins Hall 1141
	Riverside, CA 92521

Institution:	**California State University-Fullerton**
Institution Type:	Public, 4 year + graduate
Unit:	Afro-Ethnic Studies Department
Contact Person:	J. Owens Smith, Chair
Address:	800 State College Drive
	Fullerton, CA 92634
Phone:	(714) 773-3677
Fax:	(714) 773-3304
Unit Offers:	Major, minor
Degrees Offered:	B.A. in Ethnic Studies with a degree in Afro-Ethnic Studies
Majors Per Year:	10
Faculty:	6
Established:	1972

Institution:	Foothill College
Unit:	Black Studies
Address:	12345 El Monte Road
	Los Altos, CA 93022

Institution:	**University of California-Santa Barbara**
Institution Type:	Public, 4 year
Unit:	Department of Black Studies
Unit Type:	Division of Social Sciences
Contact Person:	Cedric Robinson, Chair
Address:	3631 South Hall
	Santa Barbara, CA 93106
Phone:	(805) 893-3847
Fax:	(805) 893-3597
E-mail:	robinson@alishaw.ucsb.edu
Unit Offers:	Major
Degrees Offered:	B.A.
Majors Per Year:	35
Faculty:	9
Established:	1969
Special Features:	The Department of Black Studies seeks to increase the general awareness and understanding of the black experience through an examination of its historical and contemporary manifestation in various societies. It utilizes a cross-cultural approach, incorporating the active participation of faculty, students, and the wider community. The department offers a major leading to the B.A. degree. The faculty is available to students who are pursuing graduate degrees in other departments on topics in the area of Black Studies.

Institution:	**California State University-Bakersfield**
Unit:	Black Studies
Contact Person:	Solomon O. Iyasere
Address:	Bakersfield, CA 93309

Institution:	**California State University-Fresno**
Unit:	Black Studies
Contact Person:	Lilly Small, Chair

Address:	Fresno, CA 93704
Institution:	**Fresno City College**
Institution Type:	Public, 2 year
Unit:	African American Studies/Cultural Studies Department
Unit Type:	Program, Department
Contact Person:	Kehinda Solwah
Address:	1101 E. University Avenue
	Fresno, CA 93741
Phone:	(209) 442-4600
Unit Offers:	Major
Degrees Offered:	African American Studies; Cultural Studies
Majors Per Year:	25
Faculty:	4 full-time, 11 part-time
Established:	1969
Institution:	**Canada College**
Institution Type:	Public, 2 year
Unit:	Ethnic Studies Requirement to Receive AA/AS degree
Contact Person:	Carole Bogue-Feinour, Vice President of Instruction
Address:	4200 Farm Hill Boulevard
	Redwood City, CA 94061
Phone:	(415) 306-3353
Unit Offers:	Classes
Degrees Offered:	A.A., A.S., plus transfer preparation; a class in Ethnic Studies required by some 4-year institutions
Faculty:	9
Established:	1968
Institution:	**San Francisco State University**
Unit:	Black Studies
Contact Person:	Oba T'Shaka, Chair
Address:	1600 Holloway Avenue
	San Francisco, CA 94132
Institution:	**Stanford University**
Institution Type:	Private, 4 year + graduate

Unit:	Center for African Studies
Contact Person:	Katherine Welsh, Administrator
Address:	Stanford, CA 94305-5013
Phone:	(415) 723-0295
Fax:	(415) 723-6784
Unit Offers:	Certificate, classes
Established:	1979
Special Features:	The National Resource Center for African Studies coordinates FLAS program, local and national outreach, special events, weekly discussion groups, and more.

Institution:	**College of San Mateo**
Unit:	Afro-American Studies
Address:	1700 W. Hillsdale Boulevard
	San Mateo, CA 94402

Institution:	**College of Alameda**
Unit:	Black Studies
Address:	555 Atlantic Avenue
	Alameda, CA 94501

Institution:	**California State University-Hayward**
Unit:	Afro-American Studies
Contact Person:	Michael Clark
Address:	Hayward, CA 94542

Institution:	**Laney College**
Unit:	Ethnic Studies/Black Studies
Contact Person:	Carole Ward-Allen
Address:	900 Fallon Street
	Oakland, CA 94607

Institution:	**Graduate Theological Union**
Unit:	Black Urban Religious Education
Address:	2465 Le Conte Avenue
	Berkeley, CA 94709

Institution:	**University of California-Berkeley**
Institution Type:	Public, 4 year + graduate
Unit:	Department of African American Studies

Contact Person:	Percy Hintzen, Chair
	or Marguerite Versher, Administrative Analyst
Address:	3335 Dwinelle Hall
	Berkeley, CA 94720-2572
Unit Offers:	Major, minor, classes
Degrees Offered:	A.B. with social sciences or humanities emphasis (bachelor's degree); proposed change to interdisciplinary studies for 1996
Majors Per Year:	40
Minors:	18
Faculty:	13
Established:	1970
Special Features:	In 1992, the Department of African American Studies faculty proposed that a Ph.D. program be offered at the University of California at Berkeley. The proposed graduate program in African American Studies has been approved by the Berkeley Campus. The proposal, following review proceedings by the Coordinating Committee on Graduate Affairs at the Office of the President, should receive final approval from the U.C. Regents during the 1994–95 academic year. The long approval process has required the postponement of recruitment and admissions until the next academic year. The department anticipates the first class of graduate students to begin work in the fall of 1996.

Institution:	**Contra Costa College**
Unit:	Afro-American Studies
Address:	2600 Mission Bell Drive
	San Pablo, CA 94806

Institution:	**Sonoma State University**
Institution Type:	Tribal
Unit:	Afro-American Studies/American Multi-Cultural Studies Department
Contact Person:	Jim Gray, Professor
Address:	Rohnert Park, CA 94928

Phone:	(707) 664-2486
Unit Offers:	Major, minor
Degrees Offered:	B.A. Afro-American Studies
Majors Per Year:	12–16
Minors:	22
Faculty:	3
Established:	1969

Institution:	**DeAnza College**
Unit:	Afro-American Studies
Address:	21250 Stevens Creek Boulevard
	Cupertino, CA 95014

Institution:	**University of Santa Clara**
Unit:	Black Studies
Contact Person:	Gary Okihiro
Address:	820 Alviso Street
	Santa Clara, CA 95014

Institution:	**San Jose City College**
Unit:	Black Ethnic Studies
Contact Person:	Charles Murray
Address:	2100 Moorpart Avenue
	San Jose, CA 95128

Institution:	**San Jose State University**
Institution Type:	Public, 4 year + graduate
Unit:	African-American Studies Department
Contact Person:	Kwasi Harris, Chair
Address:	One Washington Square Hall
	San Jose, CA 95192
Phone:	(408) 924-5871
Fax:	(408) 924-5892
Unit Offers:	Major, minor
Degrees Offered:	B.A. African-American Studies
Majors Per Year:	5–10
Minors:	25–30
Faculty:	8
Established:	1969

Institution:	**University of the Pacific**
Institution Type:	Private, 4 year + graduate
Unit:	Black Studies Department
Contact Person:	Mamie Darlington, Chair
Address:	3601 Pacific Avenue
	Stockton, CA 95211
Phone:	(209) 946-2245
Fax:	(209) 946-2318
Unit Offers:	Major
Degrees Offered:	B.A. Black Studies
Majors Per Year:	5
Faculty:	1
Special Features:	Black Studies utilizes a systems approach in addressing social and economic injustices against all people of color. The unique injustices based on racism against African Americans are a priority in all courses. The four objectives of this department are to: (1) understand and appreciate the social, political, economic, and artistic contributions of African Americans; (2) understand the impact of social and political forces in the United States on African Americans; (3) promote better communication among African Americans and non–African Americans; and (4) promote acquisitions of human relationship theory and skills.

Institution:	**California State University-Stanislaus**
Unit:	Black Studies
Address:	801 W. Monte Vista Avenue
	Turlock, CA 95380

Institution:	**Humboldt State University**
Unit:	Black Studies
Contact Person:	Nate Smith, Chair
Address:	Arcata, CA 95521

Institution:	**University of California-Davis**
Institution Type:	Public, 4 year + graduate
Unit:	African-American and African Studies Program
Contact Person:	John Stewart, Chair

Address:	280 Kerr Hall
	Davis, CA 95616
Phone:	(916) 752-1548
Fax:	(916) 752-9704
Unit Offers:	Major
Degrees Offered:	African-American Studies
Majors Per Year:	10
Minors:	8
Faculty:	5
Established:	1969
Special Features:	The program has five core faculty members whose research interests include African-American literature and African-American folklore. Areas in popular culture include blacks in film and video; religion and society in cinema in Africa and the diaspora; Caribbean culture and literature; comparative historical studies; African-descent intellectual history; blacks in rural America; and education in the African-American community.

Institution:	**California State University-Sacramento**
Institution Type:	Public, 4 year + graduate
Unit:	Pan-African Studies Program
Contact Person:	David Covin, Director
Address:	Ethnic Studies
	6000 J Street
	Sacramento, CA 95819-6013
Phone:	(916) 278-7570
Fax:	(916) 278-5787
Unit Offers:	Major, minor, certificate, classes
Degrees Offered:	B.A. Ethnic Studies with a concentration in Pan African Studies
Majors Per Year:	12
Faculty:	12
Established:	1969
Special Features:	The program offers an African Studies Certificate, a Cooper-Woodson College Enhancement Program, and a Black Resource Center in the Sciences.

Institution:	**Yuba College**
Unit:	Black Studies
Address:	2088 N. Beale Road
	Marysville, CA 95901

Institution:	**Santa Ana College**
Unit:	Black Studies
Address:	Santa Ana, CA 97206

COLORADO

Institution:	**Metropolitan State University**
Unit:	Afro-American Studies
Contact Person:	Rachel B. Noel
Address:	Afro-American Studies
	Metropolitan State University
	Denver, CO 80204

Institution:	**University of Colorado-Denver**
Unit:	Black Education Program, INA
Address:	Denver, CO 80217
Phone:	(303) 556-2726

Institution:	**University of Colorado-Boulder**
Institution Type:	Public, 4 year + graduate
Unit:	Afro-American Studies Program
Contact Person:	William M. King, Coordinator
Address:	Campus Box 339
	Boulder, CO 80309-0339
Phone:	(303) 492-8789
Fax:	(303) 492-7799
Unit Offers:	Major, minor, classes
Degrees Offered:	B.A. Afro-American Studies
Majors Per Year:	3–5
Minors:	7–10
Faculty:	3+
Established:	1968
Special Features:	AAS is part of the Center for Studies of Ethnicity and Race in America. It seeks to provide a grounding in the life history and culture of black

people in the United States as a base for exacting comparative study of the same with the American Indian, Asian American, and Chicano elements of the center.

Institution:	**University of Northern Colorado**
Institution Type:	Public, 4 year + graduate
Unit:	Department of Black Studies
Contact Person:	Anthonia Kalu, Chair
Address:	Michener L128
	Greeley, CO 80639
Phone:	(303) 351-1744/2685
Fax:	(303) 351-1571
E-mail:	akalu@goldng8.univnorthco.edu
Unit Offers:	Major, minor, classes
Degrees Offered:	B.A. Black Studies; B.A. Black Studies with an emphasis in Multicultural Education
Faculty:	3 full-time, 2–4 part-time
Established:	1969 (program); 1972 (department)
Special Features:	This department's new emphasis is on multicultural education. Graduates in Black Studies will be prepared to enter professional and academic careers in the humanities and social sciences. They will possess accurate information about the histories and identities of people of African descent. They will be exposed to and contribute to scholarship about people of African descent and will have a liberal arts education and those skills necessary for working in multicultural environments. They will understand the struggles of black people. As a job-related field, Black Studies fosters the intellectual and professional expertise valuable for positions in teaching (elementary, secondary, and postsecondary levels), business, criminal justice, counseling, education, and health-related fields. Additional applications include community resource development, urban planning, public and social policy analysis, law, social services, government (local, state, and federal), and international relations. Graduates also qualify for graduate work in Black Studies.

Institution:	**Central Connecticut State University**
Institution Type:	Public, 4 year + graduate
Unit:	African-American Studies Program
Contact Person:	Felton Best, Director
Address:	1615 Stanley Street
	New Britain, CT 06050-4010
Phone:	(203) 832-2817
Fax:	(203) 832-3140
Unit Offers:	Minor
Degrees Offered:	Minor in African American Studies
Minors Per Year:	114
Faculty:	5
Established:	1992

Institution:	**University of Hartford**
Unit:	African American Studies Program
Contact Person:	Harald M. Sandstrom, Director
Address:	West Hartford, CT 06119
Phone:	(203) 243-4980

Institution:	**University of Connecticut**
Unit:	Institute for African-American Studies
Contact Person:	Donald Spivey, Director
Address:	Storrs, CT 06268
Phone:	(203) 486-3630

Institution:	**Connecticut College**
Unit:	Black Studies
Contact Person:	Ernestine Brown
Address:	Box 1453
	New London, CT 06320

Institution:	**Wesleyan University**
Institution Type:	Private, 4 year + graduate
Unit:	Center for African American Studies
	African-American Studies Program
Contact Person:	Kate Rushin, Center Director,
	or Gayle Pemberton, Chair,
	African-American Studies

Address:	343 High Street
	Middletown, CT 06459
Phone:	(203) 685-2040
Fax:	(203) 685-2041
E-mail:	gpemberton@wesleyan.edu
Unit Offers:	Major, classes
Degrees Offered:	B.A.
Majors Per Year:	50
Faculty:	5 and approximately 5 affiliated with cross-listings
Special Features:	Both the Center for African-American Studies and the Program in African-American Studies offer a rich variety of programs: a lecture series on a specific topic yearly that brings top scholars to campus, a film series, brown-bag lunches, and special lecturers. In addition, the center houses a library with campus archives and materials germane to African-American Studies.

Institution:	**Southern Connecticut State University**
Unit:	Black Studies
Contact Person:	William Wright
Address:	Seabury Hall
	New Haven, CT 06515

Institution:	**University of New Haven**
Unit:	Minority Affairs
Contact Person:	Melba Lee-Hanna
Address:	300 Orange Avenue
	West Haven, CT 06516

Institution:	**Yale University**
Institution Type:	Private, 4 year + graduate
Unit:	Afro-American Cultural Center
Contact Person:	Director
Address:	211 Park Street
	New Haven, CT 06520
Phone:	(203) 432-4131
Fax:	(203) 432-8138
Special Features:	This is a student services and cultural center. Yale also has an African and African American Studies Department.

Institution:	**University of Bridgeport**
Unit:	Black Studies
Contact Person:	Ralph Forde
Address:	Bridgeport, CT 06602

DELAWARE

Institution:	**University of Delaware**
Unit:	Black American Studies
Contact Person:	James E. Newton
Address:	Newark, DE 19711

Institution:	**Delaware State College**
Unit:	Black Studies
Contact Person:	Clenora Hudson-Withers
Address:	Dover, DE 19901

DISTRICT OF COLUMBIA

Institution:	**Wesley Theological Seminary**
Unit:	Black Philosophy of Culture
Address:	4400 W. Avenue NW
	Washington, DC 20016

Institution:	**Howard University**
Institution Type:	Public, 4 year + graduate
Unit:	Afro-American Studies Program
Contact Person:	Russell L. Adams, Director
Address:	Washington, DC 20059
Phone:	(202) 806-7242

FLORIDA

Institution:	**Florida State University**
Institution Type:	Public, 4 year
Unit:	Black Studies Program
Contact Person:	William R. Jones, Director

Address:	College of Social Sciences
	172 Bellamy Building
	Tallahassee, FL 32306-4028
Phone:	(904) 644-5512
Fax:	(904) 644-7329
E-mail:	wjones@garnet.acns.fsu.edu
Unit Offers:	Minor
Degrees Offered:	Minor in Black Studies
Special Features:	Special features include: Black Abolitionists Papers Project (BAPP); the Patricia Roberts Harris Fellowship Program (PRHFP); the Summer Minority Graduate Orientation Program (SMGOP); and FSU Community/University Partnership Program (Brother of Pride).

Institution:	**Florida A&M University**
Unit:	Afro-American Studies
Address:	Tallahassee, FL 32307

Institution:	**University of Florida**
Unit:	Center for African Studies
Contact Person:	Peter R. Schmidt, Director
Address:	Gainesville, FL 32611
Phone:	(904) 392-2187

Institution:	**Rollins College**
Unit:	Afro-American Studies
Contact Person:	Alzo Reddick
Address:	601 S. Interlochen Avenue
	Winter Park, FL 32789

Institution:	**University of Miami**
Institution Type:	Public, 4 year + graduate
Unit:	Caribbean, African, and Afro-American Studies Program (CAAS)
Contact Person:	Marvin P. Dawkins, Director
Address:	P.O. Box 248245
	Coral Gables, FL 33124
Phone:	(305) 284-6340
Fax:	(305) 284-2701

Unit Offers:	Major, minor, classes
Degrees Offered:	B.A. in African-American Studies with concentrations in African-American, African, and Caribbean dimensions of the black experience
Majors Per Year:	New major effective fall 1994
Minors:	15–25
Faculty:	12
Established:	1970
Special Features:	CAAS is offered as a joint major with other undergraduate majors in the College of Arts and Sciences and other schools at the University of Miami. CAAS also cosponsors a Caribbean Writers Summer Institute with the English Department.

Institution:	**University of South Florida**
Institution Type:	Public, 4 year + graduate
Unit:	Africana Studies Program
Contact Person:	Navita Cummings James, Director
Address:	Soc 287
	Tampa, FL 33620
Phone:	(813) 974-2427
Fax:	(813) 974-2668
Unit Offers:	Major, minor, classes
Degrees Offered:	B.A. African Studies
Majors Per Year:	10
Faculty:	15
Established:	1969
Special Features:	The program's focus is on African American, African, and Afro-Caribbean Studies.

GEORGIA

Institution:	**Emory University**
Unit:	African American and African Studies
Contact Person:	Dolores Aldridge
Address:	Atlanta, GA 30304

Institution:	**Spelman College**
Unit:	Black Studies

Contact Person:	Martin Yanuck
Address:	Atlanta, GA 30314

Institution:	**Clark Atlanta University**
Institution Type:	4 year + graduate
Unit:	African and African-American Studies
Contact Person:	David Dorsey, Chair
Address:	P.O. Box 224
	Fair Street and James P. Brawley Drive, S.W.
	Atlanta, GA 30314
Phone:	(404) 880-8533 or 880-8535
Fax:	(404) 880-8222 or 880-6771
Unit Offers:	Major (graduate only), minor (undergraduate 1995), classes
Degrees Offered:	M.A. African-American Studies; M.A. African Studies; Doctor of Arts in Humanities with concentration in African-American Studies
Majors Per Year:	40
Minors:	Effective 1995
Faculty:	3, and 20 affiliates
Established:	1970
Special Features:	The program designs an individual program for each student, based on the student's particular scholarly interests, previous training, and career goals. Each student attains a master's level of competence in a traditional discipline, an overview of history and cultures of Africa and the diaspora, and in-depth knowledge of a particular area of Black Studies. Three professors are responsible for the unifying courses unique to the program; all other courses are taught by specialists in all the social science and humanities departments of the university.

The interdisciplinary Doctor of Arts in Humanities Program requires a master's degree for admission. Its interdisciplinary and pedagogical courses are complemented by equal emphasis in a concentration. African-American Studies is one of the optional concentrations.

Institution:	**Morehouse College**
Unit:	Afro-American and African Studies
Contact Person:	W. P. Smith
Address:	Atlanta, GA 30314

Institution:	**University of Georgia**
Institution Type:	Public, 4 year
Unit:	The Institute for African American Studies
Contact Person:	R. Baxter Miller, Director
Address:	164 Psychology Building
	Athens, GA 30602-1786
Phone:	(706) 542-5197
Fax:	(706) 542-3071
E-mail:	rbmiller@uga.cc.uga.edu
Unit Offers:	Certificate; major and minor pending
Faculty:	7
Established:	1990
Special Features:	The Institute for African American Studies offers several courses in the core curriculum. Students wishing to earn a certificate in African American Studies can do so by taking the courses in addition to two courses approved by the director. The intent is to be both intellectually exciting and rigorously challenging. Often, views might seem unusually innovative. Many students of the institute might well be interested in professional study and scholarly research beyond the undergraduate level. Others might begin to lay out a systematic plan for thoughtful public services.

The institute is dedicated to the production of creative research on the achievements of African Americans and to exciting instruction for a diverse community of thinkers. In addition, the institute serves as a cultural repository and resource for the citizenry of Georgia.

Institution:	**Mercer University**
Unit:	Afro-American Studies
Address:	Macon, GA 31207

Institution:	**Albany State College**
Unit:	Afro-American Studies
Contact Person:	Lois B. Hollis
Address:	504 College Drive
	Albany, GA 31705

ILLINOIS

Institution:	**Northern Illinois University**
Institution Type:	Public, 4 year + graduate
Unit:	Center for Black Studies
Contact Person:	Admasu Zike, Director
Address:	Lincoln Terrace Drive
	DeKalb, IL 60115
Phone:	(815) 753-1709
Fax:	(815) 753-9291
Unit Offers:	Minor, classes
Degrees Offered:	Minors in African-American and African Studies
Minors Per Year:	55
Faculty:	20
Established:	1970
Special Features:	The center is the home for many student organizations such as Black Student Union, Black Graduate Student Association, Organization of Black Business Students, Black Theatre Workshop, African Student Union, and Present Perfect Modeling.

Institution:	**Northeastern University**
Unit:	African American Studies
Contact Person:	William Exum
Address:	Anderson Hall
	Evanston, IL 60201

Institution:	**Prairie State College**
Unit:	Afro-American Studies
Address:	P.O. Box 487
	Chicago Heights, IL 60411

Institution:	Governor State College
Unit:	Pan-African Studies
Contact Person:	Roger Oden
Address:	Park Forest South, IL 60466
Institution:	George William College
Unit:	Afro-American College
Contact Person:	Norma C. George
Address:	Downers Grove, IL 60515
Institution:	Roosevelt University
Unit:	African/Afro-American Studies
Contact Person:	S. Miles Woods
Address:	Chicago, IL 60605
Institution:	University of Illinois-Chicago
Institution Type:	Public, 4 year + graduate
Unit:	Department of African-American Studies
Contact Person:	Mildred McGinnis, Administrative Assistant
Address:	1007 West Harrison Street
	Room 4078 BSB-M/C 069
	Chicago, IL 60607-7140
Phone:	(312) 996-2950
Fax:	(312) 996-5799
Unit Offers:	Major, minor
Degrees Offered:	Area of specialization in Liberal Arts and Sciences
Majors Per Year:	12
Minors:	6
Faculty:	9, and 6 affiliates
Established:	1972
Institution:	Chicago State University
Institution Type:	Public, 4 year + graduate
Unit:	Gwendolyn Brooks Center for Black Literature and Creative Writing
Contact Person:	Haki Madhubuti, Director
Address:	Room 210 Douglas Library
	9501 South King Drive
	Chicago, IL 60628-1598
Phone:	(312) 995-4440

Fax:	(312) 995-2077
Unit Offers:	Classes
Faculty:	3
Special Features:	This is a research center for those studying the works of poet Gwendolyn Brooks.

Institution:	**University of Chicago**
Institution Type:	Private, 4 year
Unit:	Africa and African-American Studies Program
Contact Person:	Ralph Austen, Chair
Address:	5828 South University Avenue
	Chicago, IL 60637
Phone:	(312) 702-0902
Fax:	(312) 702-2587
Unit Offers:	Minor, classes
Degrees Offered:	No degrees are offered, but courses of concentration in existing degree programs such as history, anthropology, sociology, and political science are valuable for anyone concentrating on Africa or black America in these disciplines.
Special Features:	In addition to academic courses in African and African-American civilizations, the program coordinates regular workshops in which students and faculty share their work. The program also brings to campus speakers from other institutions.

Institution:	**University of Chicago**
Institution Type:	Private, 4 year
Unit:	Committee on African and African-American Studies
Contact Person:	Ralph Austen, Professor
Address:	5828 South University Avenue
	Chicago, IL 60637
Phone:	(312) 702-8344
Fax:	(312) 702-2587
Unit Offers:	Major, classes
Degrees Offered:	B.A.
Majors Per Year:	4
Special Features:	The committee is an interdepartmental and interdivisional body concerned with promoting the

study of African and African-American culture and society from prehistoric to contemporary times. The university does not grant a degree in African or African-American Studies, and students must be admitted to one of the regular departments or programs. The University of Chicago offers broad opportunities for interdisciplinary and comparative work. Its Social Sciences and Humanities divisions and aggregate of non–Western area programs are among the strongest in the country and are organized on a flexible basis to meet a wide range of student interests. Students may work toward an M.A. degree based upon a specialization in African or African-American Studies in the Master of Arts Program in the Social Sciences, the Committee on International Relations, or the Committee on General Studies in the Humanities.

Institution:	**Western Illinois University**
Institution Type:	Public, 4 year + graduate
Unit:	African American Studies
Contact Person:	Carl Briscoe, Director
Address:	Lurren Hall AAS
	900 W. Adams Street
	Macomb, IL 61455
Phone:	(309) 298-1181
Unit Offers:	Minor
Faculty:	2
Established:	1970s

Institution:	**Bradley University**
Unit:	Black Studies
Contact Person:	Gene Young
Address:	Peoria, IL 61606

Institution:	**Illinois Wesleyan University**
Unit:	Black Studies
Contact Person:	Paul Bushnell
Address:	Bloomington, IL 61701

Institution:	**Illinois State University**
Unit:	Afro-American Arts and Studies
Address:	Normal, IL 61761

Institution:	**University of Illinois-Urbana**
Institution Type:	Public, 4 year + graduate
Unit:	Afro-American Studies and Research Program
Contact Person:	Dianne M. Pinderhughes, Director
Address:	606 S. Gregory
	Urbana, IL 61801
Phone:	(217) 333-7781
Fax:	(217) 244-4809
Unit Offers:	Minor, classes
Minors Per Year:	18
Faculty:	6, and 40 faculty affiliates
Established:	1969
Special Features:	The Afro-American Studies and Research Program (AASRP) is an academic unit within the College of Liberal Arts and Sciences. The teaching and research of AASRP focus primarily on the experiences of people of African descent in the United States, and to a lesser degree, on the rest of the hemisphere. The program has offered an Interdisciplinary Minor in Afro-American Studies since fall 1988. In 1992 the program began hosting one Chancellor's Minority Postdoctoral Fellow and a Visiting Lecturer completing a dissertation.

Institution:	**Eastern Illinois University**
Institution Type:	Public, 4 year + graduate
Unit:	Afro-American Studies Program
Contact Person:	William E. Colvin, Director
Address:	208 Blair Hall
	Charleston, IL 61920
Phone:	(217) 581-5719
Fax:	(217) 581-5188
Unit Offers:	Major, minor
Degrees Offered:	B.S.
Majors Per Year:	2

Minors:	1
Faculty:	1
Established:	1973
Special Features:	The program is an interdisciplinary one that proves to be quite versatile for various students and interests. It is highly complementary to the multicultural requirements in several departments.

Institution:	**Richland Community College**
Unit:	Black Studies
Address:	Decatur, IL 62521

Institution:	**Sangamon State University**
Institution Type:	Public, 4 year + graduate
Unit:	African American Studies Program (AAS)
Contact Person:	Maria Mootry, Director
Address:	Brookens 425
	Springfield, IL 62704
Phone:	(217) 786-7427
Unit Offers:	Major, minor, classes
Degrees Offered:	B.A., M.A.
Majors Per Year:	10
Minors:	13
Faculty:	9
Established:	1993
Special Features:	Because SSU has a special public affairs mission, being located in the capital of Illinois, many of our AAS students combine AAS curricula with study in city planning, health care, social work, and politics.

Institution:	**Southern Illinois University**
Unit:	Black American Studies
Address:	Room 4, Quigley Hall
	Carbondale, IL 62901

Institution:	**DePauw University**
Institution Type:	Private, 4 year
Unit:	Black Studies Program
Contact Person:	Mac Dixon-Fyle
Address:	Department of History
	Greencastle, IN 46135
Phone:	(317) 658-4588
Fax:	(317) 658-4177
E-mail:	macdixon@depauwbitnet
Unit Offers:	Minor, classes
Degrees Offered:	B.A., B.S.
Minors:	20
Faculty:	8
Established:	1988
Special Features:	The minor has several objectives. Courses on the African and African American experience sensitize students to the history, literature, politics, and sociology of a group that now constitutes over twenty-five percent of the United States' population. The inculcation of various theoretical and empirical perspectives sharpens the skills of students interested in graduate work, while preparing others for the challenging fields of social work, community development, journalism, elementary and high-school teaching, counseling, marketing, paralegal and probation duty, and a host of related occupations. Students gain insights to help them deal more effectively with racial matters. Through this minor, the African American student will come to a more balanced appreciation of the dynamics of Black America.

Institution:	**Indiana University-Purdue University Indianapolis**
Institution Type:	Public, 4 year + graduate
Unit:	Afro-American Studies Program
Contact Person:	Monroe Little, Director
Address:	IUPUI CA 504L
	425 University Boulevard
	Indianapolis, IN 46202

Phone:	(317) 274-8662
Fax:	(317) 274-2347
Unit Offers:	Minor, classes
Established:	1981

Institution:	**Valparaiso University**
Unit:	Afro-American Studies
Contact Person:	Bill Neal
Address:	Valparaiso, IN 46383

Institution:	**Goshen College**
Unit:	Department of Urban and Afro-American Studies
Contact Person:	Wilma Bailey
Address:	Goshen, IN 46526

Institution:	**University of Notre Dame**
Institution Type:	Private, 4 year
Unit:	African-American Studies Program
Contact Person:	Frederick Wright, Director
Address:	345 O'Shaugnessy Hall
	Notre Dame, IN 46556
Phone:	(219) 631-5628
Fax:	(219) 631-4268
Unit Offers:	Major, classes
Degrees Offered:	B.A.
Faculty:	14

Institution:	**Manchester College**
Institution Type:	4 year
Unit:	African and African-American Studies
Contact Person:	Benson Onyeji, Coordinator
Address:	History and Political Science
	North Manchester, IN 46962
Phone:	(219) 982-5337
Fax:	(219) 982-6868
Unit Offers:	Classes
Degrees Offered:	A.A., B.A., B.S.
Faculty:	4

Special Features:	Instead of a formal program, Manchester College has a variety of ethnic-based courses that can constitute an emphasis for students in a given major. There is a faculty coordinator to assist students who want to tailor their careers along ethnic studies.
Institution:	**Taylor University**
Unit:	Black Studies
Contact Person:	Nellie McGee
Address:	Upland, IN 46989
Institution:	**Ball State University**
Institution Type:	Public, 4 year + graduate
Unit:	African American Studies Program
Contact Person:	Nina Mjagki
Address:	History Department
	Muncie, IN 47306
Institution:	**Earlham College**
Unit:	Department of African and African-American Studies
Contact Person:	Phyllis Boanes, Director
Address:	Richmond, IN 47374
Phone:	(317) 983-1661
Institution:	**Indiana University**
Institution Type:	Public, 4 year + graduate
Unit:	Department of Afro-American Studies
Contact Person:	Mellonee Burnim, Chair
Address:	Memorial Hall East M39
	Bloomington, IN 47405
Phone:	(812) 855-3874
Fax:	(812) 855-4869
Unit Offers:	Major, minor, classes
Degrees Offered:	B.A., Ph.D., Minor in Afro-American Studies
Majors Per Year:	20
Minors:	60
Faculty:	15
Established:	1970

Institution:	**Indiana State University**
Unit:	Afro-American Studies
Contact Person:	Warren Swindell
Address:	Terre Haute, IN 47808

Institution:	**Purdue University**
Institution Type:	Public
Unit:	African-American Studies and Research Center
Unit Type:	Program
Contact Person:	Leonard Harris, Director
Address:	1367 Liberal Arts and Education Building
	Room 6180
	West Lafayette, IN 47906
Phone:	(317) 494-5680
E-mail:	harrisl@mace.cc.purdue.edu
Unit Offers:	Major, minor
Majors Per Year:	3
Minors:	5
Faculty:	4
Established:	1976

Institution:	**Wabash College**
Unit:	Black Cultural Center
Contact Person:	Horace Turner
Address:	Crawfordsville, IN 47933

IOWA

Institution:	**Grinnell College**
Institution Type:	Private, 4 year
Unit:	African-American Studies Concentration
Contact Person:	Kesho Y. Scott, Chair
Address:	106 Carnegie Hall
	Grinnell, IA 50112
Phone:	(515) 269-4291
Fax:	(515) 269-4285
Unit Offers:	Concentration, classes
Concentrations	
Per Year:	10

Faculty:	6–10
Special Features:	Students examine Afro-American culture as an integral part of American culture through core courses in anthropology, literature, history, and sociology. Students choose additional courses dealing with Afro-American heritage through a variety of other disciplines in the arts, the humanities, and the social sciences. This background lays the foundation for an interdisciplinary senior project that encourages students to perceive connections with related cultures and to understand essential similarities and differences.

Institution:	**Central College**
Unit:	Afro-American Studies
Address:	Pella, IA 50219

Institution:	**Luther College**
Institution Type:	4 year
Unit:	Africana Studies Department
Contact Person:	Lawrence H. Williams, Chair
Address:	Decorah, IA 52101
Phone:	(319) 387-1158
Fax:	(319) 387-2158
Unit Offers:	Major, minor, classes
Degrees Offered:	A.B. with major and/or minor in Africana Studies; A.B. with concentrations in Africana Studies
Majors Per Year:	1–2
Minors:	1–2
Faculty:	3
Established:	1968
Special Features:	The department has areas of concentration in African history and African literature and African-American history and African-American literature. Although there are few majors and minors, a large number of students take the courses to satisfy other requirements.

Institution:	**University of Iowa**
Institution Type:	4 year + graduate

Unit:	African American World Studies Program
Contact Person:	Frederick Woodard, Chair
Address:	303 EPB
	Iowa City, IA 52242
Phone:	(319) 335-0317
Fax:	(319) 335-2535
Unit Offers:	Major, minor, classes
Degrees Offered:	B.A. African American Studies; B.A. African American World Studies; B.A. African Studies; M.A. African American World Studies
Majors Per Year:	50
Minors:	100
Faculty:	5
Established:	1970
Special Features:	This is a very open and diverse program for motivated students, since it is community-oriented with room for student input and involvement. Research and teaching assistantships are available to master's students.

Institution:	**Coe College**
Institution Type:	Private, 4 year
Unit:	Afro-American Studies Program
Contact Person:	James Randall
Address:	English Department
	Cedar Rapids, IA 52402
Phone:	(319) 399-8000
Fax:	(319) 399-8748
Unit Offers:	Major, minor
Degrees Offered:	B.A. Afro-American Studies
Majors Per Year:	3
Minors:	5
Faculty:	2 full-time, 1 part-time
Established:	1973

KANSAS

Institution:	**Ottawa University**
Unit:	Black Studies

Contact Person:	Ronald Averyt
Address:	Ottawa, KS 66067

Institution:	**Kansas State University**
Unit:	Black Studies
Contact Person:	Kenneth Lewallen
Address:	Manhattan, KS 66502

Institution:	**Washburn University**
Unit:	Afro-American Studies
Contact Person:	Roderick A. McDonald
Address:	Topeka, KS 66621

Institution:	**Wichita State University**
Unit:	Black Studies
Contact Person:	R. W. Blake, Jr.
Address:	Box 81
	Wichita, KS 67208

KENTUCKY

Institution:	**University of Louisville**
Unit:	Pan-African Studies
Contact Person:	Maurice Hommel
Address:	Louisville, KY 40292

Institution:	**Berea College**
Institution Type:	Private, 4 year
Unit:	Black Cultural Center and Interracial Education Program
Unit Type:	Center
Contact Person:	Andrew Baskin, Director
Address:	CPO 134
	Berea, KY 40404
Phone:	(606) 986-9341 (ext. 6515/16)
Fax:	(606) 986-4506
Unit Offers:	Minor, classes
Minors Per Year:	0–5
Faculty:	5

Established:	1983
Special Features:	The center publishes *The Griot,* the official journal of the Southern Conference on African Studies, Inc.

Institution:	**University of Kentucky**
Institution Type:	Public, 4 year + graduate
Unit:	African American Studies and Research Program
Contact Person:	Doris Wilkinson, Director
Address:	#1769 Patterson Office Tower
	Lexington, KY 40506-0279
Phone:	(606) 257-3593
Fax:	(606) 323-1956
E-mail:	aabrp@ukcc.uky.edu
Unit Offers:	Minor, classes
Minors Per Year:	10+
Faculty:	2
Established:	1992
Special Features:	This program offers an interdisciplinary minor, a lecture series, a newsletter, and guest lecturers.

Institution:	**Kentucky State University**
Unit:	Afro-American Studies
Address:	Frankfort, KY 40601

LOUISIANA

Institution:	**Dillard University**
Unit:	Afro-American Studies
Contact Person:	Earl Smith
Address:	2601 Gentilly Boulevard
	New Orleans, LA 70122

Institution:	**Grambling State University**
Unit:	Afro-American Studies
Address:	Grambling, LA 71245

Institution:	**Bowdoin College**
Institution Type:	Private, 4 year
Unit:	Africana Studies Program
Contact Person:	Randolph Stakeman, Director
Address:	Brunswick, ME 04011
Phone:	(207) 725-3272
Fax:	(207) 725-3123
Unit Offers:	Major, classes
Degrees Offered:	B.A.
Majors Per Year:	6
Faculty:	11
Established:	1969

Institution:	**University of Maine**
Unit:	Black Studies
Contact Person:	Connie Carroll
Address:	Portland, ME 04103

Institution:	**Bates College**
Institution Type:	Private, 4 year
Unit:	African American Studies Program
Contact Person:	Charles V. Carnegie, Acting Director
Address:	Lewiston, ME 04240
Phone:	(207) 786-6079
Fax:	(207) 786-6123
Unit Offers:	Major
Degrees Offered:	B.A.
Established:	1993
Special Features:	In addition to being a program in its own right, African American Studies at Bates is at the core of American Cultural Studies. Students majoring in the latter program are required to take specified core courses in African American Studies.

Institution:	**Colby College**
Institution Type:	Private, 4 year
Unit:	African American Studies Program
Contact Person:	Cheryl Townsend Gilkes, Director

Address:	Waterville, ME 04901
Phone:	(207) 872-3133
Fax:	(207) 872-3555
E-mail:	svjones@colby.edu
Unit Offers:	Minor, classes
Minors Per Year:	4
Faculty:	13
Established:	1969
Special Features:	African American Studies courses are offered in close association with the American Studies Program. It is an interdisciplinary program designed to provide an overview and introduction to the experiences of African Americans in the United States. The courses attempt to connect the African American experiences to the literatures, histories, and cultures of Africa, Latin America, and the Caribbean. The core courses expose the student to classical and contemporary literature, issues of public policy, critical debates in social science and history, and to the main currents of historical and contemporary cultural expression.

MARYLAND

Institution:	**University of Maryland**
Unit:	Afro-American Studies
Contact Person:	Al-Tony Gilmore
Address:	College Park, MD 20740

Institution:	**Towson State University**
Institution Type:	Public, 4 year + graduate
Unit:	African-American Studies Program
Contact Person:	John M. Gissendanner
Address:	English Department
	Towson, MD 21204
Phone:	(410) 830-2863
Unit Offers:	Minor, classes
Minors Per Year:	10
Faculty:	15

Established:	1974
Special Features:	Students may choose a concentration in the program, select courses to structure a concentration within the Interdisciplinary Studies Program, or take courses as electives. Special topics and mini-master courses may be accepted toward the major.

Institution:	**University of Maryland**
Unit:	African American Studies
Contact Person:	Daphne Harrison
Address:	5401 Wilkins Avenue
	Baltimore, MD 21228

Institution:	**Morgan State University**
Unit:	Black Studies
Contact Person:	J. Carleston
Address:	Holnes 103
	Baltimore, MD 21239

MASSACHUSETTS

Institution:	**Hampshire College**
Unit:	Black Studies
Contact Person:	Eugene Terry
Address:	Amherst, MA 01002

Institution:	**Amherst College**
Institution Type:	Private, 4 year
Unit:	Black Studies Department
Contact Person:	Rhonda Cobham-Sander, Chair
Address:	Williston Hall
	Amherst, MA 01002
Phone:	(413) 542-5832
Fax:	(413) 542-5837
E-mail:	blackstudies@amherst.edu
Unit Offers:	Major
Degrees Offered:	B.A. Liberal Arts
Majors Per Year:	20

Faculty:	6
Established:	1971
Special Features:	Courses within the department are cross-cultural and interdisciplinary. They include material on Africa, the Caribbean, and African America, as well as comparative material on other United States ethnic groups. Disciplines presently covered include history, philosophy, literature, religion, fine arts, and psychology.

Institution:	**University of Massachusetts-Amherst**
Institution Type:	Public, 4 year + graduate
Unit:	W.E.B. DuBois Department of Afro-American Studies
Contact Person:	Barbara McGlynn, Office Manager
Address:	325 New Africa House
	Amherst, MA 01003-6210
Phone:	(413) 545-2751
Unit Offers:	Major, minor, certificate, classes
Degrees Offered:	B.A., Ph.D. (fall of 1995)
Majors Per Year:	20
Minors:	50
Faculty:	11
Established:	1972

Institution:	**Smith College**
Institution Type:	Private, 4 year
Unit:	African-American Studies Department
Contact Person:	Louis Wilson, Chair
Address:	Wright Hall
	Northampton, MA 01063
Phone:	(413) 585-3572/73
Fax:	(413) 585-3339
Unit Offers:	Major, minor, classes
Degrees Offered:	B.A.
Majors Per Year:	10
Minors:	10
Faculty:	3–5
Established:	1970
Special Features:	The department offers courses in history, litera-

ture, anthropology, psychology, and government, as well as study abroad.

Institution:	**Mount Holyoke College**
Unit:	Black Studies Program
Contact Person:	Walter Stewart, Director
Address:	South Hadley, MA 01075
Phone:	(413) 538-2507

Institution:	**Springfield College**
Unit:	Black Studies
Contact Person:	Al Carter
Address:	Box 1636
	Springfield, MA 01109

Institution:	**Williams College**
Institution Type:	Private, 4 year
Unit:	Afro-American Studies Program
Contact Person:	David Lionel Smith, Chair
Address:	Stetson Hall
	Williamstown, MA 01224
Phone:	(413) 597-2547
Fax:	(413) 597-4032
Unit offers:	Minor/concentration
Faculty:	8
Established:	1969
Special Features:	The program offers a concentration, which is the equivalent of a minor.

Institution:	**University of Lowell**
Unit:	Equal Opportunity/Black Studies
Contact Person:	June Gonsalves
Address:	Lowell, MA 01854

Institution:	**Salem State College**
Unit:	African American Studies Program
Contact Person:	Gerdes Fleurant, Director
Address:	Salem, MA 01970
Phone:	(617) 547-2111

Institution:	**Roxbury Community College**
Unit:	Black Studies
Contact Person:	Aggrey M'Bere
Address:	425 Dudley
	Roxbury, MA 02115

Institution:	**Northeastern University**
Unit:	African-American Studies
Contact Person:	Ozzie Edwards
Address:	Boston, MA 02115

Institution:	**University of Massachusetts-Boston**
Institution Type:	Public, 4 year + graduate
Unit:	Black Studies Department
Contact Person:	Chukwuma Azoronye, Chair
Address:	100 Morrissey Boulevard
	Boston, MA 02125
Phone:	(617) 287-6795
Fax:	(617) 287-6511
Unit Offers:	Major, minor
Degrees Offered:	B.A. with major or minor in Black Studies
Majors Per Year:	35
Minors:	15
Faculty:	7
Special Features:	

Black Studies is a multidisciplinary and interdisciplinary field of academic study aimed at exploring, in an orderly, systematic, and structurally integrated fashion, the history, environment, culture, and social systems of peoples of African descent across the world. The broad educational purpose of the department is to accumulate and disseminate a specialized body of knowledge about the black experience in Africa, the Caribbean, and the Americas with particular emphasis on the United States.

The requirements for a Black Studies major are consistent with the concept of Black Studies as a multidisciplinary plan of study designed to provide its majors with a wide range of knowledge and analytical skills, as well as a firm grounding in one of three areas of specialization, namely history, the social sciences, or the humanities. With the broad base of training provided by the department, the Black Studies major becomes equipped for graduate or professional school, or the many social-service oriented fields traditionally entered by liberal arts graduates. Students may also minor in Black Studies, or they may choose to take one course or a set of courses in Black Studies.

Institution:	**Simmons College**
Institution Type:	Private, 4 year + graduate
Unit:	African American Studies Program
Contact Person:	Michael Williams, Director
Address:	300 The Fenway
	Boston, MA 02134
Phone:	(617) 521-2255
Fax:	(617) 521-3199
Unit Offers:	Major
Degrees Offered:	B.A. African American Studies
Majors Per Year:	5
Faculty:	5
Established:	1971
Special Features:	This program produces the journal *Abafazi*.

Institution:	**Harvard University**
Institution Type:	Private, 4 year
Unit:	Afro-American Studies Department
Contact Person:	Henry L. Gates, Jr., Chair
Address:	1430 Massachusetts Avenue, 4th Floor
	Cambridge, MA 02138
Phone:	(617) 495-4113
Fax:	(617) 496-2871
Unit Offers:	Major, minor, classes
Degrees Offered:	A.B. Afro-American Studies
Majors Per Year:	50
Faculty:	24
Established:	1969

Institution:	Radcliffe College
Unit:	Afro-American Studies
Address:	10 Garden Street
	Cambridge, MA 02138

Institution:	Tufts University
Institution Type:	Private, 4 year
Unit:	African and New World Studies
Contact Person:	Rosalind Shaw, Faculty Coordinator
Address:	Anthropology and Sociology Department
	Tufts University
	Medford, MA 02155
Phone:	(617) 628-5000
Unit Offers:	Minor
Degrees Offered:	B.A., B.S.
Faculty:	20
Special Features:	African and New World Studies is an interdisciplinary minor program that gives students an opportunity to study systematically the history and culture of Afro-America, Africa, the Caribbean, and Latin America. From the perspectives of south to north, students investigate the multifaceted past and present linkages between Africa and the societies of the Americas. Students learn the historical interactions and contemporary parallels surrounding culture and development in Native America, Afro-America, the Caribbean, Latin America, and Africa. The program includes a biannual colloquium and the Walter Rodney Memorial Lecture Series. There is at present no regular major concentration in African and New World Studies, although students may propose a plan of study in this field.

Institution:	Boston College
Institution Type:	Private, 4 year + graduate
Unit:	Black Studies Program
Contact Person:	Frank F. Taylor, Director

Address:	Lyons Hall 301
	140 Commonwealth Avenue
	Chestnut Hill, MA 02167
Phone:	(617) 552-3238
Fax:	(617) 552-8828
Unit Offers:	Major, minor
Degrees Offered:	B.A. Independent Major in Black Studies
Majors Per Year:	1
Minors:	40
Faculty:	13
Established:	1969
Special Features:	Black Studies at Boston College has developed a unique and significant specialization in local African American history. A course in Boston's black history is offered annually, and the program regularly sponsors a conference on "Blacks in Boston." Started in 1983, "Blacks in Boston," the first of its kind in the region, brings together academics, community historians, students, and community people to encourage research, education, and preservation.

Institution:	**Wellesley College**
Institution Type:	Private, 4 year
Unit:	Africana Studies Department
Contact Person:	Selwyn R. Cudjoe, Chair
Address:	106 Central Street
	Wellesley, MA 02181
Phone:	(617) 283-2563
Fax:	(617) 283-3639
Unit Offers:	Major, minor, classes
Majors Per Year:	15
Minors:	7
Faculty:	5

Institution:	**Wheelock College**
Unit:	Black Studies
Contact Person:	Brunetta Wolfman
Address:	Boston, MA 02215

Institution:	**Boston University**
Unit:	Afro-American Studies
Contact Person:	Adele Gulliver
Address:	Boston, MA 02215

Institution:	**Brandeis University**
Institution Type:	Private, 4 year + graduate
Unit:	African and Afro-American Studies Department
Contact Person:	Ibrahim Sundiata, Chair
Address:	Rabb 107
	P.O. Box 9110
	Waltham, MA 02254
Phone:	(617) 736-2090
Fax:	(617) 736-3412
E-mail:	isaacs@binah.cc.brandeis.edu
Unit Offers:	Major, minor, certificate, classes
Degrees Offered:	B.A. African and Afro-American Studies
Majors Per Year:	10
Minors:	5
Faculty:	3
Established:	1969
Special Features:	The department offers an interdisciplinary examination of the relationship of Africa and the African diaspora, aimed at uniting, in one curriculum, the basic knowledge of both. It explores history, anthropology, sociology, psychology, politics, religions, economics, languages, and the arts. Pan-African in assumptions, it relates the experience and aspirations of black America to the experience and aspirations of African people elsewhere in the world—particularly in Africa, South America, and the Caribbean. It uses both traditional and innovative teaching styles, directing the full potential of academic inquiry to human needs.

Institution:	**Bridgewater State Cultural Center**
Unit:	Afro-American Society
Contact Person:	Paul A. Gray
Address:	Bridgewater, MA 02324

Institution:	**University of Michigan**
Institution Type:	Public, 4 year + graduate
Unit:	Center for Afro-American and African Studies
Contact Person:	Evans Young, Assistant Director
Address:	550 East University
	200 West Engineering Building
	Ann Arbor, MI 48109-1092
Phone:	(313) 764-5513
Fax:	(313) 763-0543
Unit Offers:	Major, minor, classes
Majors Per Year:	25
Minors:	5
Faculty:	18
Established:	1970

Institution:	**Eastern Michigan University**
Unit:	Afro-American Studies Program
Contact Person:	Ronald C. Woods, Director
Address:	Ypsilanti, MI 48197
Phone:	(313) 487-3460

Institution:	**Wayne State University**
Institution Type:	Public, 4 year + graduate
Unit:	Department of Africana Studies
Contact Person:	Michael Martin, Chair
Address:	51 W. Warren, 4th Floor
	Detroit, MI 48202
Phone:	(313) 577-2321
Fax:	(313) 577-3407
Unit Offers:	Major, minor, classes
Degrees Offered:	B.A. with a major in Africana Studies
Majors Per Year:	36
Minors:	42
Faculty:	5 full-time, 8 part-time
Established:	1990
Special Features:	The department offers two concentrations of study for majors, a study abroad summer pro-

gram, community internships, and African language instruction.

Institution:	**University of Michigan-Flint**
Institution Type:	Public, 4 year + graduate
Unit:	African American Studies Department
Contact Person:	Robert Matthews, Administrative Assistant
Address:	303 E. Kearsley Street
	446 CROB
	Flint, MI 48502-2186
Phone:	(810) 762-3353
Fax:	(810) 762-3687
E-mail:	clarkj@crob.flint.umich.edu
Unit Offers:	Major, minor, classes
Degrees Offered:	B.A. with a concentration in African American Studies
Majors Per Year:	15
Minors:	30
Faculty:	8
Established:	1972
Special Features:	This program is structured so that students can easily do double majors in African American Studies and history, political science, sociology, or English.

Institution:	**Washtenaw Community College**
Unit:	Black Studies
Address:	4800 E. Huron River Drive
	Ann Arbor, MI 48106

Institution:	**Highland Park Community College**
Unit:	Afro-American Studies
Contact Person:	Howard Lindsey
Address:	Highland Park, MI 48203

Institution:	**University of Detroit**
Unit:	Center for Black Studies
Contact Person:	Mary Helen Washington
Address:	4001 W. McNichols Road
	Detroit, MI 48221

Institution:	**Eastern Michigan University**
Unit:	Black Studies
Contact Person:	Robert Green
Address:	East Lansing, MI 48823

Institution:	**Western Michigan University**
Unit:	Black American Studies Program
Contact Person:	Le Roi Ray, Jr., Director
Address:	Kalamazoo, MI 49008-5093
Phone:	(616) 387-2664

MINNESOTA

Institution:	**Carleton College**
Unit:	African and African-American Studies Program
Contact Person:	Mary Easter, Director
Address:	Northfield, MN 55057
Phone:	(507) 663-4486

Institution:	**University of Minnesota**
Unit:	Department of Afro-American and African Studies
Contact Person:	Rose Brewer, Director
Address:	Minneapolis, MN 55455
Phone:	(612) 624-1338

MISSISSIPPI

Institution:	**University of Mississippi**
Institution Type:	Public, 4 year + graduate
Unit:	Afro-American Studies Program
Contact Person:	James F. Payne, Director
Address:	Barr Hall 303
	University, MS 38677
Phone:	(601) 236-5280
Unit Offers:	Minor
Minors Per Year:	17
Faculty:	5
Established:	1970

53

Special Features:	The Afro-American Studies Program develops and coordinates an interdisciplinary program that focuses mainly on the black experience in the United States, especially in Mississippi and the South. Its objectives are to examine the black experience, to facilitate a cultural and intellectual atmosphere on campus that will be favorable to such studies, and to develop a program of research and community service.
Institution:	**Tougaloo College**
Unit:	Afro-American Studies
Address:	Tougaloo, MS 39174
Institution:	**Jackson State University**
Unit:	Afro-American Studies
Contact Person:	Leslie B. McClemore
Address:	Jackson, MS 39217
Institution:	**Mississippi State University**
Institution Type:	Public, 4 year + graduate
Unit:	Department of History
Contact Person:	Robert L. Jenkins
Address:	Drawer H
	Mississippi State, MS 39762
Phone:	(601) 325-3604/3605
Unit Offers:	Classes
Special Features:	The university offers only individual courses in African American history. A course in racial and cultural minorities is offered in the Department of Sociology.

MISSOURI

Institution:	**St. Louis University**
Unit:	Afro-American Studies
Contact Person:	Barbara Woods
Address:	221 N. Grand Boulevard
	St. Louis, MO 63103

Institution:	**Eden Theological Seminary**
Unit:	Education for Black Urban Ministries
Address:	475 E. Lockwood Avenue
	Webster Groves, MO 63119

Institution:	**Washington University**
Institution Type:	Private, 4 year + graduate
Unit:	African and Afro-American Studies Program
Contact Person:	Gerald Early, Director
Address:	Campus Box 1109
	One Brookings Drive
	St. Louis, MO 63130-4899
Phone:	(314) 935-5690
Fax:	(314) 935-5631
E-mail:	atuchler@artsci.wustl.edu
Unit Offers:	Major, minor, classes
Degrees Offered:	B.A. African and Afro-American Studies
Majors Per Year:	10–12
Minors:	10–20
Faculty:	14
Established:	1972
Special Features:	African and Afro-American Studies at Washington University is an interdisciplinary academic program, largely concentrated in the social sciences and the humanities. It provides critical and objective instruction and opportunity for serious research for all interested students in the cultural and artistic life, and the intellectual, economic, religious, social, and political history of the various peoples in the world who so identify themselves as being African or of African descent, or who are so identified by others and who themselves attach significance or have significance attached by others to their African nationality or their descent therefrom.

Institution:	**Park College**
Unit:	Black Studies
Contact Person:	Edythe H. Grant

Address:	Kansas City, MO 64152

Institution:	**Lincoln University**
Institution Type:	Public, 4 year + graduate
Unit:	Department of Social & Behavioral Sciences
Contact Person:	A. F. Holland, Chair
Address:	820 Chestnut Street
	Jefferson City, MO 65102
Phone:	(314) 681-5145
Unit Offers:	Minor, classes
Degrees Offered:	Minor in Afro-American Studies
Special Features:	The department offers an interdisciplinary program in Afro-American Studies, offering a minor.

Institution:	**University of Missouri**
Unit:	Black Studies Program
Contact Person:	Sundiata K. Cha-Jua, Director
Address:	Columbia, MO 65211
Phone:	(314) 882-6229

MONTANA

Institution:	**University of Montana**
Institution Type:	Public, 4 year + graduate
Unit:	African-American Studies Program
Contact Person:	James Flightner, Dean
Address:	College of Liberal Arts and Sciences
	Missoula, MT 59812
Phone:	(406) 243-2632
Unit Offers:	Classes
Degrees Offered:	B.A. in Liberal Studies can include course work in African-American Studies
Faculty:	1
Established:	1968
Special Features:	African-American Studies at the University of Montana deals with African-American experiences and the development of racism's consciousness while encouraging the growth of individual identity within the process of community development.

Institution:	**Creighton University**
Institution Type:	Private, 4 year + graduate
Unit:	Black Studies Program
Contact Person:	A. W. Welch, Coordinator
Address:	Department of History
	2400 California Plaza
	Omaha, NE 68104
Phone:	(402) 280-2657
Fax:	(402) 280-4731
Unit Offers:	Minor
Minors Per Year:	5
Faculty:	8
Established:	1970
Special Features:	Black Studies is an interdisciplinary program with links in the Departments of English, Fine and Performing Arts, History, Political Science, Sociology, and Theology. It can be used as a support or minor for students majoring in any department of the College of Arts and Sciences. A number of Black Studies courses satisfy humanities and social sciences core requirements. The program focuses on Africa and the African diaspora in the Americas, especially in the United States.

Institution:	**University of Nebraska-Omaha**
Institution Type:	Public, 4 year
Unit:	Black Studies Department
Contact Person:	George R. Garrison, Chair
Address:	Omaha, NE 68164
Phone:	(402) 554-2412
Fax:	(402) 554-3296
Unit Offers:	Major, minor
Degrees Offered:	B.A. in (1) standard Black Studies; (2) African Studies; and (3) African American Studies
Faculty:	4 full-time, 8 part-time
Established:	1972
Special Features:	UNO's Black Studies Department develops undergraduate students academically and prepares them

for future research and other scholastic demands at the advanced level. Black Studies offers a major and a minor, giving students an integrated, multidisciplined, and multicultural curriculum that brings together courses that treat the experiences of all African people and their descendants—indigenous African, Afro-American, Afro-Latino, Afro-Caribbean, etc. Another important function of the Black Studies Department is to provide service courses for the university curriculum on the African and neo-African experience. In this role it acts as a conduit for our students, helping them to understand and appreciate the cultural and racial diversity in our society, and thereby enabling them to flow into the greater stream of life with minimum difficulty.

Institution:	**University of Nebraska-Lincoln**
Institution Type:	Public, 4 year + graduate
Unit:	African American and African Studies Program
Contact Person:	Keith D. Parker, Director
Address:	730 Oldfather Hall
	Lincoln, NE 68588-0320
Phone:	(402) 472-7973
Fax:	(402) 472-6070
Unit Offers:	Minor
Minors Per Year:	10
Faculty:	5
Established:	1993
Special Features:	African American and African Studies is an interdisciplinary program concentrating on the history and culture of African Americans, Africa, and the African diaspora. Students electing to minor in African American and African Studies have an opportunity to focus in several areas of study, depending on their specific interests.

NEW HAMPSHIRE

Institution:	**Dartmouth College**
Institution Type:	Private, 4 year
Unit:	African and Afro-American Studies Department
Contact Person:	Keith Walker, Chair
	or Margie Hattori, Administrative Assistant
Address:	121 Silsby
	Hanover, NH 03755
Phone:	(603) 646-3397
Fax:	(603) 646-1680
E-mail:	keith.l.walker@dartmouth.edu
	margaret.a.hattori@dartmouth.edu;
Unit Offers:	Certificate, minor
Degrees Offered:	Minor in African or Afro-American Studies; Certificate in African and Afro-American Studies
Faculty:	7
Established:	1969

NEW JERSEY

Institution:	**Bloomfield College**
Unit:	African and Afro-American Studies
Address:	Bloomfield, NJ 07003

Institution:	**Upsala College**
Unit:	Black Studies
Contact Person:	Carolyn Thorburn
Address:	345 Prospect Street
	East Orange, NJ 07017

Institution:	**Montclair State University**
Institution Type:	Public, 4 year + graduate
Unit:	African American Studies Program
Contact Person:	Dr. Saundra, Director
Address:	Valley Road and Normal Avenue
	Upper Montclair, NJ 07043

Phone:	(201) 655-7378
Fax:	(201) 655-5455
Unit Offers:	Minor, classes
Minors:	25–30
Faculty:	14
Established:	1975
Special Features:	All of the courses fulfill one or more general education requirements for graduation, making the minor attractive to all students and easy to complete without distraction from a major. The program added its first study tour to Ghana in 1995.

Institution:	**Seton Hall**
Unit:	Black Studies
Contact Person:	Julia Miller
Address:	400 S. Orange Avenue
	South Orange, NJ 07079

Institution:	**Kean College**
Unit:	Afro-American Studies
Contact Person:	Charles Tyson
Address:	Morris Avenue
	Union, NJ 07083

Institution:	**Rutgers University**
Unit:	Afro-American and African Studies Program
Contact Person:	Wendell P. Holbrook, Director
Address:	Faculty of A&S-Newark
	Newark, NJ 07102
Phone:	(201) 648-5586

Institution:	**Jersey City State College**
Unit:	Black Studies Center
Contact Person:	Dan Wiley
Address:	2039 John F. Kennedy Boulevard
	Jersey City, NJ 07305

Institution:	**Saint Peter's College**
Unit:	Afro-American Studies
Contact Person:	Michael Mitchell

Address:	2641 John F. Kennedy Boulevard
	Jersey City, NJ 07306
Institution:	**William Paterson College**
Institution Type:	Public, 4 year + graduate
Unit:	African, African-American and Caribbean
	Studies Department
Contact Person:	Ronald Parris, Chair
Address:	Matelson Hall 221
	300 Pompton Road
	Wayne, NJ 07470
Phone:	(201) 595-3027
Fax:	(201) 595-2418
Unit Offers:	Major, minor
Degrees Offered:	A.B.
Majors Per Year:	10
Minors:	20
Faculty:	5 full-time, 9 part-time
Established:	1970
Special Features:	The orientation is multidisciplinary and Pan-Africanist with a concern that goes beyond the cultural dimensions of African-American experience to include economic, political factors in history, and contemporary perspectives.
Institution:	**Richard Stockton College of New Jersey**
Institution Type:	Public, 4 year
Unit:	African American Studies Program
Contact Person:	Linda Williamson Nelson, Coordinator
Address:	Jimmie Leeds Road
	Pomona, NJ 08240
Phone:	(609) 652-4441/4542
Unit Offers:	Certificate, classes
Certified Students	
Per Year:	25
Faculty:	14
Established:	1983
Special Features:	This is an interdisciplinary program requiring five courses. Students have the opportunity to study with theorists from all disciplines and to do inde-

pendent studies and small group tutorials as well as traditional course work.

Institution:	**Princeton University**
Institution Type:	4 year + graduate
Unit:	Afro-American Studies Program
Contact Person:	Jean Washington, Program Manager
Address:	Dickinson Hall
	Princeton, NJ 08544
Phone:	(609) 258-4270
Unit Offers:	Certificate
Certified Students Per Year:	35
Faculty:	6
Established:	1971

Institution:	**Trenton State College**
Institution Type:	Public, 4 year + graduate
Unit:	Department of African-American Studies
Contact Person:	Coloria Dickinson, Chair
Address:	Hillwood Lakes CNA 700
	Trenton, NJ 08560-4700
Phone:	(609) 771-2138
Fax:	(609) 530-7694
Unit Offers:	Minor, classes
Minors Per Year:	10
Faculty:	4
Established:	1969

Institution:	**Rutgers University-New Brunswick**
Institution Type:	Public, 4 year + graduate
Unit:	Africana Studies Department
Contact Person:	Gerald Davis, Chair
Address:	112 Beck Hall
	Livingston Campus
	New Brunswick, NJ 08903
Phone:	(908) 932-3334/3335
Fax:	(908) 932-0076
E-mail:	gdavis@gandalf.rutgers.edu
Unit Offers:	Major, minor, classes

Degrees Offered:	B.A. Africana Studies
Majors Per Year:	80
Minors:	93
Faculty:	9 full-time, 6 part-time
Established:	1966

NEW MEXICO

Institution:	**University of New Mexico**
Unit:	African American Studies Division
Contact Person:	Shiame Okunor, Director
Address:	Albuquerque, NM 87131
Phone:	(505) 277-5644

Institution:	**New Mexico State University**
Unit:	Black Programs
Contact Person:	Andrew L. Wall, Director
Address:	Box 4188
	Las Cruces, NM 88003
Phone:	(505) 646-4208

Institution:	**Eastern New Mexico University**
Unit:	Black Studies
Contact Person:	Michael Davies
Address:	Portales, NM 88130

NEW YORK

Institution:	**New York University**
Unit:	Institute of Afro-American Affairs
Contact Person:	Earl S. Davis, Director
Address:	New York, NY 10003
Phone:	(212) 998-2130

Institution:	**City University of New York (CUNY)-John Jay College of Criminal Justice**
Institution Type:	4 year + graduate
Unit:	Department of African-American Studies

Contact Person:	Jannette Domingo, Chair
Address:	445 West 59th Street
	New York, NY 10019
Phone:	(212) 237-8757/8764
Fax:	(212) 237-8747
Unit Offers:	Minor, classes
Minors:	20
Faculty:	5
Established:	1970
Special Features:	The African-American Studies Department offers an interdisciplinary approach to the study of African-American, Caribbean, and African histories, cultures, and experiences.

Institution:	**Manhattan Community College**
Unit:	Department of Black Studies
Address:	134 West 51st Street
	New York, NY 10020

Institution:	**Hunter College-CUNY**
Institution Type:	Public, 4 year + graduate
Unit:	Department of Black and Puerto Rican Studies
Contact Person:	Jose M. Torres-Santiago, Chair
Address:	695 Park Avenue, Room 1111W
	New York, NY 10021
Phone:	(212) 772-5035
Fax:	(212) 772-5138
Unit Offers:	Major, minor
Degrees Offered:	B.A.
Majors Per Year:	69
Minors:	200
Faculty:	26
Established:	1967
Special Features:	The Department of Black and Puerto Rican Studies prepares students for careers in government, education, and community organizations; for entrance to professional schools such as law, social work, and urban planning; and for graduate study and research in the social sciences and humanities. Graduates of the department have followed ca-

reers in journalism, counseling, and teaching. Some work in museums; others have entered politics; still others have careers in private industry or in human services as self-employed professionals.

Institution:	**City College of New York**
Unit:	African and Afro-American Studies
Address:	160 Convent Avenue
	New York, NY 10031

Institution:	**Bronx Community College**
Unit:	Black Studies Program
Contact Person:	Glen Ray
Address:	Bronx, NY 10453

Institution:	**Fordham University**
Unit:	Afro-American Studies
Contact Person:	Claud Mangum
Address:	644 Commonwealth Avenue
	Bronx, NY 10458

Institution:	**Lehman College-CUNY**
Unit:	Black Studies Program
Contact Person:	James A. Jervis, Director
Address:	Bronx, NY 10468
Phone:	(212) 960-7803

Institution:	**New York City Technical College**
Institution Type:	Public, 2 year
Unit:	African American Studies Department
Contact Person:	Diane Wilson, Chair
Address:	300 Jay Street, Room A 643
	Brooklyn, NY 11201
Phone:	(718) 260-5205
Unit Offers:	Minor, classes
Faculty:	3 full-time, 4 part-time
Established:	1970
Special Features:	This is an African American and Caribbean Studies curriculum offered in an urban technical college. Courses in the humanities, performing arts, and

social sciences are used to fulfill requirements leading toward a degree (A.A. or A.S.) in Liberal Arts.

Institution:	**Brooklyn College-CUNY**
Institution Type:	Public, 4 year + graduate
Unit:	Africana Studies Department
Contact Person:	Regine Latortue, Chair
Address:	2900 Bedford Avenue
	Brooklyn, NY 11210
Phone:	(718) 951-5597/5598
Fax:	(718) 951-4707
Unit Offers:	Major, minor, classes
Degrees Offered:	B.A. Africana Studies with emphasis on (1) history and political science; or (2) literature, culture and the arts; or (3) society and the economy
Majors Per Year:	10
Minors:	12–15
Faculty:	6 full-time, 3–6 part-time
Established:	1970

Institution:	**Medgar Evers College**
Unit:	Black Studies
Contact Person:	Edna Edet
Address:	1150 Carroll Street
	Brooklyn, NY 11225

Institution:	**Queens College**
Unit:	Africana Institute
Contact Person:	W. Ofuatey Kodjoe
Address:	6530 Kissena Boulevard
	Flushing, NY 11367

Institution:	**York College-CUNY**
Institution Type:	Public, 4 year
Unit:	Afro-American Studies Program
Contact Person:	Celestine Anderson, Coordinator
Address:	94-20 Guy R. Brewer Boulevard
	Jamaica, NY 11451
Phone:	(718) 262-2617/2605
Fax:	(718) 262-2027

Unit Offers:	Major, classes
Degrees Offered:	B.A.
Minors:	5
Faculty:	2
Established:	1972

Institution:	**Adelphi University**
Institution Type:	Private, 4 year
Unit:	Center for African American Studies Programs
Contact Person:	Robert F. Hood, Director
Address:	Harvey Hall, Room 219
	Garden City, NY 11530
Phone:	(516) 877-4980
Fax	(516) 877-4097
Unit Offers:	Minor
Minors Per Year:	2
Faculty:	4
Established:	1969
Special Features:	This program emphasizes Afro-Caribbean culture, literature, religion, and anthropology as well as Afro-American. These are undergraduate programs.

Institution:	**Nassau Community College**
Institution Type:	Public, 2 year
Unit:	African American Studies Department
Contact Person:	Kenneth Jenkins, Chair
Address:	Garden City, NY 11530
Phone:	(516) 572-7158
Unit Offers:	Major, classes
Degrees Offered:	A.A.
Majors Per Year:	20
Faculty:	7 (full-time and adjunct)
Established:	1972
Special Features:	Special features include African and African American culture, history, and literature courses; theatre, dance, and music performance courses; community outreach; and a teacher certificate program is pending.

Institution:	**Hofstra University**
Institution Type:	Private, 4 year
Unit:	NOAH Program
Contact Person:	Dean Frank Whelan Smith, Assistant Provost
Address:	Gallon Wing, Room 132
	113 Hofstra University
	Hempstead, NY 11550-1090
Phone:	(516) 463-6976
Unit Offers:	Major, minor, classes
Degrees Offered:	B.A. African Studies

Institution:	**State University of New York-Stony Brook**
Unit:	Africana Studies Program
Contact Person:	Amiri Baraka, Director
Address:	Stony Brook, NY 11790
Phone:	(516) 632-7470

Institution:	**State University of New York-Albany**
Institution Type:	Public, 4 year
Unit:	Department of Africana Studies
Contact Person:	Joseph A. Sarfoh, Acting Chair
Address:	1400 Washington Avenue BA 115
	Albany, NY 12222
Phone:	(518) 442-4730
Fax:	(518) 442-2569
Unit Offers:	Major, minor
Degrees Offered:	M.A.
Majors Per Year:	85
Minors:	60
Faculty:	8 full-time, 6 adjunct
Established:	1971
Special Features:	In addition to a large number of students majoring in African and African American Studies, the department also offers a master's degree in Africana Studies.

Institution:	**State University of New York-New Paltz**
Institution Type:	Public, 4 year + graduate
Unit:	Department of Black Studies
Contact Person:	Margaret Wade Lewis, Chair

Address:	College Hall F-105
	New Paltz, NY 12561
Phone:	(914) 257-2760
Fax:	(914) 257-3009
Unit Offers:	Major, minor
Degrees Offered:	B.A. Liberal Arts; B.S. Elementary Education
Majors Per Year:	60
Minors:	40
Faculty:	5 full-time, 7 part-time
Established:	1969
Special Features:	The department offers Voice of Unity Gospel Choir, New Day Ensemble Theatre Group, *Eghart Newspaper,* and the Black Studies Student Organization.

Institution:	**Vassar College**
Institution Type:	Private, 4 year
Unit:	Program in Africana Studies
Contact Person:	Joyce Bickerstaff, Director
Address:	P.O. Box 262
	Poughkeepsie, NY 12601
Phone:	(914) 437-7490
Fax:	(914) 437-7187
Unit Offers:	Major, minor, classes
Degrees Offered:	B.A. Africana Studies
Majors Per Year:	8–10
Minors:	2–3
Faculty:	7
Established:	1969
Special Features:	Students who major in Africana Studies are encouraged to participate in a cross-cultural field research and study experience in Africa, the Afro-Caribbean, or in the southern region of the United States at one of four historic black colleges: Fisk University, Howard University, Spelman College, and Morehouse College. The program also offers the Third World Festival Events of Arts and Culture.

Institution:	**State University of New York-Plattsburgh**
Unit:	Afro-American Studies
Address:	Plattsburgh, NY 12901

Institution:	**State University of New York-Cortland**
Institution Type:	Public, 4 year + graduate
Unit:	African American Studies Program
Contact Person:	Samuel L. Kelley
Address:	Cortland, NY 13045
Phone:	(607) 753-4201
Unit Offers:	Major, minor
Degrees Offered:	B.A., B.S. African American Studies
Special Features:	Students majoring in AAS may concentrate in Africa and African American history, African American sociological, political, and community development, African American literature, and the humanities. They may also qualify for provisional certification in secondary social studies.

Institution:	**State University of New York-Oswego**
Unit:	Afro-American Studies
Address:	Oswego, NY 13126

Institution:	**Syracuse University**
Unit:	Afro-American Studies
Contact Person:	Harry Morgan
Address:	735 Ostrom Avenue
	Syracuse, NY 13244

Institution:	**Colgate University**
Institution Type:	Private, 4 year
Unit:	Africana and Latin American Studies Program
Contact Person:	Roy S. Bryce-Laporte, Director
Address:	13 Oak Drive
	Hamilton, NY 13346-1398
Phone:	(315) 824-7546
Fax:	(315) 824-7726
E-mail:	mkeys@center.colgate.edu
Unit Offers:	Major, minor, classes
Degrees Offered:	B.A. Africana Studies; B.A. Latin American Studies

Majors Per Year:	15–18
Minors:	5–6
Faculty:	38
Established:	1983
Special Features:	This is an interdisciplinary program with majors and minors in Africana and in Latin American Studies. Three minors are offered: African, African and African American, and Latin American Studies. Soon a Caribbean Studies minor and study group will be offered. There are also study groups going to Central America/Mexico, the Dominican Republic, and Africa.

Institution:	**State University of New York-Oneonta**
Unit:	Department of Black Studies
Contact Person:	Rashid Hamid
Address:	Oneonta, NY 13820

Institution:	**State University of New York-Binghamton University**
Institution Type:	Public, 4 year + graduate
Unit:	Department of Africana Studies
Contact Person:	Isidore Okpewho, Chair
Address:	Binghamton, NY 13902
Phone:	(607) 777-2635/2636
Fax:	(607) 777-2280
Unit Offers:	Major, minor
Degrees Offered:	B.A. Africana Studies
Majors Per Year:	35
Minors:	30
Faculty:	12
Established:	1970
Special Features:	Previously called the Department of Afro-American and African Studies, the department has just been rechristened the Department of Africana Studies in line with our desire to adopt a unified or synoptic approach to the study of all peoples of African descent across the world (especially the African and the Atlantic diasporas).

Institution:	**State University of New York-Buffalo**
Institution Type:	Public, 4 year
Unit:	African American Studies Department
Contact Person:	Lynn R. Taylor
Address:	732 Clemen Hall
	Buffalo, NY 14260
Phone:	(716) 645-2082/2083
Fax:	(716) 645-5976
E-mail:	amslynn@ubvm.buffalo.edu
Unit Offers:	Major, minor, classes
Degrees Offered:	B.A. and B.A. (honors) in the Faculty of Arts and Letters
Faculty:	7, 7 adjunct faculty
Established:	1969
Special Features:	African American Studies is a unique academic unit consisting of three interrelated geo-historical and cultural areas of study: Africa, the Caribbean, and African America. Through the study of the histories and cultures of peoples of African descent, students address interdisciplinary issues facing African peoples in the diaspora from the vantage point of the African American experience.

Institution:	**State University of New York-Brockport**
Institution Type:	Public, 4 year
Unit:	Department of African and Afro-American Studies
Contact Person:	Ena L. Farley, Chair
Address:	Brockport, NY 14420
Phone:	(716) 395-2470
Fax:	(716) 395-2172
E-mail:	efarley@acsprl.acs.brockport.edu
Unit Offers:	Major, minor
Degrees Offered:	B.A., minor
Majors Per Year:	20
Minors:	23
Faculty:	4 faculty, 3 adjuncts, 4 regularly cross-listed courses from other units
Special Features:	The Department of African and Afro-American Studies affirms the scholarly importance of stud-

ies relating to the African, African American, and Caribbean presence in the world. It seeks to promote the kind of analysis that emphasizes the African and African American perspective, which includes the contributions of peoples of African descent to world civilization and which sensitizes all students to many realities of the lives of persons of African descent.

The department shares with the college a global thrust. Its teaching, research, and service explore the impact of several political, economic, and social issues on the African continent (food insecurity, human rights violations, development and underdevelopment, political stability, and mismanagement of national resources, to name a few), and deal with the impact on the world of the African aesthetic (dance, literature, music, and art). The department calls attention to the highlighted issues through ongoing teaching, as well as through a series of forums, a Martin Luther King Faculty Seminar, films, videotapes, a newsletter, research, and community involvement.

Institution:	**Hoburt and William Smith Colleges**
Institution Type:	Private, 4 year
Unit:	Africana and Latino Studies Program
Contact Person:	Professor Jimenez, Director
Address:	Geneva, NY 14456
Phone:	(315) 781-3791/3793
Fax:	(315) 781-3793
Unit Offers:	Major, minor, classes
Degrees Offered:	B.A. African-American Studies, African Studies, Africana Studies, Latin American Studies, Latino Studies
Majors Per Year:	3
Minors:	2
Faculty:	1 half-time (others teach within their departments)
Established:	1976

Institution:	**Colgate Rochester Divinity School**
Institution Type:	Private
Unit:	Program of Black Church Studies
Contact Person:	Walter Glucker, Dean
Address:	1100 South Goodman Street
	Rochester, NY 14620-2592
Phone:	(716) 271-1320
Unit Offers:	Classes
Faculty:	3
Established:	1969
Special Features:	The program is a part of the degree requirements for the Master of Divinity Degree in Theology. Special features include the Howard Thurman Papers Project; the National Resource Center for the Development of Ethical Leadership from the Black Church Tradition (NRC); and the Program of Education and Action for Responsible Leadership (PEARL).

Institution:	**Cornell University**
Unit:	Africana Studies and Research Center
Contact Person:	Locksley Edmondson, Director
Address:	310 Triphammer Road
	Ithaca, NY 14850
Phone:	(607) 255-5218
Fax:	(607) 255-0784
Special Features:	The Africana Studies and Research Center is concerned with the examination of the history, culture, intellectual development, and social organization of black people and cultures in the Americas, Africa, and the Caribbean. Its program is structured from an interdisciplinary and comparative perspective and presents a variety of subjects in focal areas of history, literature, social sciences, and Swahili languages including Swahili, Yoruba, and Mandinka.

The center offers a unique and specialized program of study that leads to an undergraduate degree through the College of Arts and Sciences and a graduate degree, the Master of Professional

Studies (African and Afro-American), through the university's Graduate School. A student may major in Africana studies; however, another attractive alternative is the center's joint major program. This program enables the student to complete a major in any of the other disciplines represented in the college while at the same time fulfilling requirements for a major in Africana Studies.

NORTH CAROLINA

Institution:	**Bennett College**
Unit:	Afro-American Studies
Contact Person:	P. E. Adotey
Address:	900 E. Washington Street
	Greensboro, NC 27401

Institution:	**University of North Carolina at Greensboro**
Institution Type:	Public, 4 year + graduate
Unit:	African American Studies Program
Contact Person:	Angela Rhone, Chair
Address:	200 Foust Building
	Greensboro, NC 27412-5001
Phone:	(919) 334-5673
Unit Offers:	Minor, classes
Faculty:	2
Established:	1985

Institution:	**University of North Carolina at Chapel Hill**
Institution Type:	Public, 4 year + graduate
Unit:	African and Afro-American Studies Curriculum
Contact Person:	Julius E. Nyang'oro, Chair
Address:	CB# 3395
	Chapel Hill, NC 27599-3395
Phone:	(919) 966-5496
Fax:	(919) 962-2694
Unit Offers:	Major, minor, classes
Degrees Offered:	B.A. African Studies; B.A. Afro-American Studies
Majors Per Year:	20

Minors:	30+
Faculty:	8
Established:	1969
Special Features:	The undergraduate curricula in African and Afro-American Studies are interdisciplinary programs leading to the B.A. degree administered through the College of Arts and Sciences at UNC-CH. The aim of the curriculum is to enable students to examine the experiences of Afro-Americans and the cultures of Africa.

Institution:	**Saint Augustine's College**
Unit:	Black Studies
Contact Person:	Julius F. Nimmons
Address:	1315 Oakwood Avenue
	Raleigh, NC 27610

Institution:	**Shaw University**
Institution Type:	Private, 4 year
Unit:	African American Studies Minor Program
Contact Person:	Hazel A. Ervin, Chair
Address:	111 E. South Street
	Raleigh, NC 27611
Phone:	(919) 546-8254
Fax:	(919) 546-8301
Unit Offers:	Minor
Minors:	10
Faculty:	6
Established:	1993
Special Features:	Courses used to complete a minor are taught in various departments (English, history, theatre, music, and philosophy).

Institution:	**North Carolina Central University**
Institution Type:	Public, 4 year + graduate
Unit:	History and Social Science Department
Contact Person:	Sylvia M. Jacobs, Chair
Address:	Durham, NC 27707
Phone:	(919) 560-6271
Fax:	(919) 560-5361

Unit Offers:	Major, minor, certificate, classes
Degrees Offered:	B.A. History and Social Science; M.A. History
Majors Per Year:	225
Minors:	20
Faculty:	15
Established:	1948
Special Features:	This department offers concentrations in African American history, African history, and African diasporic history.

Institution:	**Duke University**
Institution Type:	Private, 4 year
Unit:	African and Afro-American Studies Program
Contact Person:	George C. Wright, Director
	or Edwinda Daye, Program Coordinator
Address:	408 Old Chem
	Box 90252
	Durham, NC 27710-0252
Unit Offers:	Major, certificate
Majors Per Year:	18–20
Faculty:	25
Special Features:	Students may choose one of the following two options: a North American focus or an African/ Caribbean focus. Students who are not majoring in African and Afro-American Studies may complete a certificate in the field by satisfactorily completing five courses.

Institution:	**University of North Carolina**
Unit:	Black Studies Center
Contact Person:	Bertha Maxwell
Address:	Charlotte, NC 28233

Institution:	**Fayetteville State University**
Unit:	Black Studies
Contact Person:	Shia-Ling Lio
Address:	1200 Murchison Road
	Fayetteville, NC 28301

Institution:	**Appalachian State University**
Institution Type:	Public, 4 year
Unit:	College of Arts and Sciences/Black Studies Minor
Contact Person:	Donald W. Sink, Dean
Address:	Boone, NC 28608
Phone:	(704) 262-3078
Unit Offers:	Minor
Minors Per Year:	10
Faculty:	6–10
Established:	Early 1980s

OHIO

Institution:	**Ohio Wesleyan University**
Institution Type:	Private, 4 year
Unit:	Department of Black World Studies
Contact Person:	Emmanuel K. Twesigye
Address:	Delaware, OH 43015
Phone:	(614) 368-3827
Unit Offers:	Major, minor, classes
Degrees Offered:	B.A.
Majors Per Year:	8
Minors:	10
Faculty:	6
Established:	1970
Special Features:	The program is divided into four components: Africa, African-American, cross-cultural, and integrative theory. It prepares students for entry into law school, graduate school, theology/ministry, social services, and community leadership. The program publishes *Zumari: A Journal of Black World Studies*.

Institution:	**Denison University**
Institution Type:	Private, 4 year
Unit:	Center for Black Studies
Contact Person:	John L. Jackson, Director
Address:	Granville, OH 43023

Phone:	(614) 587-6594
Fax:	(614) 587-6417
Unit Offers:	Major, minor, classes
Degrees Offered:	B.A.
Majors Per Year:	4
Minors:	4
Faculty:	14 part-time
Established:	1970
Special Features:	This center enjoys the distinction of having established a minority/women studies general education requirement in 1978, touted by the *Chronicle of Higher Education* as the first college in the country to establish such a requirement.

Institution:	**Ohio State University**
Institution Type:	Public, 4 year + graduate
Unit:	Department of Black Studies
Contact Person:	Ted McDaniel, Chair
Address:	486 University Hall
	230 North Oval Mall
	Columbus, OH 43210
Phone:	(614) 292-3700
Unit Offers:	Major, minor
Degrees Offered:	B.A. African American Studies and African Studies; M.A. African American Studies and African Studies
Majors Per Year:	30
Minors:	90
Established:	1972
Special Features:	The department offers a comprehensive interdisciplinary curriculum that includes courses in literature, music, art, history, theatre, economics, dance, psychology, sociology, community development, geography, and political sciences. The department offers courses in five African languages and cultures. The total program is designed to acquaint students with the social and intellectual experiences of African people throughout the world.

Institution:	**University of Toledo**
Unit:	Minority Affairs
Contact Person:	Leon Carter
Address:	2801 Bancroft Street
	Toledo, OH 43606

Institution:	**Muskingum College**
Unit:	Afro-American Affairs
Contact Person:	Dorothy Belenga
Address:	New Concord, OH 43762

Institution:	**Oberlin College**
Institution Type:	Private, 4 year
Unit:	Department of African American Studies
Contact Person:	Adrienne Jones, Chair
Address:	Rice Hall 214
	Oberlin, OH 44074
Phone:	(216) 775-8923
Fax:	(216) 775-8124
Unit Offers:	Major
Majors Per Year:	35
Minors:	100
Faculty:	6

Institution:	**Case Western Reserve University**
Unit:	Afro-American Studies
Address:	11075 East Boulevard
	Cleveland, OH 44106

Institution:	**Cleveland State University**
Unit:	Black Studies Program
Contact Person:	Howard A. Mims, Director
Address:	2121 Euclid Avenue
	U.C. 103
	Cleveland, OH 44115
Phone:	(216) 687-5461
Fax:	(216) 687-5446
Unit Offers:	Minor
Faculty:	36
Established:	1969

Institution:	**Cuyahoga Community College**
Institution Type:	Public, 2 year
Unit:	Martin Luther King Center for Human Relations
Contact Person:	Dorothy Salem, Professor
Address:	2900 Community College Avenue
	Cleveland, OH 44115
Phone:	(216) 987-4515/4527
Fax:	(216) 987-4404
Special Features:	The resource center has print and nonprint materials and serves as the center for multicultural presentations (brown bag lectures at lunch time). The center also has an African Heritage Program that issues a certificate.

Institution:	**Ohio University-Cleveland**
Unit:	Center for Afro-American Studies
Contact Person:	Francis C. Childs
Address:	Cleveland, OH 44115

Institution:	**Hiram College**
Unit:	Black Studies Program
Contact Person:	Ronald Daniels
Address:	Hiram, OH 44234

Institution:	**Kent State University**
Institution Type:	Public, 4 year + graduate
Unit:	Department of Pan-African Studies
Address:	117 Oscar Ritchie Hall
	Center of Pan-African Culture
	Kent, OH 44242-0001
Phone:	(216) 672-2300/7938
Fax:	(216) 672-4837
Unit Offers:	Major, minor, certificate, classes
Degrees Offered:	B.A. Pan-African Studies; Minor in Pan-African Studies
Majors Per Year:	4
Minors:	3
Faculty:	6 full-time, 3 adjunct, 3 assistant professors, 5 part-time
Established:	1979

| Special Features: | The department offers educational support ser-vices, the Center of Pan-African Culture, the Institute for African American Affairs, an African language program (Kiswahili I, II, III, IV), a communication skills and arts program (English), and African community theatre. |

Institution:	**University of Akron**
Institution Type:	Public, 4 year
Unit:	Black Cultural Center
Unit Type:	Program
Contact Person:	W. Neal Holmes
	William Lewis, III, Director
Address:	East Hall 202
	Afro-American Program Studies
	Akron, OH 44325-1801
Phone:	(216) 972-7030
Fax:	(216) 972-6990
Unit Offers:	Certificate, classes
Faculty:	1
Established:	1973
Special Features:	This is an Afro-American Studies Program with courses in other disciplines. The Black Cultural Center also has programs outside the classroom.

Institution:	**Youngstown State University**
Institution Type:	Public, 4 year + graduate
Unit:	Black Studies Program
Contact Person:	Sarah Brown-Clark, Director
Address:	410 Wick Avenue
	Youngstown, OH 44555-0001
Phone:	(216) 742-3097
Fax:	(216) 742-1998
Unit Offers:	Major, minor
Majors Per Year:	10
Minors:	25
Faculty:	5
Established:	1970
Special Features:	The purpose of this interdisciplinary major is to facilitate academic investigation and analysis of

the historical, social, and aesthetic impact of people of African descent on American society and the world. It also provides for the systematic study of problems confronting the modern multiethnic world.

Institution:	**The College of Wooster**
Institution Type:	Private, 4 year
Unit:	Black Studies Program
Contact Person:	Josephine Wright, Chair
Address:	Department of Music
	Wooster, OH 44691
Phone:	(216) 263-2044
Unit Offers:	Major, minor
Degrees Offered:	B.A.
Majors Per Year:	4–5
Minors:	10–13
Faculty:	5, adjunct staff
Special Features:	The Black Studies curriculum is designed to provide students with an Afrocentric perspective on the history and culture of African American people. It aims to help them gain insight and understanding of the experiences of black women and men in today's world and develop the ability to examine, analyze, and interpret these experiences within the context of a liberal arts program. To this end, the curriculum is interdisciplinary in focus inasmuch as the study of the black experience cannot be compartmentalized within traditional academic disciplines. The program is administered by the Director of Black Studies and the Black Studies Curriculum Committee.

Institution:	**Heidelberg College**
Unit:	Black Studies
Contact Person:	Leslie Fishel
Address:	Tiffin, OH 44883

Institution:	**Miami University**
Institution Type:	Public, 4 year + graduate

Unit:	Black World Studies Program
Contact Person:	Rodney D. Coates
Address:	157 Upham Hall
	Oxford, OH 45056
Phone:	(513) 529-1235
Fax:	(513) 529-3841
Unit Offers:	Major, minor, classes
Degrees Offered:	B.S. Black World Studies
Majors Per Year:	20
Minors:	20
Faculty:	15
Established:	1976

Institution:	**University of Cincinnati**
Unit:	Afro-American Studies Department
Address:	Cincinnati, OH 45221
Phone:	(513) 556-0350

Institution:	**Central State University**
Unit:	Black Studies
Contact Person:	Carolyn Wright
Address:	Wilberforce, OH 45384

Institution:	**Wright State University**
Unit:	Black Cultural Resource Center
Contact Person:	Pamela Pritchard
Address:	Dayton, OH 45435

Institution:	**University of Dayton**
Unit:	Afro-American Studies
Contact Person:	Faith E. Johnson
Address:	Dayton, OH 45469

Institution:	**Ohio University**
Unit:	African Studies Program
Contact Person:	William Stephen Howard, Director
Address:	Athens, OH 45701
Phone:	(614) 593-1834

OKLAHOMA

Institution:	**University of Oklahoma**
Institution Type:	Public, 4 year + graduate
Unit:	African and African American Studies Program
Contact Person:	Charles E. Butler, Director
Address:	804 Dale Hall Tower
	Lindsay and Elms Street
	Norman, OK 73019
Phone:	(405) 325-2327
Fax:	(405) 325-0842
Unit Offers:	Major, minor
Degrees Offered:	B.A. African and African American Studies
Faculty:	22
Year Established:	1978
Special Features:	This program, though established in 1978, was approved to offer a major and minor in January of 1994. It is an interdisciplinary program with the bulk of the courses offered by established departments.

OREGON

Institution:	**Reed College**
Unit:	Black Studies
Contact Person:	W. H. McClendon
Address:	3203 SE Woodstock Boulevard
	Portland, OR 97202

Institution:	**Portland State University**
Institution Type:	Public, 4 year + graduate
Unit:	Black Studies Department and Center
Contact Person:	Darrell Millner, Chair
Address:	P.O. Box 751
	Portland, OR 97207-0751
Phone:	(503) 725-3472
Fax:	(503) 725-4882
Unit Offers:	Minor, certificate, classes

Faculty:	4 full-time, 6 associated in other departments
Established:	1969
Special Features:	This is an interdisciplinary program with overseas research and study opportunities and an innovative undergraduate curriculum.

Institution:	**University of Oregon**
Unit:	Black Studies
Contact Person:	Monica H. Gordon
Address:	Eugene, OR 97403

PENNSYLVANIA

Institution:	**Allegheny Community College**
Unit:	Black Studies
Address:	808 Ridge Avenue
	Pittsburgh, PA 15212

Institution:	**Chatham College**
Institution Type:	Private, 4 year
Unit:	African/African American Studies Program
Contact Person:	Emma Lucas, Associate Vice President for Academic Affairs
Address:	Woodland Road
	Library—3rd floor
	Pittsburgh, PA 15232
Phone:	(412) 365-1207
Fax:	(412) 365-1505
E-mail:	lucas@brumpy.chatham.edu
Unit Offers:	Minor, classes
Minors Per Year:	3
Faculty:	1
Established:	1970
Special Features:	A study of the history, experience, and literature of peoples of African descent, this program is designed to foster understanding of the culture of a significant segment of the population.

Institution:	**University of Pittsburgh**
Institution Type:	Public, 4 year + graduate
Unit:	Black Studies Department
Contact Person:	Brenda F. Berrian, Chair
Address:	3701 Forbes Quadrangle
	Pittsburgh, PA 15260
Phone:	(412) 648-7540
Fax:	(412) 648-7214
E-mail:	bberrian@vms.cis.pitt.edu
	bjgrier@vms.cis.pitt.edu
Unit Offers:	Major
Degrees Offered:	B.S., B.A.
Majors Per Year:	45
Minors:	70
Faculty:	10
Established:	1969
Special Features:	The department has an interdisciplinary curriculum in the humanities and social sciences on African American, African, and Caribbean experience.

Institution:	**Allegheny College**
Unit:	Black Studies
Address:	Meadville, PA 16335

Institution:	**Pennsylvania State University**
Institution Type:	Public, 4 year + graduate
Unit:	African/African American Studies Department
Contact Person:	David McBride, Chair
Address:	236 Grange Building
	University Park, PA 16802
Phone:	(814) 863-4243
Unit Offers:	Major, minor
Degrees Offered:	B.A. African/African American Studies
Majors Per Year:	3
Minors:	20
Faculty:	2
Established:	1973

Institution:	**Dickson College**
Unit:	Afro-American Studies
Contact Person:	James Cox
Address:	Carlisle, PA 17013
Institution:	**Pennsylvania State University-Middletown**
Unit:	Afro-American Studies
Address:	Capital Campus, Route 230
	Middletown, PA 17057
Institution:	**Shippensburg State College**
Unit:	Afro-American Studies
Address:	Shippensburg, PA 17257
Institution:	**Gettysburg College**
Unit:	Black Studies
Contact Person:	Janet Gemmill
Address:	Box 2068
	Gettysburg, PA 17325
Institution:	**Haverford College**
Unit:	Black Studies
Address:	Haverford, PA 19041
Institution:	**Swarthmore College**
Unit:	Black Cultural Center
Contact Person:	Leandre Jackson
Address:	Swarthmore, PA 19081
Institution:	**University of Pennsylvania**
Institution Type:	Private, 4 year + graduate
Unit:	Afro-American Studies Program
Contact Person:	John W. Roberts, Director
Address:	204 Bennett Hall
	Philadelphia, PA 19104
Phone:	(215) 898-4965
Fax:	(215) 573-2052
Unit Offers:	Major, minor
Degrees Offered:	B.A.
Majors Per Year:	10
Minors:	25

Faculty:	20
Established:	1972

Institution:	**Temple University**
Institution Type:	Public, 4 year + graduate
Unit:	African American Studies Department
Contact Person:	M. Asante, Chair
Address:	809 Gladfelter Hall
	Philadelphia, PA 19122
Phone:	(215) 204-3451
Fax:	(215) 204-3731
Unit Offers:	Major, minor, classes
Degrees Offered:	B.A., M.A., Ph.D. African American Studies
Majors Per Year:	40
Minors:	30
Faculty:	16
Established:	1973
Special Features:	The department sustains a full Afrocentric analysis of African phenomena. The program provides eighteen teaching assistantships and two fellowships.

Institution:	**Cheyney University of Pennsylvania**
Unit:	Afro-American Studies
Contact Person:	Edward Richards
Address:	Cheyney, PA 19319

Institution:	**Lincoln University**
Unit:	Institute for Black Studies, INA
Address:	Lincoln University, PA 19352

Institution:	**West Chester State College**
Unit:	Afro-American Studies
Address:	West Chester, PA 19383

RHODE ISLAND

Institution:	**University of Rhode Island**
Unit:	African and Afro-American Studies Program

Contact Person:	Cynthia M. Hamilton, Director
Address:	Kingston, RI 02881
Phone:	(401) 792-2536

Institution:	**Rhode Island College**
Institution Type:	Public, 4 year + graduate
Unit:	African/Afro-American Studies Program
Contact Person:	Richard Lobban, Director
Address:	Providence, RI 02908
Phone:	(401) 456-8784
Fax:	(401) 456-8379
E-mail:	faclobban@ric.edu
Unit Offers:	Major, minor
Degrees Offered:	B.A.; individualized M.A.
Majors Per Year:	5–10
Minors:	10–20
Faculty:	15
Established:	1971

Institution:	**Brown University**
Institution Type:	Private, 4 year + graduate
Unit:	Afro-American Studies Program
Contact Person:	Paget Henry, Director
Address:	155 Angell Street, 2nd Floor
	Box 1904
	Providence, RI 02912
Phone:	(401) 863-3137
Fax:	(401) 863-3700
Majors Per Year:	10–16
Faculty:	10
Established:	1968
Special Features:	The Afro-American Studies Program focuses on the scholarly exploration of the history, culture, psychology, and literature of Afro-Americans, embracing North, Central and South America and the Caribbean and their historic and present linkages to continental Africa. The program's course offerings and other academic activities are supplemented by extracurricular activities that emphasize the global reach and implications of Afro-

America without losing sight of the specific concerns of Afro-America-U.S.A. An important outgrowth of the global nature of the program's concerns is the emphasis placed on the acquisition of competency in those languages in addition to English that are spoken in the Afro-Americas—French, Portuguese, and Spanish. Since all these languages are taught at Brown, concentrators are strongly urged to acquire competency, that is, a minimum of two semesters' study, to enable them to avail themselves of the extensive written material on the Afro-Americas available in these languages. While no continental African language is presently offered at Brown, students who study abroad and acquire certified competency in any African language could petition the program for credit.

SOUTH CAROLINA

Institution:	**South Carolina State College**
Unit:	Black Studies
Address:	Orangeburg, SC 29115

Institution:	**University of South Carolina**
Institution Type:	Public, 4 year + graduate
Unit:	African American Studies Program
Contact Person:	Thomas E. Terrill
Address:	History Department
	Gambrell Hall
	Columbia, SC 29208
Phone:	(803) 777-7248/6026
Fax:	(803) 777-4494
Unit Offers:	Major, minor
Degrees Offered:	B.A.
Majors Per Year:	15
Minors Per Year:	25
Faculty:	3
Established:	1971

Institution:	**Clemson University**
Institution Type:	Public, 4 year
Unit:	African American Studies (AAS) Minor
Contact Person:	H. Lewis Suggs
Address:	P.O. Box 1168
	Clemson, SC 29633
Phone:	(803) 656-5372
Fax:	(803) 656-5377
Unit Offers:	Minor
Faculty:	8
Established:	1994
Special Features:	Fifteen hours are required for the minor.

TENNESSEE

Institution:	**Austin Peay State University**
Institution Type:	Public
Unit:	African American Studies Program
Contact Person:	A. J. Stovall
Address:	P.O. Box 4715
	Clarksville, TN 37044
Phone:	(615) 648-6274
Fax:	(615) 648-7475
Unit Offers:	Minor
Faculty:	6
Special Features:	At present, only a minor in African American Studies is offered. The program is a unique opportunity for students who desire a structured program of study. The program seeks to strengthen the ties between the university and the African American community through its programs and activities. The program consists of twenty-four hours of courses, including required courses in Contemporary Black Thought and Movements; Afro-American Writers; and African American Families in the United States. In the Study Abroad in Africa Program, a student may earn six semester hours of credit.

Institution:	**Southern Methodist University**
Unit:	African American Studies Program
Contact Person:	Kenneth Hamilton, Director
Address:	Dallas, TX 75275
Phone:	(214) 692-2195

Institution:	**Stephen F. Austin State University**
Unit:	Afro-American Studies
Address:	Nacogdoches, TX 75962

Institution:	**University of Houston-University Park**
Institution Type:	Public, 4 year + graduate
Unit:	African American Studies Program
Contact Person:	Linda Reed, Director
Address:	4800 Calhoun Road
	Houston, TX 77204-3783
Phone:	(713) 743-2811
Fax:	(713) 743-2818
Unit Offers:	Minor, classes
Minors Per Year:	60
Faculty:	15
Established:	1968
Special Features:	The African American Studies Program's mission is reflected in the larger vision of the University of Houston's commitment to increase both the appreciation of the contributions of diverse cultures and the regard of individual differences. AAS develops, promotes, and enhances the educational opportunities congruent with such a society through teaching, research, and community service projects.

Institution:	**Prairie View College**
Unit:	Black Studies
Contact Person:	Howard J. Jones
Address:	Box 2545
	Prairie View, TX 77443

Institution:	University of Texas at Austin
Institution Type:	Public
Unit:	Center for African and African American Studies
Contact Person:	Sheila S. Walker, Director
Address:	Jester Center A232A
	Austin, TX 78705
Phone:	(512) 471-1784
Unit Offers:	Major, minor
Degrees Offered:	Bachelor degree offered with special emphasis in any academic discipline, primarily in liberal arts; also in communications, natural sciences, social work, and education
Majors Per Year:	8
Faculty:	25
Established:	1969
Special Features:	The University of Texas/University of Ghana Exchange Program was established in 1993 and implemented in fall 1993. The center established and offers substantial support to the Graduate Program in Anthropology of the African Diaspora; this program is unique in the United States, and, possibly, in the world.

Institution:	Abilene Christian University
Unit:	Afro-American Studies
Contact Person:	B. F. Speck
Address:	Box 8245
	Abilene, TX 79601

UTAH

Institution:	University of Utah
Unit:	African American Studies Program
Contact Person:	Wilfred D. Samuels, Director
Address:	Salt Lake City, UT 84112
Phone:	(801) 581-5206

VIRGINIA

Institution:	**George Mason University**
Unit:	African American Studies Program
Contact Person:	Marilyn Sanders Mobley, Director
Address:	Fairfax, VA 22030
Phone:	(703) 993-1199

Institution:	**University of Virginia**
Institution Type:	Public, 4 year + graduate
Unit:	Afro-American and African Studies Program
Contact Person:	Adria LaViolette, Director
Address:	Carter G. Woodson Institute for Afro-American and African Studies
	1512 Jefferson Park Avenue
	Charlottesville, VA 22903
Phone:	(804) 924-8892
Fax:	(804) 924-3109
Unit Offers:	Major, minor, classes
Degrees Offered:	B.A. (an interdisciplinary program)
Majors Per Year:	20
Minors:	5
Faculty:	40
Established:	1981
Special Features:	The major consists of two introductory core courses, four elective courses from any contributing departments, and five courses from a single department, the latter providing a disciplinary focus for the major. The program provides a broad range of courses each semester, allowing students to focus on African Studies, Afro-American Studies, or to remain generalized between the two areas.

Institution:	**Virginia Commonwealth University**
Institution Type:	Public, 4 year + graduate
Unit:	African American Studies Program
Contact Person:	Ann Creighton-Zollar, Interim Director
Address:	312 N. Shafer Street
	Richmond, VA 23284-2509

Phone:	(804) 367-1384
Fax:	(804) 367-1027
E-mail:	acreight@cabell.vcu.edu
Unit Offers:	Minor, classes
Degrees Offered:	Minor in African American Studies
Minors Per Year:	40
Faculty:	25
Established:	1971

Institution:	**Hampton University**
Institution Type:	Private, 4 year + graduate
Unit:	History Department
Address:	126 Martin Luther King Hall
	Hampton, VA 23668
Phone:	(804) 727-5349
Unit Offers:	Major, minor
Degrees Offered:	B.A. History; B.A. History with Teacher Education Endorsement
Majors Per Year:	80
Faculty:	6 full-time, 12 adjuncts
Special Features:	The department has an active history club, emphases in African American and African history, and is developing a cross-cultural/ international studies emphasis.

Institution:	**Hampden-Sydney College**
Institution Type:	Private, 4 year
Unit:	Afro-American Studies
Contact Person:	George F. Bagby
Address:	English Department
	Hampden-Sydney, VA 23943
Phone:	(804) 223-6247
Fax:	(804) 223-6345
Unit Offers:	Classes
Faculty:	3
Established:	1972
Special Features:	Hampden-Sydney is a small liberal arts college. Although it does not have a program in Afro-American Studies, it offers courses on a regular basis: Introduction to Afro-American Literature

in the English Department (occasionally supple-
mented by advanced courses), plus Black America
and the Civil Rights Movement in the History
Department.

WASHINGTON

Institution:	**Central Washington University**
Unit:	Black Studies
Address:	Ellensburg, WA 98926

Institution:	**Eastern Washington University**
Institution Type:	Public, 4 year + graduate
Unit:	Black Education Program
Contact Person:	Felix Boateng, Director
Address:	Mail Stop 164
	Cheney, WA 99004
Phone:	(509) 359-2205
Fax:	(509) 359-6927
E-mail:	fboateng@ewu.edu
Unit Offers:	Minor, classes
Minors Per Year:	25
Faculty:	4
Established:	1972
Special Features:	The Black Education Program is an academic and student service program in the College of Educa-tion and Human Development. The program's primary objectives and responsibilities are to teach Black Studies courses, conduct research into the black experience, and administer recruiting and retention service for African American stu-dents.

Institution:	**Washington State University**
Institution Type:	Public, 4 year + graduate
Unit:	African American Student Center
Contact Person:	Francyenne Ashley
Address:	Pullman, WA 99164-2326
Phone:	(509) 335-2626

Fax:	(509) 335-8368
Unit Offers:	Major, minor
Faculty:	2

WEST VIRGINIA

Institution:	**West Virginia University**
Institution Type:	Public, 4 year + graduate
Unit:	Center for Black Culture and Research
Contact Person:	Erin Crum, Administrative Secretary
Address:	590 Spruce Street
	P.O. Box 6417
	Morgantown, WV 26506
Phone:	(304) 293-7029
Fax:	(304) 293-2967
Unit Offers:	Certificate, classes
Degrees Offered:	Certificate in Africana Studies through the Africana Studies Program
Certificates Per Year:	10
Faculty:	11
Established:	1987
Special Features:	The African and African-American Studies Certificate Program (AAAS) is sponsored by the Center for Black Culture and Research at West Virginia University. The AAAS Certificate Program is devoted to the exploration and analysis of the history and culture of African people in the United States, the Caribbean, and Africa. It seeks to explore the black experience from an Afrocentric rather than a Eurocentric perspective, to illuminate the contributions of African people to world culture, and to correct a traditional approach to the study of world history that has tended to bypass the African experience.

The objective of the AAAS Certificate Program is to provide comprehensive programs aimed at greater understanding for all people of the African experience. Students from all racial, religious, and ethnic backgrounds are exposed to academic experiences beyond those found in traditional college curricula.

WISCONSIN

Institution:	**University of Wisconsin-Whitewater**
Unit:	Black Studies Program
Contact Person:	Lloyd A. Binagi
Address:	Baker Hall
	Whitewater, WI 53190

Institution:	**University of Wisconsin-Madison**
Institution Type:	4 year + graduate
Unit:	Department of Afro-American Studies
Contact Person:	Nellie McKay, Chair
Address:	4231 Humanities
	455 N. Park Street
	Madison, WI 53706
Phone:	(608) 263-1642
Unit Offers:	Major, classes
Degrees Offered:	B.A., M.A.
Majors Per Year:	30
Faculty:	16
Established:	1969
Special Features:	Undergraduate and M.A. programs in culture, history, and society are offered. The department cooperates with African Studies and diaspora programs with American Indian, Chicano, Asian American, and Comparative Ethnic Studies.

Institution:	**University of Wisconsin-Green Bay**
Unit:	Black Studies
Address:	2420 Nicolet Drive
	Green Bay, WI 54311

ASIAN AMERICAN/PACIFIC ISLAND STUDIES

ARIZONA

Institution:	**Arizona State University**
Institution Type:	Public, 4 year + graduate
Unit:	Center for Asian Studies
Contact Person:	Stephen R. MacKinnon, Director
Address:	Tempe, AZ 84287-1702
Phone:	(602) 965-7184
Fax:	(602) 965-8317
E-mail:	icsrm@asuvm.inre.asu.edu
Unit Offers:	Certificate
Majors Per Year:	30
Faculty:	61
Established:	1966

CALIFORNIA

Institution:	**University of California-Los Angeles**
Institution Type:	Public, 4 year + graduate
Unit:	Asian American Studies Center
Contact Person:	Don T. Nakanishi, Director
Address:	3230 Campbell Hall
	Los Angeles, CA 90024-1546
Phone:	(310) 825-2974
Fax:	(310) 206-9844
E-mail:	iyi4dtn@ucla.mvs.bitnet
Unit Offers:	Major, minor, classes

Degrees Offered:	B.A., M.A. Asian American Studies
Majors Per Year:	150
Minors:	200
Faculty:	25
Established:	1969
Special Features:	This is one of the oldest and most distinguished Asian American Studies Programs in the country, with extensive research, publications, archival collections, teaching, and community outreach activities.

Institution:	**Los Angeles City College**
Unit:	Asian American Studies
Address:	855 N. Vermont Avenue
	Los Angeles, CA 90029

Institution:	**California State University-Dominguez Hills**
Institution Type:	Public, 4 year + graduate
Unit:	Asian American Studies
Contact Person:	Donald Hata, Director
Address:	Department of History
	1000 E. Victoria Street
	Carson, CA 90743
Phone:	(310) 516-3326
Unit Offers:	Major, minor
Degrees Offered:	B.A.
Majors per year:	40
Minors:	80
Faculty:	8
Established:	1972

Institution:	**California State University-Long Beach**
Institution Type:	Public, 4 year + graduate
Unit:	Asian and Asian American Studies Department
Contact Person:	Arnold P. Kaminsky, Chair
Address:	1250 Bellflower Boulevard
	Long Beach, CA 90840
Phone:	(310) 985-4645
Fax:	(310) 985-1535

Unit Offers:	Minor, certificate, classes
Degrees Offered:	B.A. Asian Studies; M.A. Asian Studies; B.A. Japanese; minor in Asian American Studies; certificates in Asian Studies, Japanese, and Asian American Studies
Majors Per Year:	35 (B.A.), 20 (M.A.) in Asian Studies, 3 in Japanese Studies
Minors:	2 in Asian American Studies
Faculty:	8 (2 Asian Studies specialists)
Established:	1987
Special Features:	The department has three major responsibilities: Area Studies (Asian); Ethnic Studies (Asian American); and Language Studies (Chinese, Japanese).

Institution:	**Pasadena City College**
Institution Type:	Public, 2 year
Unit:	Asian American Studies Program
Contact Person:	Susie Ling
	Social Sciences Department
Address:	1570 E. Colorado Boulevard
	Pasadena, CA 91106-2003
Phone:	(818) 585-7248/7335
Unit Offers:	Classes
Faculty:	2

Institution:	**Southwestern College**
Institution Type:	Public, 2 year
Unit:	Asian American Studies
Contact Person:	Felix Tuyay
Address:	900 Otay Lakes Road
	Chula Vista, CA 91910
Unit Offers:	Major, classes
Degrees Offered:	A.A. Asian American Studies

Institution:	**University of California-Irvine**
Institution Type:	Public, 4 year + graduate
Unit:	Asian American Studies
Contact Person:	R. Bin Wong, Director
Address:	Irvine, CA 92717

Institution:	**University of California-Santa Barbara**
Institution Type:	Public, 4 year + graduate
Unit:	Asian American Studies Department
Contact Person:	Sucheng Chan, Chair
Address:	Santa Barbara, CA 93106-4090
Phone:	(805) 893-2371
Unit Offers:	Major, minor
Degrees Offered:	B.A. Asian American Studies
Majors Per Year:	20
Minors:	30
Faculty:	7
Established:	1969
Special Features:	This program offers a wider array of courses in the humanities and arts as they relate to Asian Americans than any other Asian American Studies program or department in the country. Instead of focusing mainly on history and community studies, it is trying to offer a truly multidisciplinary degree program. Almost all our courses meet one or more general education requirements.

Institution:	**California State University-Bakersfield**
Institution Type:	Public, 4 year + graduate
Unit:	Asian Studies Program
Contact Person:	Charles A. Litzinger
Address:	9001 Stockdale Highway
	Bakersfield, CA 93304
Phone:	(805) 664-2235
Unit Offers:	Minor, classes
Minors Per Year:	5
Faculty:	5

Institution:	**Foothill College**
Unit:	Asian Studies
Address:	12345 El Monte Road
	Los Altos, CA 94022

Institution:	**Canada College**
Unit:	Asian American Studies
Address:	4200 Farm Hill Boulevard
	Redwood City, CA 94061

Institution:	**San Francisco State University**
Institution Type:	Public, 4 year + graduate
Unit:	Asian American Studies Department
Contact Person:	Marlon K. Hom, Chair
Address:	1600 Holloway Avenue
	San Francisco, CA 94132
Phone:	(415) 338-2698
Unit Offers:	Minor, classes
Degrees Offered:	B.A. in conjunction with Liberal Studies Program

Institution:	**Pacific and Asian American Center for Theology and Strategies (PACTS)**
Institution Type:	Public
Contact Person:	Julia Matsui-Estrella
Address:	2452 Virginia Street
	Berkeley, CA 94709
Phone:	(510) 849-0653
Unit Offers:	Classes
Established:	1972
Special Features:	The Pacific and Asian American Center for Theology and Strategies (PACTS) is an ecumenical center for research, resourcing, recruiting, training, and consciousness-raising, with focus on Pacific Islander and Asian American constituencies, to promote the fulfillment of God's mission through the ministries of the churches and the service of community groups.

Institution:	**University of California-Berkeley**
Institution Type:	Public, 4 year + graduate
Unit:	Asian American Studies Program
Contact Person:	Michael A. Omi, Coordinator
Address:	3407 Dwinelle
	Berkeley, CA 94720
Phone:	(510) 642-6195/6555
Fax:	(510) 642-6456
Unit Offers:	Major, minor
Degrees Offered:	B.A.
Majors Per Year:	18
Faculty:	6 ladder-rank, 13 lecturers

Established:	1969
Special Features:	The Asian American Studies Program is one of three programs under the Department of Ethnic Studies, along with Chicano Studies and Native American Studies. (African American Studies is a separate department.) AAS offers courses on history, community studies, and the humanities on Chinese, Filipino, Japanese, Korean, South Asian, and Southeast Asian Americans. Some of the courses are ethnic-specific; others treat the Asian American experience collectively. Many students are involved in community service for credit.

Institution:	**San Jose State University**
Institution Type:	Public, 4 year + graduate
Unit:	Asian American Studies Program
Contact Person:	Alexander Yamato, Coordinator
Address:	One Washington Square
	San Jose, CA 95192-0110
Phone:	(408) 924-5750
Fax:	(408) 924-5753
Unit Offers:	Minor, classes
Minors Per Year:	20
Faculty:	7
Established:	1973
Special Features:	The courses meet general education and American institution requirements.

Institution:	**University of California-Davis**
Institution Type:	Public, 4 year + graduate
Unit:	Asian American Studies Program
Contact Person:	Isao Fujimoto, Director
Address:	Davis, CA 95616
Phone:	(916) 752-6727
Fax:	(916) 752-9260
Unit Offers:	Minor, classes
Degrees Offered:	Minor in Asian American Studies
Minors Per Year:	15
Faculty:	3
Established:	1970

Special Features:	The Asian American Studies Program at UC Davis is formally an academic unit within the College of Letters and Science. It performs teaching, research, and service activities that advance the cultural persistence of the Asian American ethnic community within the context of a society striving for racial equality and cultural pluralism.
	The program offers an interdisciplinary curriculum that brings multiple perspectives and insights to bear on the understanding of the Asian American experience and how this relates to a broader understanding of national and international social and cultural interactions. Our current courses focus on historical foundations; contemporary perspectives; cultural studies and language (Cantonese); and social change and community development. There are a number of resources available in the program's George Kagiwada Library.
Institution:	**California State University-Sacramento**
Institution Type:	Public, 4 year + graduate
Unit:	Asian American Studies Program
Contact Person:	John C. Hwang, Director
Address:	6000 J Street
	Sacramento, CA 95819
Phone:	(916) 278-5856
Unit Offers:	Major, minor, classes
Degrees Offered:	B.A.
Majors Per Year:	2
Minors:	5
Faculty:	2
Established:	1969
Special Features:	This program offers a B.A. in Ethnic Studies with a concentration in Asian American Studies. It also provides community services.
Institution:	**Yuba College**
Unit:	Asian American Studies
Address:	2088 N. Beale Road
	Marysville, CA 95901

COLORADO

Institution:	**Colorado State University**
Unit:	Asian American Student Service
Contact Person:	Linda Ahuna, Director
Address:	Fort Collins, CO 80521

Institution:	**University of Colorado at Denver**
Unit:	Asian-American Education Program
Contact Person:	Peggy L. Lore, Director
Address:	Denver, CO 80217
Phone:	(303) 871-2927

HAWAII

Institution:	**University of Hawaii-Manoe**
Unit:	Asian American Studies
Contact Person:	Daviana McGregor, Chair
Address:	Honolulu, HI 96822

Institution:	**Kauai Community College**
Unit:	Asian American Studies
Address:	Kauai, HI 96766

ILLINOIS

Institution:	**University of Chicago**
Institution Type:	Private, 4 year + graduate
Unit:	Center for East Asian Studies
Address:	Pick Hall 121
	5828 S. University Avenue
	Chicago, IL 60637
Phone:	(312) 702-8647
Fax:	(312) 702-8260
E-mail:	dance@cicero.spu.uchicago.edu
Unit Offers:	Major, minor, classes
Degrees Offered:	M.A./M.B.A offered through the center directly (specializing in East Asian); the Social Sciences and Humanities Divisions both offer B.A.s, M.A.s, and

Ph.D.s in East Asian Studies, Chinese, Japanese, Korean, and East Asian language and civilization

Special Features: The center itself offers no degree except the M.A./ M.B.A. (in conjunction with the Business School). B.A., M.A., and Ph.D. degree-seekers would have to contact the Department of East Asian Languages and Civilizations directly. The center is an administrative body aiding in lectures, community outreach, fellowships and scholarships, and job placement.

Institution: **Mundelein College**
Unit: Asian Studies
Address: 6363 Sheridan Road
Chicago, IL 60660

KANSAS

Institution: **Kansas State University**
Institution Type: Public, 4 year + graduate
Unit: South Asia Center
Contact Person: Lelah Dushkin, Director
Address: Fairchild 304
Manhattan, KS 66506
Phone: (913) 532-5990
Fax: (913) 532-6550
E-mail: dushkin@ksuvm.ksu.edu
Unit Offers: Certificate, classes
Degrees Offered: Secondary Major in International Studies
Faculty: 12
Established: 1967
Special Features: This program offers an interdisciplinary course (under six departments) in South Asian civilizations as well as courses in various departments. It has a South Asia media center for use by grade- and high-school teachers. The center collaborates with local South Asians for various "ethnic" events.

MARYLAND

Institution:	**Towson State University**
Unit:	Asian Studies
Contact Person:	Wayne McWilliams
Address:	Baltimore, MD 21204

MASSACHUSETTS

Institution:	**Harvard University**
Institution Type:	Private, 4 year + graduate
Unit:	The Edwin O. Reischauer Institute of Japanese Studies
Contact Person:	Nancy Deptula, Executive Director
Address:	1737 Cambridge Street
	Coolidge Hall, Room 319
	Cambridge, MA 02140
Phone:	(617) 495-3220
Fax:	(617) 496-8083
Special Features:	The institute was established by former U.S. ambassador to Japan Edwin Oldfather Reischauer to promote greater understanding between the United States and Japan. This is a research organization and not an academic degree program.

MINNESOTA

Institution:	**Bemidji State University**
Unit:	Asian Studies
Address:	Bemidji, MN 56601

NEW MEXICO

Institution:	**University of New Mexico**
Institution Type:	Public, 4 year + graduate
Unit:	Asian Studies Program
Contact Person:	Noel Pugach, Chair

Address:	Department of History
	Albuquerque, NM 87131-1181
Phone:	(505) 277-2701/2451
Fax:	(505) 277-6023
Unit Offers:	Major, minor
Degrees Offered:	B.A. Asian Studies
Majors Per Year:	6
Minors:	8
Faculty:	15
Established:	1979

NEW YORK

Institution:	**Hunter College**
Unit:	Asian American Studies
Contact Person:	Franklin Odo, Chair
Address:	695 Park Avenue
	New York, NY 10021

Institution:	**The City College of New York, City University of New York**
Institution Type:	Public, 4 year + graduate
Unit:	Department of Asian Studies
Contact Person:	Thomas Lee, Chair
Address:	Convent Avenue at 137th Street
	New York, NY 10031
Phone:	(212) 650-6378
Fax:	(212) 650-6970 (ext. 6378)
Unit Offers:	Major, minor, classes
Degrees Offered:	B.A. Asian Studies with emphasis on China; B.A. Asian Studies with emphasis on Japan
Majors Per Year:	3–4
Minors:	5–6
Faculty:	3 full-time, 3 adjunct professors
Established:	1974
Special Features:	The department offers courses in three main categories: area studies, Asian languages and literatures, and Asian American studies. Our Area Studies Program focuses on China, Japan, and

India with occasional courses offered on Korea. The Asian Languages and Literatures Program offers language and literature courses of China, Japan, and India. Film and cultural courses are also offered. Asian American Studies offers social history courses on Asian immigrants and their communities.

Institution:	**Cornell University**
Institution Type:	Private, 4 year + graduate
Unit:	Asian American Studies Program
Contact Person:	Gary Y. Okihiro, Director
Address:	292 Caldwell Hall
	Ithaca, NY 14853
Phone:	(607) 255-3320
Fax:	(607) 255-3320
E-mail:	apai@cornell.edu
Special Features:	The Asian American Studies Program, the only one among Ivy League Schools, is the study of minority groups in America. Also housed within the program is a resource center that holds print and media material pertinent to the study of Asian Americans.

NORTH CAROLINA

Institution:	**Appalachian State University**
Institution Type:	Public, 4 year
Unit:	Interdisciplinary Studies/Asian Studies Department
Contact Person:	Kay H. Smith, Chair
Address:	Boone, NC 28608
Phone:	(704) 262-3177
E-mail:	smithkh@appstate
Unit Offers:	Major, minor
Degrees Offered:	B.A.
Majors Per Year:	3
Minors:	10
Faculty:	6–10

Established:	1990 (major); 1986 (minor)
Special Features:	Asian Studies is a twenty-four hour concentration within the Department of Interdisciplinary Studies. Students take courses in several departments.

UTAH

Institution:	**Weber State University**
Unit:	Asian Studies Alliance
Contact Person:	Dean W. Collinwood, Director
Address:	Ogden, UT 84408
Phone:	(801) 626-7203

VIRGINIA

Institution:	**University of Virginia**
Unit:	East Asian Language and Area Center
Contact Person:	Ronald G. Dimberg, Director
Address:	Charlottesville, VA 22903
Phone:	(804) 924-6411

WASHINGTON

Institution:	**University of Washington**
Unit:	Asian American Studies Department
Contact Person:	Shawn Wong, Director
Address:	Seattle, WA 98193
Phone:	(206) 543-5401

Institution:	**Western Washington University**
Unit:	Asian American Studies
Contact Person:	Hyung-chan Kim, Chair
Address:	Bellingham, WA 98227

Institution:	**Central Washington University**
Unit:	Asian American Studies
Address:	Ellensburg, WA 98926

Institution:	**Washington State University**
Institution Type:	Public, 4 year + graduate
Unit:	Asia Program
Contact Person:	Alice Spitzer, Acting Director
Address:	Pullman, WA 99164-4030
Phone:	(509) 335-3267
Fax:	(509) 335-4171
Unit Offers:	Major, minor, classes
Degrees Offered:	B.A. Asian Studies (can take options in China, Japan, South Asia, Middle East, or Comprehensive)
Majors Per Year:	5
Minors:	5
Faculty:	10 affiliates
Established:	1975
Special Features:	The Asia Program is designed to provide a broad, systematic knowledge of Asia through interdisciplinary study and is intended to serve four major objectives: (1) to prepare students intending to teach courses on Asia in the public schools; (2) to provide academic background for those planning to pursue graduate work on Asia; (3) to prepare students for business careers dealing with Asia; and (4) to train those interested in governmental and various private career opportunities related to Asia.

WISCONSIN

Institution:	**University of Wisconsin-Madison**
Unit:	Center for South Asia
Contact Person:	Joseph Elder, Director
Address:	8131 Social Science Building
	Madison, WI 53706
Phone:	(608) 262-2782
Fax:	(608) 251-5457
E-mail:	elder@ssc.wisc.edu
Unit Offers:	Major
Degrees Offered:	Ph.D., B.A., M.A.

Majors Per Year: 5
Faculty: 13
Established: 1959

Hispanic (Chicana/o, Latina/o, Puerto Rican) American Studies

ARIZONA

Institution:	**South Mountain Community College**
Unit:	Southwest Studies Program
Address:	7050 S. 24th Street
	Phoenix, AZ 85040

Institution:	**Scottsdale Community College**
Unit:	Southwest Studies Program
Address:	9000 East Chaparral
	Scottsdale, AZ 85256

Institution:	**Arizona State University**
Institution Type:	Public, 4 year + graduate
Unit:	Center for Latin American Studies
Contact Person:	K. Lynn Stoner, Director
Address:	Box 872401
	Tempe, AZ 85287-2401
Phone:	(602) 965-5127
Fax:	(602) 965-6679
E-mail:	atkls@asuvm.inre.asu.edu
Unit Offers:	Minor, certificate, classes
Minors Per Year:	10
Faculty:	87 affiliates
Established:	1965
Special Features:	The Latin American Studies Program at ASU is designed to give students an understanding of public affairs, culture, and trends in Latin American

nations in combination with a degree program in seven specific departments. The Latin American emphasis, combined with study in the student's major field, provides the graduate with two areas of specialization that widen employment opportunities in matters of international relations.

Institution:	**Arizona State University**
Institution Type:	Public, 4 year + graduate
Unit:	Hispanic Research Center
Contact Person:	Felipe Castro, Director
Address:	Box 872702
	Tempe, AZ 85287-2702
Phone:	(602) 965-3990
Fax:	(602) 965-0315

Institution:	**University of Arizona**
Institution Type:	Public, 4 year
Unit:	Mexican American Studies and Research Center
Contact Person:	Antonio Estrada, Acting Director
Address:	Douglass Building 315
	Tucson, AZ 85721
Phone:	(602) 621-7551
Fax:	(602) 621-7966
Unit Offers:	Major, minor
Majors Per Year:	15
Minors:	20
Faculty:	7
Established:	1981
Special Features:	The Mexican American Studies and Research Center (MASRC) is a research and publishing center, an instructional unit, and a strong university-community outreach program. The center provides and promotes an interdisciplinary approach to research, instruction, publications, and service that effectively addresses issues impacting Mexican Americans. It responds to the needs of the Hispanic student population, scholars from the university and other institutions of higher education, Mexican scholars and institutions, the Tuc-

son community, and the greater Mexican American community in Arizona. While offering students an interdisciplinary course of study on many facets of Mexican American culture, it is also an intellectual center and clearinghouse for researchers and educators at the U of A and in the greater Southwest. The center publishes a journal entitled *Perspectives in Mexican American Studies,* edited by Juan García.

Institution:	**Pima Community College**
Unit:	Southwest Studies Program
Address:	2202 West Anklam Road
	Tucson, AZ 85745

CALIFORNIA

Institution:	**University of California-Los Angeles**
Institution Type:	Public, 4 year + graduate
Unit:	Chicano Studies Research Center
Contact Person:	Guillermo Hernandez, Acting Director
	or Antonio Serrata, Administrative Assistant
Address:	180 Haines Hall
	Los Angeles, CA 90024
Phone:	(310) 825-2363
Fax:	(310) 206-1784
E-mail:	serrata@others.sscnet.ucla.edu
Established:	1969
Special Features:	The center provides research and library resources and offers a yearly post-doctoral fellowship. It also publishes *Aztlán* and is developing a Chicano/Latino net for information: e-mail salinas@latino.sscnet.ucla.edu.

Institution:	**California State University-Los Angeles**
Institution Type:	Public, 4 year + graduate
Unit:	Department of Chicano Studies
Contact Person:	Irene I. Blea, Chair
	or Jessica Murillo, Secretary

Address:	5151 State University Drive
	King Hall Room C3095
	Los Angeles, CA 90032-8221
Phone:	(213) 343-2190
Unit Offers:	Major, minor, certificate, classes
Degrees Offered:	M.A. Chicana/Latina Studies
Majors Per Year:	30
Minors:	22
Faculty:	5 full-time
Established:	1969
Special Features:	CSU has the first and oldest department in the nation creating areas of specialization on Chicana/Latina with certification. CSU is legislated by the state of California to administer the Cultural Literacy Exam. This exam is required for all teachers, especially those majoring in bilingual education.

Institution:	**Loyola Marymount University**
Institution Type:	Private, 4 year
Unit:	Department of Chicano Studies
Contact Person:	Fernando J. Guerra, Chair
Address:	7101 W. 80th Street
	Los Angeles, CA 90045
Phone:	(310) 338-4565
Fax:	(310) 338-2706
Unit Offers:	Major, minor, classes
Degrees Offered:	B.A. Chicano Studies
Majors Per Year:	11
Minors:	15
Faculty:	4
Established:	1973

Institution:	**California State University-Dominguez Hills**
Institution Type:	Public, 4 year + graduate
Unit:	Mexican American Studies Program
Contact Person:	Miguel Dominguez, Director
Address:	1000 E. Victoria Street
	Carson, CA 90747
Phone:	(310) 516-3326
Unit Offers:	Major, minor

Degrees Offered:	B.A.
Majors Per Year:	40
Minors:	80
Faculty:	8
Established:	1972

Institution:	**California State University-Long Beach**
Unit:	Chicano and Latino Studies Department
Contact Person:	Adela de la Torre
Address:	Long Beach, CA 90840
Phone:	(310) 985-4644

Institution:	**California State University-Northridge**
Institution Type:	Public, 4 year
Unit:	Chicano Studies Department
Contact Person:	Juana Mora, Chair
Address:	18111 Nordhoff Street
	Northridge, CA 91330
Phone:	(818) 885-2734
Fax:	(818) 885-4902
Unit Offers:	Major, minor
Degrees Offered:	B.A., M.A. Chicano Studies
Majors Per Year:	150
Established:	1969
Special Features:	Chicano Studies was established in 1969 in response to the educational needs of Chicano/a students. It was designed to provide students with an awareness of the social, political, economical, historical, and cultural realities in our society. Since 1969 the number of other Latino/a students has increased. The department has expanded its curriculum and its services to help meet the needs of all Latino students.

Institution:	**Los Angeles Valley College**
Institution Type:	Public, 2 year
Unit:	Chicano Studies Department
Contact Person:	G. E. Miranda, Chair
Address:	5800 Fulton Avenue
	Van Nuys, CA 91401-4096

Phone:	(818) 781-1200
Unit Offers:	Major, classes
Degrees Offered:	A.A.
Majors Per Year:	2–3
Faculty:	1 full-time
Established:	1969
Special Features:	The department offers students general education courses and classes for future Chicano Studies majors.

Institution:	**Claremont Colleges**
Institution Type:	Private, 4 year
Unit:	Intercollegiate Department of Chicano Studies
Contact Person:	Deena J. Gonzalez, Chair
Address:	919 N. Columbia Avenue
	Claremont, CA 91711
Phone:	(909) 621-8044/8000 (ext. 3710)
Unit Offers:	Major, classes
Degrees Offered:	Special concentration in Chicano Studies composed of courses in the social sciences, sciences, humanities, and the arts
Majors Per Year:	10–20
Special Features:	The Claremont Colleges are a consortium of highly selective liberal arts colleges. They share the Chicano Studies Program, which consists of a student services center and a curriculum administered by eleven faculty members jointly appointed in traditional disciplines and in Chicano Studies.

Institution:	**Mount San Antonio College**
Unit:	Mexican American Literature and History of the Mexican American
Address:	Walnut, CA 91711

Institution:	**Southwestern College**
Institution Type:	Public, 2 year
Unit:	Mexican American Studies
Contact Person:	Victor Chavez
Address:	900 Otay Lakes Road
	Chula Vista, CA 91910

Unit Offers:	Major, classes
Degrees Offered:	A.A. Mexican American Studies

Institution:	**Palomar College**
Unit:	Chicano Studies
Address:	1140 W. Mission
	San Marcos, CA 92069

Institution:	**San Diego City College**
Unit:	Chicano Studies
Address:	1313 Twelfth Avenue
	San Diego, CA 92101

Institution:	**San Diego Mesa College**
Unit:	Chicano Studies
Contact Person:	Michael Ornelas
	or Cesar Gonzales
Address:	San Diego, CA 92111

Institution:	**San Diego State University**
Institution Type:	Public, 4 year + graduate
Unit:	Mexican American Studies Department
Contact Person:	Isidro D. Ortiz, Chair
Address:	San Diego, CA 92182
Phone:	(619) 594-6452
Unit Offers:	Major, minor, certificate, classes
Degrees Offered:	B.A. Mexican American Studies
Majors Per Year:	12
Minors:	20–25
Faculty:	6 full-time, 6 part-time
Special Features:	This is an interdisciplinary department emphasizing the study of the Chicano/a experience and the development of the U.S.-Mexico border region.

Institution:	**Pasadena Community College**
Unit:	Chicano Studies
Address:	1570 E. Colorado Boulevard
	Pasadena, CA 92206

Institution:	**Riverside City College**
Unit:	Chicano Studies

| Address: | 4800 Magnolia Avenue |
| | Riverside, CA 92506 |

Institution:	**California State University-Fullerton**
Institution Type:	Public, 4 year + graduate
Unit:	Latin American Studies Program
Contact Person:	Dr. S. Maram, Coordinator
Address:	800 N. State College
	Fullerton, CA 92670
Phone:	(714) 773-2685
Fax:	(714) 449-5989
Unit Offers:	Major, minor
Majors Per Year:	17
Minors:	13
Special Features:	The Latin American Studies Program is designed to provide an in-depth, interdisciplinary understanding of Latin America. Majors develop language proficiency in both Spanish and Portuguese and choose the remainder of their curriculum from a broad range of courses in anthropology, economics, foreign languages and literature, geography, history, and political science. Students of Latin American Studies learn about the fundamental economic and social problems facing many Latin American countries and begin to develop the knowledge necessary to contribute to helping our Latin American neighbors solve those problems. The program also prepares the student for graduate work in Latin American Studies or in other disciplines involving a specialization in Latin America. A minor in Latin American Studies also is offered.

Institution:	**University of California-Irvine**
Institution Type:	Public, 4 year + graduate
Unit:	Chicano/Latino Studies Program
Contact Person:	Maria Herrera-Sobek, Director
Address:	Irvine, CA 92717
Phone:	(714) 856-7180
Fax:	(714) 856-8762
E-mail:	mherrera@uci.edu

Unit Offers:	Minor, classes
Minors Per Year:	15
Faculty:	20
Established:	1990

Institution:	**Moorpark College**
Unit:	Chicano Studies
Address:	7075 Campus Road
	Moorpark, CA 93021

Institution:	**Foothill College**
Unit:	Mexican American Studies
Address:	12345 El Monte Road
	Los Altos, CA 93022

Institution:	**University of California-Santa Barbara**
Institution Type:	Public, 4 year + graduate
Unit:	Chicano Studies Department
Address:	Santa Barbara, CA 93106
Phone:	(805) 893-4076
Unit Offers:	Major
Degrees Offered:	B.A. Chicano Studies
Majors Per Year:	30
Faculty:	7

Institution:	**California State University-Bakersfield**
Unit:	Chicano Studies Committee
Address:	Bakersfield, CA 93311

Institution:	**California State University-Fresno**
Unit:	Chicano/Latino Studies Program
Address:	Fresno, CA 93740

Institution:	**Fresno City College**
Institution Type:	Public, 2 year
Unit:	Chicano-Latino Studies Program
Contact Person:	Art Amaro
Address:	1101 E. University Avenue
	Fresno, CA 93741
Phone:	(209) 442-4600
Unit Offers:	Major

Degrees Offered:	A.A. Chicano-Latino Studies
Majors Per Year:	10
Faculty:	2 full-time, 8 part-time
Established:	1970
Special Features:	This program offers a large number of classes including Chicano history, Chicano literature, and Chicano sociology.

Institution:	**Canada College**
Unit:	Mexican American Studies
Address:	4200 Farm Hill Boulevard
	Redwood City, CA 94061

Institution:	**City College of San Francisco**
Institution Type:	Public, 2 year
Unit:	Latin American Studies Department
Address:	50 Phelan Avenue
	Box S-76
	San Francisco, CA 94112
Phone:	(415) 239-3126
Unit Offers:	Major, minor, classes
Degrees Offered:	A.A.
Majors Per Year:	15
Minors:	100
Faculty:	4
Established:	1968
Special Features:	The program has a major focus on the history, art, and politics of Latin America from pre-Columbian to the present. It also has a Chicano history and sociology course. All courses are transferable to the university system in California.

Institution:	**San Francisco State University**
Institution Type:	Public, 4 year + graduate
Unit:	La Raza Studies Department
Contact Person:	Jose B. Cuellar, Chair
Address:	School of Ethnic Studies
	1600 Holloway Avenue
	San Francisco, CA 94132
Phone:	(415) 338-2700

Fax:	(415) 338-1739
Unit Offers:	Major, minor, classes
Degrees Offered:	B.A. La Raza Studies
Majors Per Year:	60
Minors:	120
Faculty:	5 full-time, 4 part-time
Established:	1969
Special Features:	The general goal of the La Raza Studies major is to provide cultural, historical, and social knowledge relevant to the La Raza experience as a living whole. Emphasis will be on the historical analysis of the relationships between social institutions, their philosophies, and their effects on the La Raza individual and his or her place in society. Objectives of La Raza Studies are to provide an opportunity for the integrated liberal arts major in La Raza Studies for those students interested in the education and development of the La Raza community; to provide the student with a better understanding of the La Raza economic, cultural, and social heritage; to develop the student's abilities to deal effectively with the complex problems of modern society; and to train and prepare the student for careers and professions requiring expertise on different aspects of the La Raza experience.

Institution:	**Stanford University**
Institution Type:	4 year + graduate
Unit:	Chicano Fellows Program
Contact Person:	Luis Fraga, Professor
	or Claudia M. Carrillo, Program Administrator
Address:	Building 590
	Stanford, CA 94305-3044
Phone:	(415) 723-3091
E-mail:	saldivar@leland.stanford.edu
Unit Offers:	Classes
Faculty:	1 visiting professor, 2 graduate fellows, 5 professors teaching cross-listed classes.

Special Features:	The Chicano Fellows/Undergraduate Studies Program offers courses in Chicano Studies taught by an annual visiting professor and two graduate teaching fellows. The visiting faculty and fellows offer courses focusing on their respective research areas. The program also serves the campus and surrounding communities by sponsoring academic and cultural programs that serve to increase awareness about Chicano and Mexican cultures and society in the United States.
Institution:	**California State University-Hayward**
Unit:	La Raza Studies Department
Contact Person:	Juan L. Gonzales
Address:	Hayward, CA 94542
Phone:	(510) 881-3255
Institution:	**University of California-Berkeley**
Unit:	Chicano Studies Program
Address:	3335 Dwinelle Hall
	Berkeley, CA 94720
Institution:	**Contra Costa College**
Institution Type:	Public, 2 year
Unit:	La Raza Studies Department
Contact Person:	Alfred I. Zuniga, Chair
Address:	2600 Mission Bell Drive
	San Pablo, CA 94806
Phone:	(510) 235-7800 (ext. 357)
Unit Offers:	Major, classes
Degrees Offered:	A.A. La Raza Studies
Faculty:	1
Established:	1970
Special Features:	This is an interdisciplinary department that offers courses in several disciplines (e.g., history, political science, etc., under the name of La Raza Studies).
Institution:	**Sonoma State University**
Unit:	Mexican-American Studies

Address:	Rohnert Park, CA 94928

Institution:	**San Jose City College**
Unit:	Mexican American Studies
Address:	2100 Moorpart Avenue
	San Jose, CA 95128

Institution:	**San Jose State University**
Institution Type:	Public, 4 year + graduate
Unit:	Mexican American Studies Department
Address:	One Washington Square
	San Jose, CA 95192-0118
Phone:	(408) 924-5760
Fax:	(408) 924-5892
Unit Offers:	Minor
Degrees Offered:	Minor program; Master's program with emphasis on Bilingual/ Bicultural Studies, Policy Studies, Cross-Cultural Studies
Faculty:	5

Institution:	**University of Pacific**
Unit:	Mexican-American Studies
Address:	Stockton, CA 95211

Institution:	**California State University-Stanislaus**
Unit:	Chicano Studies
Contact Person:	Richard Luevano, Director
Address:	801 W. Monte Vista
	Turlock, CA 93580

Institution:	**University of California-Davis**
Unit:	Chicano Studies
Contact Person:	Beatriz Pesquera
Address:	Davis, CA 95616

Institution:	**D-Q University**
Unit:	Chicano Studies
Address:	Box 409
	Davis, CA 95616

Institution:	**California State University-Sacramento**
Institution Type:	Public, 4 year
Unit:	Chicano Studies Program
Contact Person:	Sam Rios, Jr., Director
Address:	6000 J Street
	Sacramento, CA 95819
Phone:	(916) 278-6645
Unit Offers:	Major, minor
Degrees Offered:	B.A.
Majors Per Year:	10
Minors:	10
Faculty:	30
Established:	1969

Institution:	**Yuba College**
Unit:	La Raza Studies
Address:	2088 N. Beale Road
	Marysville, CA 95901

Institution:	**Cerritos College**
Unit:	Chicano Studies Program
Address:	11110 East Alondra Boulevard
	Norwalk, CA 96050

Institution:	**Santa Ana College**
Unit:	Chicano Studies
Address:	Santa Ana, CA 97206

COLORADO

Institution:	**Metropolitan State College**
Unit:	Chicano Studies
Address:	1006 11th Street
	Denver, CO 80202

Institution:	**University of Colorado-Denver**
Unit:	Mexican-American Education Program
Contact Person:	Danny E. Martinez, Director
Address:	Denver, CO 80217

Institution:	**University of Colorado-Boulder**
Unit:	Chicano Studies Program
	Center for Ethnicity and Race in America
Contact Person:	Evelyn DuHart
Address:	Boulder, CO 80309

Institution:	**Colorado State University**
Unit:	El Centro Hispano-American Studies
Contact Person:	Victor Baez, Director
Address:	Fort Collins, CO 80523
Phone:	(303) 491-5722

Institution:	**Adams State College**
Institution Type:	Public, 4 year
Unit:	Southwestern Studies Program
Contact Person:	Priscilla Falcon
Address:	Department of History
	Alamosa, CO 81101
Phone:	(719) 589-7176
Fax:	(719) 589-7522
Unit Offers:	Minor
Minors Per Year:	2
Faculty:	1

CONNECTICUT

Institution:	**Connecticut College**
Institution Type:	Private, 4 year
Unit:	Department of Hispanic Studies
Contact Person:	Julia A. Kushigian, Chair
Address:	New London, CT 06320-4196
Phone:	(203) 439-2239
Unit Offers:	Major, minor, classes
Degrees Offered:	B.A.
Majors Per Year:	30
Minors:	10
Faculty:	5

Institution:	**Northern Illinois University**
Institution Type:	Public, 4 year + graduate
Unit:	Center for Latino and Latin American Studies
Contact Person:	Margaret A. Villanueva, Assistant Director
Address:	De Kalb, IL 60115
Phone:	(815) 753-1351
Fax:	(815) 753-1651
Unit Offers:	Minor, classes
Degrees Offered:	B.A. minor in Latino/Latin American Studies
Minors Per Year:	15
Faculty:	2 within center, 28 faculty associates
Established:	1985 (formerly Latino Affairs, established 1978)
Special Features:	The center is an interdisciplinary research and teaching unit offering programs for students, faculty, and the community. It assists faculty associates with funding, sponsors talks by recognized scholars, and offers a minor that combines studies on Latino issues in the United States with courses on Latin American society and culture.

Institution:	**University of Illinois at Chicago**
Unit:	Latin American Studies Program
Contact Person:	Rafael Nuñez-Cedeño, Director
Address:	Chicago, IL 60607-7115
Phone:	(312) 996-2445
Fax:	(312) 996-1796
E-mail:	u22136@uicvm.uic.edu
Unit Offers:	Major, minor
Faculty:	8

Institution:	**Depaul University**
Unit:	Center for Hispanic Research
Address:	2323 North Seminary Avenue
	Chicago, IL 60614

Institution:	**Illinois State University**
Unit:	Chicano and Puerto Rican Studies
Address:	Normal, IL 61761

Institution:	University of Notre Dame
Institution Type:	4 year + graduate
Unit:	Latin American Area Studies Program
Contact Person:	Michael Francis
Address:	Hesburgh Center 312
	Notre Dame, IN 46556-0368
Phone:	(219) 631-6469
Fax:	(631) 237-6717
E-mail:	michael.j.frances.@nd.edu
Unit Offers:	Certificate
Certificates	
Per Year:	15
Faculty:	25
Established:	1963
Special Features:	The Latin American Area Studies Program at the University of Notre Dame (LAASP) is coordinated by the Helen Kellogg Institute for International Studies and the College of Arts and Letters. It is open to all Notre Dame undergraduates, and the Area Studies Certificate Program, the Senior Essay competition, and the International Study Programs are also open to students from St. Mary's College. The purpose of the program is to promote opportunities for students to deepen their understanding of Latin America through a wide variety of courses, campus activities, internships, and firsthand overseas learning experiences. The LAASP seeks to make resources available to interested students to orient and enrich their scholarly interests in fields related to Latin America. An appropriate course structure is available to students who wish to concentrate their interest upon a cultural or geographic area as well as upon an interdisciplinary approach. Such programs can be especially useful to students who plan a career in international business, international organizations, or government service.

Institution:	**Indiana University**
Unit:	Chicano-Riqueño Studies
Contact Person:	Luis Dávila, Director
Address:	Bloomington, IN 47405
Phone:	(812) 855-5257

KANSAS

Institution:	**Kansas State University**
Unit:	Latin American Studies Department
Contact Person:	Marcial Antonio Riquelme, Director
Address:	Manhattan, KS 66502
Phone:	(913) 532-5990

MASSACHUSETTS

Institution:	**Smith College**
Institution Type:	Private, 4 year + graduate
Unit:	Latin American Studies Program
Contact Person:	Marina Kaplan
Address:	Department of Spanish and Portuguese
	Neilson A/11
	Northampton, MA 01063
Phone:	(413) 585-3462
Fax:	(413) 585-3593
E-mail:	mkaplan@smith.smith.edu
Unit Offers:	Major, minor, classes
Degrees Offered:	B.A.
Majors Per Year:	20
Minors:	5
Faculty:	14
Established:	1986
Special Features:	This program has small classes, good library resources, and a great diversity of course offerings by scholars active in their fields.

Institution:	**Westfield State College**
Unit:	Latin American Studies Department

Contact Person: John A. Loughney
Address: Westfield, MA 01085
Phone: (413) 568-3311

MICHIGAN

Institution:	**Wayne State University**
Unit:	Chicano-Boricua Studies
Address:	Detroit, MI 48202

MINNESOTA

Institution:	**Saint Olaf College**
Institution Type:	Private, 4 year
Unit:	Hispanic Studies Program
Contact Person:	Gwen Barnes-Karol, Director
Address:	1520 Saint Olaf Avenue
	Northfield, MN 55057
Phone:	(507) 646-3380
Fax:	(507) 646-3549/3690
E-mail:	barnesg@stolaf.edu
Unit Offers:	Major, classes
Degrees Offered:	B.A. Hispanic Studies
Majors Per Year:	15
Faculty:	14
Established:	1974
Special Features:	The Hispanic Studies Program is an interdisciplinary major that offers an academic structure for the systematic study of Latin America and Spain and people of Hispanic heritage in the United States. Students design their own major in consultation with the director of Hispanic Studies by choosing among designated courses in economics, Spanish and Latin American literature and culture, history, political science, religion, sociology/ anthropology, etc. Several of the designated courses in history and the behavioral sciences offer optional Spanish-language tracks through the

St. Olaf Languages Across the Curriculum Program. Many students apply courses from study-abroad programs in Spain, Costa Rica, Columbia, Ecuador, Guatemala, Nicaragua, and Puerto Rico toward their Hispanic Studies major. A concentration in Latin American/Latino Studies is also offered.

Institution:	**University of Minnesota**
Institution Type:	Public, 4 year
Unit:	Chicano Studies Department
Contact Person:	Guillermo Rojas, Chair
Address:	102 Scott Hall
	72 Pleasant Street, SE
	Minneapolis, MN 55455
Phone:	(612) 624-6309
Fax:	(612) 624-3858
Unit Offers:	Major, minor, classes
Degrees Offered:	B.A. Chicano Studies
Majors Per Year:	30
Minors:	15
Faculty:	4

NEBRASKA

Institution:	**University of Nebraska-Lincoln**
Institution Type:	Public, 4 year + graduate
Unit:	Latino and Latin American Studies Program
Contact Person:	Ralph Grajeda, Director
Address:	141 Andrews Hall
	Lincoln, NE 68588-0335
Phone:	(402) 472-9983/1850
Fax:	(402) 472-1123
E-mail:	rgrajeda@unl.edu
Unit Offers:	Major, minor, classes
Degrees Offered:	B.A. Latin American Studies; minor in Latin American Studies; minor in Chicano Studies
Majors Per Year:	5
Minors:	20–25

Faculty:	5
Established:	1972

NEW JERSEY

Institution:	**Rutgers University**
Institution Type:	Public, 4 year + graduate
Unit:	Department of Spanish and Portuguese
Contact Person:	Thomas M. Stephens
Address:	New Brunswick, NJ 08903-0270
Phone:	(908) 932-9323
Fax:	(908) 932-9837
E-mail:	stephens@zodiac.rutgers.edu
Unit Offers:	Major, minor
Degrees Offered:	B.A. Spanish and Portuguese; M.A. Spanish Literature; M.A.T. Spanish; M.A. Option in Translation; Ph.D. Spanish Literature
Majors Per Year:	300
Minors:	200
Faculty:	16
Established:	1981 (as a unified department)
Special Features:	Not only does this department offer a Ph.D. and M.A. in literature, but it also offers M.A.s in translation, a unique program, and in teaching. Its undergraduate population is divided between Hispanics/Latinos and non-Hispanics, which directly results from the ethnic diversity of the state of New Jersey.

Institution:	**Rutgers University**
Institution Type:	Public, 4 year + graduate
Unit:	Department of Puerto Rican and Hispanic Caribbean Studies
Contact Person:	Pedro Caban, Chair
Address:	Tillett Hall 231
	Livingston Campus
	New Brunswick, NJ 08903
Phone:	(908) 932-3820
Fax:	(908) 932-0012

E-mail:	caban@gandalf.rutgers.edu
Unit Offers:	Major, minor, classes
Degrees Offered:	B.A. Puerto Rican and Hispanic Caribbean Studies
Majors Per Year:	40
Minors:	15
Faculty:	4
Established:	1970

NEW MEXICO

Institution:	**University of New Mexico**
Unit:	Chicano Studies Department
Contact Person:	Christine Sierra, Coordinator
Address:	Albuquerque, NM 87131

Institution:	**University of New Mexico**
Unit:	Southwest Hispanic Research Institute
Contact Person:	Oswaldo Baca, Director
Address:	Albuquerque, NM 87131

Institution:	**New Mexico Highlands University**
Unit:	Mexican-American Studies
Contact Person:	Gabino Rendár
Address:	Las Vegas, NM 87701

Institution:	**New Mexico State University**
Institution Type:	Public, 4 year + graduate
Unit:	Chicano Programs Office
Contact Person:	Louis Sarabia, Director
Address:	Box 30001—Dept. 4188
	Las Cruces, NM 88003
Phone:	(505) 646-4206
Fax:	(505) 646-5291
Unit Offers:	Major (supplementary major—student must have a major in another field)
Majors Per Year:	4–5
Faculty:	8
Established:	1974

Special Features:	This program offers an interdisciplinary major through the College of Arts and Sciences. Students must also have a major in another academic area.

NEW YORK

Institution:	**New York University**
Unit:	Center for Latin American and Caribbean Studies
Contact Person:	Christopher Mitchell
Address:	New York, NY 10003
Phone:	(212) 998-8686

Institution:	**Baruch College**
Unit:	Black and Hispanic Studies
Address:	17 Lexington Avenue
	New York, NY 10010

Institution:	**John Jay College of Criminal Justice**
Institution Type:	Public, 4 year + graduate
Unit:	Puerto Rican Studies Department
Unit Type:	Program, Department
Contact Person:	Migdalia Dejesús-Torres, Chair
Address:	Room 3235 N
	445 West 59th Street
	New York, NY 10019
Phone:	(212) 237-8749/50
Fax:	(212) 237-8742
Unit Offers:	Minor, certificate, classes
Minors Per Year:	110
Faculty:	10
Established:	1971
Special Features:	The program and minor offer an inter/transdisciplinary approach to courses in the humanities, social sciences, and professional studies. The program and minor seek to complement the college's mission with courses that integrate areas of study of vital importance to criminal justice education. Six credits in Ethnic Studies core

courses are taught of which students are required to take three credits (ETH 124 and ETH 125).

Institution:	**Manhattan Community College**
Unit:	Puerto Rican Studies
Contact:	Salvador Ocasio
Address:	134 West 51st Street
	New York, NY 10020

Institution:	**Hunter College**
Institution Type:	Public, 4 year + graduate
Unit:	Centro de Estudios Puertorriquenos
Contact Person:	Juan Flores
Address:	695 Park Avenue
	New York, NY 10021
Phone:	(212) 772-5686
Fax:	(212) 650-3673
E-mail:	rbphc@cuny.vm.bitnet
Established:	1973
Special Features:	Several interinstitutional programs of academic and research collaborations operate from the Centro. They include INTERCAMBIO, linking the City University of New York and the University of Puerto Rico; and the CUNY-Caribbean Exchange, covering several Caribbean nations. Faculty, graduate students, and undergraduates are active in these exchanges. The Inter-University Program for Latino Research (IUP) has been headquartered at the Centro since 1988. This consortium now brings together eight U.S. university-based Latino research centers focused on social policy concerns on the national and international levels.

Institution:	**The City College of New York-CUNY**
Institution Type:	Public, 4 year + graduate
Unit:	Department of Latin American and Hispanic Caribbean Studies
Contact Person:	Sherrie L. Baver, Chair
Address:	NAC 6/108
	New York, NY 10031

Phone:	(212) 650-6763
Fax:	(212) 650-6970
Unit Offers:	Major, minor, classes
Degrees Offered:	B.A. Latin American Area Studies; B.A. Puerto Rican Studies
Majors Per Year:	10
Minors:	10
Faculty:	6
Established:	1969

Institution:	**Fordham University**
Institution Type:	Private, 4 year + graduate
Unit:	Latin American Studies Program
Contact Person:	Ronald Méndez-Clark, Director
Address:	Department of Modern Languages
	Bronx, NY 10458
Phone:	(718) 817-2676
Unit Offers:	Minor, classes
Degrees Offered:	Minor in Latin American Studies
Faculty:	13
Special Features:	This interdisciplinary program integrates a series of courses designed to acquaint the student with the Latin American experience in the United States and other countries. It provides students with the background to understand important contemporary developments and social issues in the Latin American community, and it examines how these issues affect major areas of American life.

Institution:	**Lehman College-CUNY**
Institution Type:	Public, 4 year + graduate
Unit:	Department of Puerto Rican Studies
Contact Person:	Ceterino Carrasqaillo, Chair
Address:	250 Bedford Park Boulevard West
	Bronx, NY 10473
Phone:	(718) 960-8280
Unit Offers:	Major, minor
Degrees Offered:	Major and minors in Puerto Rican Studies/Latin American Studies

Majors Per Year:	30
Minors:	20
Faculty:	13
Established:	1970
Special Features:	This department also runs the Bilingual Program, which allows students with limited English proficiency to take college courses while learning English as a second language.

Institution:	**New York City Technical College**
Institution Type:	Public, 2 year or 4 year
Unit:	Puerto Rican and Latin American Studies Program
Contact Person:	John D. Vasquez, Program Coordinator
Address:	300 Jay Street A642
	Brooklyn, NY 11201
Phone:	(718) 260-5202
Fax:	(718) 260-5198
Faculty:	4
Established:	1970
Special Features:	This is the only technical college in the CUNY system.

Institution:	**Brooklyn College -CUNY**
Institution Type:	Public, 4 year
Unit:	Department of Puerto Rican Studies
Contact Person:	V. Sanchez Korrol, Chair
Address:	2900 Bedford Avenue
	Brooklyn, NY 11210
Phone:	(718) 951-5561
Unit Offers:	Major, minor, classes
Degrees Offered:	B.A., B.S., M.A., M.S.
Majors Per Year:	30
Minors:	50
Faculty:	8
Established:	1971

Institution:	**Queens College-CUNY**
Institution Type:	Public, 4 year
Unit:	Puerto Rican Studies
Contact Person:	Jesse Vasquez

Address:	65-30 Kissena Boulevard
	Flushing, NY 11367
Phone:	(718) 520-7519
Fax:	(718) 997-5222
Unit Offers:	Major, minor, classes
Degrees Offered:	B.A.
Majors Per Year:	10
Faculty:	4–5
Established:	1972

Institution:	**York College-CUNY**
Institution Type:	Public, 4 year
Unit Type:	Puerto Rican and Latin American Studies Certificate
Contact Person:	Gloria Waldman, Chair
Address:	Department of Foreign Languages/ESL/Humanities
	94-20 Guy R. Brewer Boulevard
	Jamaica, NY 11451
Phone:	(718) 262-2430
Fax:	(718) 262-2027
Unit Offers:	Certificate
Degrees Offered:	B.A. in major with Certificate in Latin American and Puerto Rican Studies
Faculty:	10
Established:	1970s

Institution:	**State University of New York-Albany**
Institution Type:	Public, 4 year + graduate
Unit:	Department of Latin American and Caribbean Studies
Contact Person:	Carlos E. Santiago, Chair
Address:	1400 Washington Avenue
	Social Science 250
	Albany, NY 12222
Phone:	(518) 442-4890
Fax:	(518) 442-4790
Unit Offers:	Major, minor, certificate, classes
Degrees Offered:	B.A. Latin American and Caribbean Studies; B.A. Puerto Rican Studies; M.A. Latin American and Caribbean Studies

Majors Per Year:	20
Minors:	10
Faculty:	24
Established:	1980
Special Features:	This department offers an excellent opportunity to benefit from the advantages of interdisciplinary studies, with the flexibility to accommodate diverse career and advanced study plans. The program is a new alternative for those students interested in a program relevant and responsive to some of the major international issues and concerns of our time.

Institution:	**Mount Saint Mary College**
Institution Type:	Private, 4 year
Unit:	Hispanic Studies Program
Contact Person:	Karen Eberle-McCarthy
Address:	Aquinas Hall
	330 Powell Avenue
	Newburgh, NY 12550
Phone:	(914) 569-3174
Fax:	(914) 562-MSMC
Unit Offers:	Major, minor, classes
Degrees Offered:	B.A.
Majors Per Year:	7
Minors:	5
Faculty:	1 full-time, 2 adjuncts
Established:	1981
Special Features:	Special topics reflect interests of students such as Hispanic film and Hispanic women and media in the Spanish-speaking world.

Institution:	**State University of New York-Binghamton**
Unit:	Latin American and Caribbean Area Studies Program
Contact Person:	William Luis, Director
Address:	Binghamton, NY 13902
Phone:	(607) 777-4868

NORTH CAROLINA

Institution:	**Appalachian State University**
Institution Type:	Public, 4 year
Unit:	Interdisciplinary Studies/Latin America Studies Department
Contact Person:	Kay H. Smith, Chair
Address:	Boone, NC 28608
Phone:	(704) 262-3177
E-mail:	smithkh@appstate
Unit Offers:	Major, minor
Degrees Offered:	B.A.
Majors Per Year:	3–5
Minors:	10
Faculty:	6–10
Established:	1986 (minor); 1990 (major)
Special Features:	Latin American Studies is a twenty-four-hour concentration within the Department of Interdisciplinary Studies. Students take courses in several departments.

OHIO

Institution:	**Denison University**
Institution Type:	Private, 4 year
Unit:	Latin American Area Studies Program
Contact Person:	Eduardo Jaramillo, Coordinator
Address:	Modern Language Department
	Granville, OH 43023
Phone:	(614) 587-6731
Fax:	(614) 587-6417
E-mail:	jaramillo@cc.denison.edu
Unit Offers:	Major, minor
Degrees Offered:	B.A.
Majors Per Year:	4
Minors:	1
Faculty	2
Established:	1980s

Special Features:	This program offers summer study in Cuernavaca, Mexico.

Institution:	**University of Cincinnati**
Institution Type:	Public, 4 year + graduate
Unit:	Department of Romance Languages and Literatures
Contact Person:	Connie L. Scarborough, Undergraduate Advisor for Spanish
Address:	ML 377
	Cincinnati, OH 45221
Phone:	(513) 556-1835
Fax:	(513) 556-2577
Unit Offers:	Major, minor, certificate, classes
Degrees Offered:	M.A., Ph.D.
Majors Per Year:	75
Minors:	30
Faculty:	8 full-time and adjunct instructors
Special Features:	Students may specialize in culture (Spanish Studies) or literatures. The department offers opportunities for study in Spain (each spring quarter) and Mexico (summer) as well as a summer M.A. program. A certificate program in business Spanish and a Ph.D. in Spanish are also offered.

PENNSYLVANIA

Institution:	**West Chester State College**
Unit:	Hispanic American Studies
Address:	West Chester, PA 19380

RHODE ISLAND

Institution:	**University of Rhode Island**
Unit:	Latin American Studies Program
Contact Person:	Tom Morin
Address:	Kingston, RI 02881
Phone:	(401) 792-4706

Institution:	**Southern Methodist University**
Unit:	Mexican-American Studies Department
Contact Person:	Anthony Cortese, Director
Address:	Dallas, TX 75275
Phone:	(214) 768-2195

Institution:	**University of Texas at Arlington**
Unit:	Center for Chicano Aged
Address:	Arlington, TX 76019

Institution:	**University of Houston**
Institution Type:	Public, 4 year
Unit:	Mexican American Studies Program
Contact Person:	Tatcho Mindiola, Jr., Director
Address:	4800 Calhoun
	Room 323 AH
	Houston, TX 77204-3783
Phone:	(713) 743-3134
Fax:	(713) 743-3130
Unit Offers:	Minor, classes
Minors Per Year:	50
Faculty:	11
Established:	1974
Special Features:	The Mexican American Studies Program (MAS) at the University of Houston was established in 1974 as an interdisciplinary program encompassing the humanities, fine arts, and social sciences. Its mission is to advance the educational and intellectual development of the Mexican American community by designing and teaching courses, undertaking research projects of various kinds, and engaging in a broad spectrum of public service activities.

Institution:	**Texas Lutheran College**
Institution Type:	Private, 4 year
Unit:	Center for Mexican American Studies (MASC)
Contact Person:	Juan Rodriguez, Director

Address:	1000 West Court Street
	Seguin, TX 78155
Phone:	(210) 372-6059
Fax:	(210) 372-8096
Unit Offers:	Certificate, classes
Faculty:	3
Established:	1971

Institution:	**Texas A&M University-Kingsville**
Institution Type:	Public, 4 year + graduate
Unit:	Southwest Borderlands Cultural Studies and Research Center
Contact Person:	Rosario Torres Raines
Address:	CB 177
	Psychology/Sociology Department
	Kingsville, TX 78363
Phone:	(512) 595-2701
Unit Offers:	Minor, classes
Special Features:	Texas A&M University is located within the United States-Mexican borderlands region currently undergoing significant sociocultural, economic, and demographic change. This complex of changes has had much favorable impact but has also simultaneously produced a multiplicity of social problems along the entire length of the borderlands region. The Southwest Borderlands Cultural Studies and Research Center at Texas A&M University is committed to the practical investigation of those problems and to the development of specialized courses of study that focus on the area, its residents, and its student body.

Institution:	**Corpus Christi State University**
Unit:	Chicano Studies
Address:	P.O. Box 6010
	Corpus Christi, TX 78412

Institution:	**Texas Southmost College**
Unit:	South Texas Institute of Latin and Mexican American Research

| Address: | Brownsville, TX 78520 |

Institution:	**University of Texas-Austin**
Institution Type:	Public, 4 year + graduate
Unit:	Center for Mexican American Studies
Contact Person:	Gilberto Cardenas, Director
Address:	Austin, TX 78712
Phone:	(512) 471-4557
Fax:	(512) 471-9639
Unit Offers:	Major, minor, classes
Degrees Offered:	B.A. Ethnic Studies/Mexican Studies
Majors Per Year:	10
Minors:	5
Faculty:	12
Established:	1970

Institution:	**University of Texas-El Paso**
Institution Type:	Public, 4 year + graduate
Unit:	Chicano Studies Program
Contact Person:	Dennis Bixler-Márquez, Director
Address:	Graham Hall 104
	El Paso, TX 79968
Phone:	(915) 747-5462
Fax:	(915) 747-6501
Unit Offers:	Major, minor, classes
Degrees Offered:	B.A.
Majors Per Year:	10
Minors:	300
Faculty:	52
Established:	1970
Special Features:	Chicano Studies sponsors a wide range of cultural activities and film and lecture series. It sponsors research on issues of importance to the Chicano community and publishes an Occasional Paper Series.

UTAH

Institution:	**University of Utah**
Unit:	Chicano Studies Program
Contact Person:	José Macias, Director
Address:	Salt Lake City, UT 84112
Phone:	(801) 581-5206

WASHINGTON

Institution:	**University of Washington**
Unit:	Chicano Studies Program
Contact Person:	Johnella Butler
	or Erasmo Gamboa
Address:	Seattle, WA 98195
Phone:	(206) 543-5401

Institution:	**Central Washington University**
Unit:	Chicano Studies
Address:	Ellensburg, WA 98926

Institution:	**Washington State University**
Unit:	Chicano Studies Program
Contact Person:	Fernando V. Padilla, Director
Address:	Pullman, WA 99165

WISCONSIN

Institution:	**University of Wisconsin-Whitewater**
Unit:	Chicano Studies Program
Address:	Whitewater, WI 53190

Institution:	**University of Wisconsin-Madison**
Institution Type:	Public, 4 year
Unit:	Chicano Studies Program
Contact Person:	Jim Escalante, Director
Address:	175 Science Hall
	550 N. Park Street
	Madison, WI 53706

Phone:	(608) 263-4486
E-mail:	chicano@macc.wisc.edu
Unit Offers:	Classes
Faculty:	5
Established:	1975
Special Features:	Designed to enrich the university community at large, this program offers a broad selection of courses exploring the varied Chicano/Mexican American experience throughout the United States. The Chicano Studies Program will soon offer students the opportunity to pursue a program certificate in Chicano Studies.

Native American/American Indian Studies

ALASKA

Institution:	**University of Alaska-Fairbanks**
	College of Kuskokwim
Unit:	Yup'ik Language Center
Contact Person:	Gerald S. Domnick, Coordinator
Address:	Bethel, AK 99559
Phone:	(907) 543-4555
Institution:	**University of Alaska-Fairbanks**
Unit:	Alaskan Native Studies Department
Contact Person:	Michael Gaffney, Chair
Address:	508 Gruening
	Fairbanks, AK 99775
Phone:	(907) 474-7181
Unit Offers:	Minor
Degrees Offered:	B.A.
Majors Per Year:	5
Minors:	20
Special Features:	This program emphasizes social science and humanistic approaches to Alaskan Native cultures. The curriculum, degree requirements, and special activities are shaped largely by five organizing principles: emphasis on changing conditions of Alaskan Native life, recognition of Alaskan Native cultural pluralism and varieties of historical experiences, inquiry into Alaskan Native encounters with culturally different aspects of American life and institu-

tions, and understanding the developing Alaskan Native humanities in a changing world.

Institution: **University of Alaska-Douglas Community College**
Unit: Native People of Alaska
Address: Box 135
                 Auke Bay, AK 99821

ARIZONA

Institution: **University of Arizona**
Institution Type: Public, 4 year + graduate
Unit: American Indian Studies Program
Contact Person: Joseph (Jay) H. Stauss, Director
Address: Harvill Building, Room 430
                    Tucson, AZ 85721
Phone: (602) 621-7108
Fax: (602) 621-7952
Unit Offers: Major, minor, classes
Degrees Offered: M.A. American Indian Studies
Majors Per Year: 35
Minors: 8
Faculty: 22
Established: 1982
Special Features: The American Indian Studies Program (AINS) at the University of Arizona enjoys a national reputation as a leader in the field. As the nation's first program to offer an interdisciplinary graduate master's degree in American Indian Studies, AINS is affiliated with one of the most distinguished groups of faculty and scholars in the nation. Because AINS seeks to develop a wider scope of understanding of American Indian peoples, their traditions, and their aspirations for self-determination, AINS is relevant as an academic discipline for both Indians and non-Indians alike.

In carrying out the land grant mission of the University of Arizona, AINS plays a vital role in enhancing the knowledge of Arizona's rich Southwest heritage through developing course work and supporting scholarly research relevant to the indigenous peoples of the state and the nation. As an intellectual discipline, AINS is committed to a deeper understanding of cultural diversity through exploring continuing contributions and governing institutions of American Indian peoples in a complex multicultural society.

Institution:	**Northern Arizona University**
Institution Type:	Public, 4 year + graduate
Unit:	Native American Studies Program
Contact Person:	Lawrence Gishey, Director
Address:	Babbit Administration Center 106
	Box 4085
	Flagstaff, AZ 86011
Phone:	(602) 523-9295
Fax:	(602) 523-1075
Unit Offers:	Minor, classes
Minors Per Year:	30–40
Faculty:	12
Special Features:	The NASM consists of eighteen hours and provides a multidisciplinary understanding of American Indian histories, religions, and cultures in the past and present.

Institution:	**Yavapai College**
Unit:	American Indian Studies
Contact Person:	Anne Highum
Address:	1101 E. Sheldon
	Prescott, AZ 86301

Institution:	**College of Ganado**
Unit:	Native American Studies
Address:	Ganado, AZ 86505

Institution:	**Navajo Community College**
Unit:	Navajo and Indian Studies Program
Address:	Tsaile Rural Post Office
	Tsaile, AZ 86556

Phone: (602) 724-3311
Unit Offers: Courses

CALIFORNIA

Institution:	**University of California-Los Angeles**
Institution Type:	Public, 4 year
Unit:	American Indian Studies Center
Unit Type:	Organized Research Unit
Contact Person:	Dwight Youpee
Address:	3220 Campbell Hall
	Los Angeles, CA 90024
Phone:	(310) 825-7315
Fax:	(310) 206-7060
Unit Offers:	Minor, classes
Degrees Offered:	Master's degrees in American Indian Studies: history, social sciences, literature, arts, music; an undergraduate minor.
Faculty:	10
Established:	1972
Special Features:	The UCLA American Indian Studies offers a two-year master's degree program with a liberal arts orientation. In 1994 the center began to offer an undergraduate minor. The center carries on research, has a postdoctoral program, a predoctoral fellowship, and awards small research grants to faculty and students.

Institution:	**California State University-Long Beach**
Institution Type:	Public, 4 year + graduate
Unit:	American Indian Studies Program
Contact Person:	Mary Ann Jacobs, Director
Address:	1250 Bellflower Boulevard
	Long Beach, CA 90840-3603
Phone:	(310) 985-5293
Fax:	(310) 985-1535
Unit Offers:	Minor, certificate, classes
Degrees Offered:	B.A. with a concentration in American Indian Studies

Minors Per Year:	15–20
Established:	1967
Special Features:	This program offers academic advising, admission assistance, assistance with BIA aid, financial aid/grant listings, information on grades and transfer credit referrals to other campuses and community services, and academic, social, and personal support.

Institution:	**California State University-Northridge**
Unit:	American Indian Studies
Address:	18111 Nordoff Street
	Northridge, CA 91330
Phone:	(818) 885-3331

Institution:	**Palomar College**
Institution Type:	Public, 2 year
Unit:	American Indian Studies
Contact Person:	Steven Crouthamel, Chair
Address:	1140 W. Mission Road
	San Marcos, CA 92069
Phone:	(619) 744-1150 (ext. 2425)
Fax:	(619) 744-8123
Unit Offers:	Certificate, classes
Degrees Offered:	Certificate
Certificates	
Per Year:	6–8
Faculty:	9
Established:	1969–70
Special Features:	This program offers about twenty classes in American Indian Studies and has recently expanded to add American Studies (introductory survey courses). Tenured faculty includes a sociologist, an anthropologist, and a historian. Nearly half of the faculty is Native American.

Institution:	**San Diego State University**
Institution Type:	Public, 4 year + graduate
Unit:	Department of American Indian Studies
Contact Person:	Linda S. Parker, Chair

Address:	College Avenue
	San Diego, CA 92182-0387
Phone:	(619) 594-6991
Fax:	(619) 594-4998
Unit Offers:	Minor
Degrees Offered:	Minor in College of Arts and Letters
Minors Per Year:	40
Faculty:	2 full-time, 4 part-time
Established:	1976 (department); 1970 (program)

Institution:	**Riverside City College**
Unit:	Native American College
Address:	4800 Magnolia Avenue
	Riverside, CA 92506

Institution:	**California State University-Fullerton**
Unit:	American Indian Studies Program
Contact Person:	Carl Jackson, Director
Address:	Fullerton, CA 92634
Phone:	(714) 773-3677

Institution:	**California State University-Fresno**
Institution Type:	Public, 4 year + graduate
Unit:	American Indian Studies Program
Contact Person:	Delores J. Huff, Director
Address:	2225 E. San Ramon
	Fresno, CA 93740-0100
Phone:	(209) 278-3277
Fax:	(209) 278-7664
E-mail:	delores.huff@csufresno.edu
Special Features:	This program offers a full range of American Indian courses including contemporary Indian affairs and seminars in Indian law and the politics of Indian education.

Institution:	**Fresno City College**
Unit:	Native American Studies Program
Contact Person:	Wendy Rose, Coordinator
Address:	1101 University Avenue
	Fresno, CA 93741

Phone:	(209) 442-8210
Institution:	**San Francisco State University**
Unit:	American Indian Studies
Address:	1600 Holloway Avenue
	San Francisco, CA 94132
Phone:	(415) 469-2046
Institution:	**California State University-Hayward**
Unit:	Native American Studies Program
Contact Person:	Roxanne Dunbar Ortiz
Address:	Hayward, CA 94542
Phone:	(510) 881-3255
Institution:	**University of California-Berkeley**
Institution Type:	Public, 4 year + graduate
Unit:	Native American Studies Program
Contact Person:	Karen Biestman, Coordinator
Address:	3415 Dwinelle Hall
	Berkeley, CA 94720
Phone:	(510) 642-6717
Fax:	(510) 643-8084
E-mail:	ojibwa@uclinkberkeley.edu
Unit Offers:	Major, minor
Degrees Offered:	A.B. Native American Studies
Majors Per Year:	25
Minors:	12
Faculty:	8
Institution:	**Sonoma State University**
Unit:	Native American Studies Program
Address:	1801 East Cotati Avenue
	Rohnert Park, CA 94928
Phone:	(707) 664-2450
Institution:	**Humboldt State University**
Unit:	Native American Studies Program
Contact Person:	Jack Norton, Director
Address:	Ethnic Studies
	Arcata, CA 95521

Phone:	(707) 826-4329/3711
Unit Offers:	Major, minor
Degrees Offered:	B.A., M.A.
Special Features:	Humboldt State University offers a B.A. with a Native American Studies major and a minor in Native American Studies. An M.A. is offered through Social Sciences in Native American Studies/Anthropology.

Institution:	**University of California-Davis**
Institution Type:	Public, 4 year + graduate
Unit:	Native American Studies Program
Contact Person:	Jack D. Forbes, Director
Address:	Davis, CA 95616
Phone:	(916) 752-3237
Fax:	(916) 752-7097
Unit Offers:	Major, minor, classes
Degrees Offered:	A.B. North America, Meso-America, South America Studies; designated emphasis in conjunction with several UC-Davis Ph.D. programs
Majors Per Year:	12–20
Minors:	40–50
Faculty:	8
Established:	1969
Special Features:	The program focuses upon the entire Americas, North and South, as well as upon indigenous peoples elsewhere to some degree. We have a highly regarded faculty of top scholars and artists and creative persons. We have been approved by the campus to become a department, subject to a systemwide review. We offer graduate seminars and a Ph.D. in the form of a "designated emphasis in Native American Studies."

Institution:	**D-Q University**
Institution Type:	Private, tribal, 2 year
Unit:	Native American Studies Program
Contact Person:	Carlos Cordero, President or Annzell Loufas, Vice President

Address:	P.O. Box 409
	Davis, CA 95617
Phone:	(916) 758-0470
Fax:	(916) 758-4891
Unit Offers:	Major, certificate, classes
Degrees Offered:	A.A. Indigenous Studies, Native American Fine Arts, Community Development
Special Features:	D-Q University is an intertribal college. California's only tribally controlled college, D-Q University is accredited and is dedicated to the continued progress of indigenous communities.

Institution:	**California State University-Sacramento**
Unit:	Native American Studies Program
Contact Person:	Frank Lapena, Director
Address:	6000 Jay Street
	Sacramento, CA 95819
Phone:	(916) 278-6645 or (916) 454-6452

Institution:	**Yuba College**
Unit:	Native American Studies
Address:	2088 N. Beale Road
	Marysville, CA 95901

Institution:	**Chico State University**
Institution Type:	Public, 4 year + graduate
Unit:	American Indian Studies Program
Contact Person:	Lisa E. Emmerich, Coordinator
Address:	Department of History
	Chico, CA 95929-0735
Phone:	(916) 898-6338/5249
Fax:	(916) 898-6824
Unit Offers:	Minor, classes
Degrees Offered:	B.A. in Ethnic Studies with a minor in American Indian Studies
Minors Per Year:	5–10
Faculty:	1
Established:	1976

COLORADO

Institution:	**University of Colorado**
Unit:	Native American Education Program
Contact Person:	Vivian Locust
Address:	Denver, CO 80202

Institution:	**University of Denver**
Unit:	American Indian Studies
Contact Person:	J. Donald Hughes
Address:	Denver, CO 80208

Institution:	**Fort Lewis College**
Unit:	Division of Intercultural Studies Program
Contact Person:	Mary Jean Moseley, Chair
Address:	Intercultural Center
	Durango, CO 81301
Phone:	(303) 247-7221
Unit Offers:	Major
Degrees Offered:	B.A. Southwest Studies
Special Features:	This program offers a variety of courses related to the cultures of the Southwest, including Navajo Language, Native Americans in the Modern World, and many others.

HAWAII

Institution:	**University of Hawaii-Hilo**
Unit:	Hawaiian Studies
Contact Person:	William Wilson, Director
Address:	Hilo, HI 96720
Phone:	(808) 933-3454

ILLINOIS

Institution:	**Northern Illinois University**
Unit:	American Indian Studies
Address:	Dekalb, IL 60115

Institution:	**Native American Educational Services (NAES) College**
Institution Type:	Private, 4 year
Unit:	Tribal Research Center
Contact Person:	Faith Smith, President
	or David Beck, Director
Address:	2838 W. Peterson
	Chicago, IL 60650
Phone:	(312) 761-5000
Fax:	(312) 761-3808
Unit Offers:	Major, minor, classes
Majors Per Year:	1
Minors:	3
Faculty:	5
Established:	1974

Institution:	**University of Illinois-Chicago**
Unit:	Native American Studies Program
Contact Person:	Mary Glenn Wiley, Associate Dean
Address:	College of Liberal Arts and Sciences (m/c 312)
	Box 4348
	Chicago, IL 60680
Phone:	(312) 996-5383
Unit Offers:	Minor
Special Features:	Students wishing to minor in Native American Studies must complete eighteen semester hours of course work appropriate to the Native American Studies Option chosen in consultation with an adviser. Courses include Archaeology of North America, The First Americans, American Indian Religion and Philosophy, North and South American Indians, Introduction to Native American Literatures and Studies in Native American Literatures, and Introduction to Native American History.

INDIANA

Institution:	**Ball State University**
Unit:	Native American Studies
Address:	Muncie, IN 47306
Phone:	(317) 285-1575
Unit Offers:	Minor

IOWA

Institution:	**Iowa State University**
Institution Type:	4 year + graduate
Unit:	American Indian Studies Program
Contact Person:	Jerry Stubben, Chair
Address:	506 C Ross Hall
	Ames, IA 50011
Phone:	(515) 294-1853
Fax:	(515) 294-1003
Unit Offers:	Minor, classes
Degrees Offered:	B.A. Distributive Studies
Minors:	12
Faculty:	5
Established:	1975
Special Features:	The American Indian Studies Program is a cross-disciplinary program in the College of Liberal Arts and Science and offers to all Iowa State University students an opportunity to learn more about the cultural heritage of American Indians, their historical relationship with non-Indians, and their participation in contemporary American society. This program serves both American Indian and non-Indian students and emphasizes perspectives from anthropology, history, literature, art and design, and political science.

Institution:	**Morningside College**
Institution Type:	Private, 4 year
Unit:	Indian Studies Department
Unit Type:	Program, Department

Contact Person:	Denny Smith, Director
Address:	1501 Morningside Avenue
	Sioux City, IA 51106
Phone:	(712) 274-5000
Fax:	(712) 274-5101
Unit Offers:	Major, minor, classes
Degrees Offered:	Indian Studies major (general); Tribal Management major
Majors Per Year:	5
Minors:	7
Faculty:	1 full-time, 1 part-time
Established:	1975
Special Features:	This department offers an active student Indian club (American Indian Alliance) and offers an annual Indian Awareness Day, including speakers, cultural activities, and a pow-wow.

KANSAS

Institution:	**Haskell Indian Junior College**
Contact Person:	Mary Mae Norton, Chair
Address:	Lawrence, KS 66047
Phone:	(913) 749-8472
Special Features:	Haskell is operated by the Bureau of Indian Affairs.

MASSACHUSETTS

Institution:	**Harvard University**
Unit:	Native American Program
Contact Person:	Jeffrey Hamley, Director
Address:	Read House
	Graduate School of Education
	Appian Way
	Cambridge, MA 02138
Phone:	(617) 495-4923
Fax:	(617) 496-3312

MICHIGAN

Institution:	**Michigan State University**
Unit:	Native American Institute
	Department of Urban Affairs
Contact Person:	George Cornell, Director
Address:	West 104 Owen Hall
	East Lansing, MI 48824
Phone:	(517) 353-6632

Institution:	**Northern Michigan University**
Institution Type:	Public, 4 year + graduate
Unit:	Native American Studies Program
Contact Person:	James Spresser, Melissa Hearn, Co-Directors
Address:	c/o English Department
	Marquette, MI 49855
Phone:	(906) 227-2779 (Spresser)
	(906) 227-1633 (Hearn)
Unit Offers:	Minor, classes
Degrees Offered:	Interdisciplinary minor in Native American Studies
Minors Per Year:	15
Faculty:	7
Established:	1991
Special Features:	The minor includes two courses in beginning Ojibwa language and culture taught as part of the Weekend College Program. Also offered is a course entitled Native American Experience that deals with Native cultures and issues in North America.

MINNESOTA

Institution:	**United Theological Seminary of Twin Cities**
Institution Type:	Private (graduate school), 2 year
Unit:	Diploma in Indian Ministries
Unit Type:	Program
Contact Person:	Wilson Yates, Dean of the Seminary
Address:	3000 5th Street, N.W.
	New Brighton, MN 55112

Phone:	(612) 633-4311
Fax:	(612) 633-4315
Majors Per Year:	New program effective 1994–95
Special Features:	The program has been jointly designed by the Seminary and the Minnesota Committee on Indian Work (MCIW) with the support of the Episcopal Council of Indian Ministries, the Bishop, and the Standing Committee. The faculty and supervisors will include persons from both institutions. The program represents a new model for theological education in the education of Native American clergy with strong focus on special issues and needs that arise in Indian ministries.

Institution:	**Minneapolis College of Art and Design**
Unit:	Native American Arts Program
Address:	200 E. 25th Street
	Minneapolis, MN 55404

Institution:	**Augsburg College**
Institution Type:	Private, 4 year + graduate
Unit:	American Indian Support Program
Contact Person:	Bonnie Wallace, Director
Address:	2211 Riverside Avenue
	Minneapolis, MN 55407
Phone:	(612) 330-1138
Fax:	(612) 330-1606
Unit Offers:	Minor, classes
Degrees Offered:	Minor in American Indian Studies
Faculty:	2 full-time, 8 part-time American Indian faculty
Special Features:	AISP has the highest retention and graduation rate (eighty-five percent) of American Indian students in postsecondary institutions in Minnesota.

Institution:	**University of Minnesota-Minneapolis**
Institution Type:	Public, 4 year + graduate
Unit:	American Indian Studies Department
Contact Person:	David Born, Chair

Address:	102 Scott Hall
	72 Pleasant Street, S.E.
	Minneapolis, MN 55455
Phone:	(612) 624-1338
Fax:	(612) 624-3858
E-mail:	dborn@maroon.tc.umn.edu
Unit Offers:	Major, minor
Degrees Offered:	B.A.
Majors Per Year:	30
Minors:	10
Faculty:	10
Special Features:	Students may take a six-quarter sequence in Ojibwa or Dakota to complete the undergraduate second language requirement.

Institution:	**College of St. Scholastica**
Institution Type:	Private, 4 year
Unit:	American Indian Studies Department
Contact Person:	Barbara King, Chair
Address:	1200 Kenwood Avenue
	Duluth, MN 55811-4199
Phone:	(218) 723-6170
Fax:	(218) 723-6290
Unit Offers:	Minor, classes
Minors Per Year:	4–6
Faculty:	2
Established:	1970s
Special Features:	The department offers numerous courses including history, philosophy, art and music, law and public policy, literature, and an introduction to Indian Studies. It has close ties with a Bilingual Teacher Training Program that offers Ojibwe language courses and works with the social work program and offers a joint certificate that focuses on social work practice with American Indians.

Institution:	**University of Minnesota, School of Medicine**
Unit:	American Indian Studies Program
Contact Person:	Robert Divers
Address:	Duluth, MN 55812

Institution:	University of Minnesota-Duluth
Institution Type:	Public, 4 year + graduate
Unit:	American Indian Studies Department
Contact Person:	Robert E. Powless, Chair
Address:	209 Bohannon Hall
	10 University Drive
	Duluth, MN 55812-2496
Phone:	(218) 726-8771
Fax:	(218) 726-6386
Unit Offers:	Minor, classes
Minors Per Year:	8
Faculty:	5
Established:	1972
Special Features:	Special features include: (1) an American Indian Education/Culture Project at Federal Correctional Institution at Sandstone, MN; (2) Ojibwe Language Immersion Program during summers; and (3) a concentration in American Indian law.

Institution:	Moorhead State University
Unit:	American Indian Studies Program
Contact Person:	Donna Rush, Director
Address:	P.O. Box 111
	Moorhead, MN 56563
Phone:	(218) 236-4043
Unit Offers:	Minor
Special Features:	A minor requires twenty-four credits in courses such as the following: Traditional American Indian Culture, Contemporary American Indians, American Indian Belief Systems, American Indian Cultural Origins, Plains Indian Culture, Ojibwe Culture, Indian Education/North Dakota, Indians of the Southwest, Readings on the American Indian, Minnesota Prehistoric People, North American Archaeology, Introduction to American Ethnic Literature, and others.

Institution:	Bemidji State University
Institution Type:	Public, 4 year + graduate
Unit:	Indian Studies Program

Contact Person:	Kent Smith, Director
Address:	1500 Birchmont Drive
	Bemidji, MN 56601-2699
Phone:	(218) 755-3977
Fax:	(218) 755-4115
Unit Offers:	Major, minor, classes
Degrees Offered:	B.A. Indian Studies
Majors Per Year:	15
Minors:	25
Faculty:	6
Established:	1969

MONTANA

Institution:	**Little Big Horn College**
Institution Type:	Tribal, 2 year
Contact Person:	Janine Pease-Windy Boy, President
Address:	P.O. Box 370
	Crow Agency, MT 59022
Phone:	(406) 638-7211
Fax:	(406) 638-7213
Unit Offers:	Major, minor
Degrees Offered:	A.A. Crow Studies
Majors:	10
Minors:	15
Faculty:	2
Established:	1983
Special Features:	The Department of Crow Studies offers courses in the humanities and social sciences that include introductory courses to Native American Studies and the Montana Indian, but it predominantly offers courses in the scholarship of the Crow people: socio-family kinships, Crow language I to III, history of the Ariets, oral history of the Crows, music and dance of the Crow people, Crow Indian history post-settlement, etc.

Institution:	**Dull Knife Memorial College**
Contact Person:	Arthur MacDonald

Address:	P.O. Box 1174
	Kalispell, MT 59901
Phone:	(406) 477-6219

Institution:	**Eastern Montana College**
Unit:	Native American Studies Program
Contact Person:	Ruey-Lin Lin, Chair
Address:	1500 N. 30th Street
	Billings, MT 59101
Phone:	(406) 657-2311
Unit Offers:	Minor
Special Features:	Courses include Native American Literature, Social Issues of the Native American, The Indian and the Law, Montana Indian Groups Prior to 1862 and to Present, Native American Psychology, Shamanism and Social Medicine, and Survey of American Indian Art.

Institution:	**Fort Peck Community College**
Contact Person:	James Shanley
Address:	P.O. Box 575
	Poplar, MT 59255
Phone:	(406) 768-5155

Institution:	**College of Great Falls**
Institution Type:	Private, 4 year
Unit:	Department of Human Services
Contact Person:	Deborah Kottel, Head
Address:	Division of Human Service
	1301 20th Street South
	Great Falls, MT 59405
Phone:	(406) 761-8210 (ext. 303)
Fax:	(406) 771-7008
Unit Offers:	Minor
Minors Per Year:	20
Faculty:	3
Established:	1978
Special Features:	The department offers an interdisciplinary minor with a strong emphasis on field experience.

Institution:	**Blackfeet Community College**
Contact Person:	Gordon Belcourt
Address:	P.O. Box 819
	Browning, MT 59417
Phone:	(406) 338-5441

Institution:	**Northern Montana College**
Institution Type:	Public, 4 year + graduate
Unit:	Native American Studies Program
Contact Person:	S. G. Sylvester, Chair
Address:	305 Cowan Hall—NMC
	Havre, MT 59501
Phone:	(406) 265-4169
Fax:	(406) 265-3777
Unit Offers:	Major, minor
Majors Per Year:	20
Minors:	30
Faculty:	3
Established:	1992

Institution:	**Fort Belknap Community College**
Contact Person:	Margaret Perez
Address:	P.O. Box 547
	Harlem, MT 59526
Phone:	(406) 353-2205 (ext. 241)

Institution:	**Caroll College**
Unit:	Native American Studies
Address:	Helena, MT 59601

Institution:	**Montana State University**
Institution Type:	Public, 4 year + graduate
Unit:	Center for Native American Studies
Contact Person:	Wayne J. Stein, Director
Address:	2-152 Wilson Hall
	Bozeman, MT 59717-0234
Phone:	(406) 994-3881
Unit Offers:	Minor
Degrees Offered:	Minor in Native American Studies
Minors Per Year:	30

Faculty:	5
Established:	1975
Special Features:	Special features include a four-part mission: academic instruction, Native American student support, research, and service. We have very strong ties to the tribal colleges in Montana and the region.

Institution:	**University of Montana**
Institution Type:	Public, 4 year + graduate
Unit:	Native Studies Program
Contact Person:	Bonnie Craig, Director
Address:	600 University
	Missoula, MT 59801
Phone:	(406) 243-5831
Fax:	(406) 243-4076
Unit Offers:	Minor, classes
Minors Per Year:	40
Faculty:	4
Established:	1969
Special Features:	This program offers classes taught from a Native perspective.

Institution:	**Salish-Kootenai Community College**
Unit:	Native American Studies
Contact Person:	Joe McDonald
Address:	Box 117
	Pablo, MT 59855
Phone:	(406) 675-4800

Institution:	**Flathead Valley Community College**
Institution Type:	Public, 2 year
Unit:	Native American Studies Class
Contact Person:	Evelyn Pool, Instructor
Address:	777 Grandview Drive
	Kalispell, MT 59901
Phone:	(406) 756-3822
Fax:	(406) 756-3815
Unit Offers:	Classes
Faculty:	2

Special Features:	This class provides exposure to Indian art, music, celebrations, and personalities, emphasizing current government, education, and health care and their impact on individuals, families, and tribes. The class also gives the student an awareness of social patterns, prejudices, and practices exemplified by these people and in our own lives.

NEBRASKA

Institution:	**Nebraska Indian Community College**
Contact Person:	Thelma Thomas
Address:	P.O. Box 752
	Winnebago, NE 68071
Phone:	(402) 878-2414

Institution:	**University of Nebraska-Lincoln**
Institution Type:	Public, 4 year
Unit:	Native American Studies Program
Contact Person:	Charles Ballard, Director
Address:	301 Burnett Hall
	P.O. Box 880335
	Lincoln, NE 68588-0335
Phone:	(402) 472-1663
Unit Offers:	Minor
Minors Per Year:	13
Faculty:	8
Established:	1967

Institution:	**American Indian Satellite Community College**
Address:	801 E. Benjamin Avenue
	Norfolk, NE 68701
Established:	1973

NEW HAMPSHIRE

Institution:	**Dartmouth College**
Institution Type:	Private, 4 year

Unit:	Native American Studies Department
Contact Person:	Linda M. Welch, Administrative Assistant
Address:	306 Bartlett Hall (HB 6152)
	Hanover, NH 03755
Phone:	(603) 646-3530
Fax:	(603) 646-3115
Unit Offers:	Minor, classes
Minors Per Year:	10
Faculty:	9
Established:	1972
Special Features:	As of fall 1993, Dartmouth students may achieve minor status in Native American Studies, or may design a special major in Native American Studies. Many Native and non-Native students at Dartmouth participate in a term-long internship experience sponsored by a Native American government or support organization. Native American Studies also hosts annual symposia on subjects of Native American interest to scholars around the country.

NEW MEXICO

Institution:	**University of New Mexico**
Institution Type:	Public, 4 year + graduate
Unit:	Native American Studies Program
Contact Person:	Ted Jojola, Director
Address:	1812 Las Lomas, N.E.
	Albuquerque, NM 87131
Phone:	(505) 277-3917
Fax:	(505) 277-1818
Unit Offers:	Classes
Established:	1970
Special Features:	Native American Studies is the academic component of the Native American Studies Center. The center's other components include a research and publication program, the Institute for Native American Development (INAD), and an academic support program, the Native American Academic

Intervention Project. Presently, a degree option at the B.A. level is being pursued. Courses cosponsored with Native American Studies are offered through various academic departments.

Institution: **Southwestern Indian Polytechnic Institute**
Contact Person: Robert G. Martin
Address: P.O. Box 10146
                    9169 Coors Road, NW
                    Albuquerque, NM 87184
Phone: (505) 766-8418/3763

Institution: **Navajo Community College**
Address: P.O. Box 580
                    Shiprock, NM 87420
Phone: (505) 368-5291

Institution: **Institute of American Indian Arts**
Address: College of Santa Fe Campus
                    St. Michael's Drive
                    Santa Fe, NM 87501-9990

Institution: **New Mexico Highlands University**
Unit: Native American Studies
Address: Las Vegas, NM 87701

Institution: **New Mexico State University**
Unit: American Indian Program
Contact Person: Harry A. Lujan, Director
Address: Las Cruces, NM 88003
Phone: (505) 646-4207

NEW YORK

Institution: **State University of New York**
Unit: Native Northeastern Studies
Contact Person: Dean R. Snow
Address: Department of Anthropology
                    Albany, NY 12222
Phone: (518) 442-4700

Institution:	**State University of New York-New Paltz**
Institution Type:	4 year
Unit:	American Indian Studies Program
Contact Person:	L. Hauptman, Professor
Address:	Department of History
	New Paltz, NY 12561
Phone:	(914) 257-3523/3545
Fax:	(914) 257-3009
Unit Offers:	Minor
Minors Per Year:	5
Faculty:	3
Established:	1975–76

Institution:	**State University of New York-Oswego**
Unit:	Native American Studies
Address:	Oswego, NY 13126

Institution:	**Colgate University**
Institution Type:	Private, 4 year
Unit:	Native American Studies Program
Contact Person:	Jordan E. Kerber, Director
Address:	Department of Sociology and Anthropology
	Hamilton, NY 13346
Phone:	(315) 824-7559
Fax:	(315) 824-7974
Unit Offers:	Major, minor, classes
Degrees Offered:	B.A.
Majors Per Year:	4
Minors:	2
Faculty:	9
Established:	1982
Special Features:	This program offers a comparative and historical study of the pre-Columbian, colonial, and contemporary Native American cultures of the Americas from a wide range of disciplines including art, archaeology, history, geography, and religion.

Institution:	**State University of New York-Buffalo**
Unit:	Native American Studies Program
Contact Person:	Oren Lyons, Coordinator

Address:	1010 Clemens Hall
	Buffalo, NY 14260
Phone:	(716) 645-2546
Fax:	(716) 645-5977

Institution:	**Ithaca College**
Unit:	American Indian Studies Program
Contact Person:	Raymond Fougnier
Address:	Cornell, 215 Stone Hall
	Ithaca, NY 14850

Institution:	**Cornell University**
Unit:	American Indian Studies
Address:	Ithaca, NY 14853
Phone:	(607) 255-5137

NORTH CAROLINA

Institution:	**Pembroke State University**
Institution Type:	Public, 4 year + graduate
Unit:	American Indian Studies Department
Contact Person:	Linda E. Oxendine, Chair
Address:	Pembroke, NC 28372
Phone:	(919) 521-6266
Fax:	(919) 521-6547
Unit Offers:	Major, minor
Degrees Offered:	B.A. American Indian Studies
Majors Per Year:	8–10
Minors:	5
Faculty:	1 full-time, 5 adjunct from other departments, 2 part-time
Established:	1984
Special Features:	Pembroke State University began in 1887 as an institution for American Indians. Located in the heart of the Lumbee Indian community, PSU today serves a multiracial student body. Through the American Indian Studies Department, PSU offers a program to educate students about the rich diversity of American Indian history and cul-

ture, to promote research and scholarship concerning American Indian issues, and to prepare students for professional or scholarly careers.

Institution:	Western Carolina University
Institution Type:	Public, 4 year + graduate
Unit:	Cherokee Center
Unit Type:	Program
Contact Person:	L. H. Arney, Director
Address:	520 HF Robinson Building
	Cullowhee, NC 28723
Phone:	(704) 227-7151
Fax:	(704) 227-7424
Unit Offers:	Minor
Degrees Offered:	A Cherokee minor may be taken along with any of a number of academic majors.
Minors Per Year:	3
Faculty:	4
Established:	before 1978
Special Features:	Some of the classes are taken at the university, while others may be taken on the Cherokee Reservation, twenty-five miles away.

NORTH DAKOTA

Institution:	University of North Dakota
Institution Type:	Public, 4 year + graduate
Unit:	Department of Indian Studies
Contact Person:	Mary Jane Schneider, Chair
Address:	Box 7103
	Grand Forks, ND 58202
Phone:	(701) 777-4315
Unit Offers:	Major, minor
Degrees Offered:	B.A. Indian Studies
Majors Per Year:	25
Minors:	6
Faculty:	3
Established:	1977
Special Features:	This is an interdisciplinary department oriented

around traditional and contemporary Northern Plains Indian culture. It also provides a good general background in history and culture of other North American tribes, offering languages, literature, and studies in tribal government.

Institution:	**Turtle Mountain Community College**
Institution Type:	Tribal, 2 year
Contact Person:	Larry Belgarda, Dean of Instruction
Address:	P.O. Box 340
	Belcourt, ND 58316
Phone:	(701) 477-5605
Fax:	(701) 477-5028
Unit Offers:	Classes
Degrees Offered:	A.A. Arts; A.A. Science; A.A. Applied Science; "Ethnic" Studies is integrated throughout the curriculum in all degree programs and in all courses.
Majors Per Year:	500
Minors:	500
Faculty:	36
Established:	1972
Special Features:	TMCC requires each course syllabus to reflect integration of American Indian, especially Chippewa, contents and focus. Nearly 100 percent (90 to 95 percent generally) of our student body is Indian.

Institution:	**Little Hoop Community College**
Contact Person:	Merril Berg
Address:	P.O. Box 269
	Fort Totten, ND 58335
Phone:	(701) 766-4415

Institution:	**United Tribes Technical College**
Contact Person:	David Gipp
Address:	3315 University Drive
	Bismarck, ND 58501

Institution:	**University of Mary**
Institution Type:	Private, 4 year + graduate

Unit:	Indian Studies Program
Contact Person:	Carole Barrett
Address:	7500 University Drive
	Bismarck, ND 58504
Phone:	(701) 255-7500 (ext. 337)
Fax:	(701) 255-7687
Unit Offers:	Minor, classes
Degrees Offered:	Minor in Indian Studies offered through the Division of Social and Behavioral Sciences
Minors Per Year:	12
Faculty:	1
Established:	1975
Special Features:	The courses in the Indian Studies area are taken by a large number of students. Indian Studies coursework is required for education majors according to state law. Social work majors at the University of Mary are required to take Indian Studies. The concentration is on Northern Plains tribes.

Institution:	**Standing Rock Community College**
Unit:	Lakota Studies
Contact Person:	Jack Barrdew
Address:	HC #1, Box 4
	Fort Yates, ND 58538
Phone:	(701) 854-3861

Institution:	**Minot State College**
Unit:	American Indian Studies
Address:	Minot, ND 58701

OKLAHOMA

Institution:	**University of Science and Arts of Oklahoma**
Institution Type:	Public, 4 year
Unit:	American Indian Studies Program
Contact Person:	Howard Meredith
Address:	Chickasha, OK 73018-0001
Phone:	(405) 224-3140

Fax:	(405) 521-6244
Unit Offers:	Major, minor
Degrees Offered:	B.A. American Indian Studies
Majors Per Year:	3
Minors:	3
Faculty:	3
Special Features:	American Indian Studies is designed to advance the university's interdisciplinary, liberal arts mission. The program works regularly with area tribes including Comanche, Kiowa, Apache, Wichita, Caddo, Delaware, Cheyenne, Arapaho, and Chickasaw.

Institution:	**University of Oklahoma**
Unit:	Native American Studies
Address:	Norman, OK 73069

Institution:	**Oscar Rose Junior College**
Unit:	Native American Studies
Contact Person:	Carolyn Poole
Address:	Midwest City, OK 73110

Institution:	**Murray State College**
Unit:	American Indian Studies
Contact Person:	Sue McGilbray
Address:	Tishomingo, OK 73460

Institution:	**Oklahoma State University**
Institution Type:	Public, 4 year + graduate
Unit:	Native American Area Studies Certificate
Contact Person:	John R. Cross
Address:	Sociology Department
	CLB 033
	Stillwater, OK 74078
Phone:	(405) 744-6121
Fax:	(405) 744-5780
Unit Offers:	Certificate, classes
Faculty:	8
Special Features:	The Native American Area Studies Certificate Program (NAASCP) enables the student to de-

velop an expertise in Native American Studies while majoring in an approved degree program at OSU. The specialization can contribute to the academic preparation of individuals who plan to work in occupations related to Native American communities and programs, such as public administration, business administration, teaching, or social sciences. The certificate program also provides a basic background for students who plan graduate study or research on Native American topics.

Institution:	**Bacone College**
Unit:	American Indian Studies
Contact Person:	Will Freeman
Address:	Muskogee, OK 74401

Institution:	**Northeastern State University**
Institution Type:	Public, 4 year
Unit:	Native American Studies Program
Contact Person:	William Corbett, Chair
Address:	History Department
	College of Social and Behavioral Sciences
	Tahlequah, OK 74464-2399
Phone:	(918) 456-5511 (ext. 3500)
Unit Offers:	Major, minor
Degrees Offered:	B.A. Native American Studies
Majors Per Year:	15
Minors:	10
Faculty:	5
Established:	1970
Special Features:	The Native American Studies degree at Northeastern State University is an interdisciplinary program. The major consists of thirty-six hours of coursework drawn from the fields of anthropology/archaeology, history, literature, political science, and sociology. The emphasis of the program is to inform students about the historical experience and social and cultural heritage of the American Indian.

Institution:	**Southeastern Oklahoma State University**
Unit:	Choctaw/Native American Studies
Contact Person:	E. Sturch
Address:	Durant, OK 74701

Institution:	**East Central State University**
Unit:	Bilingual/Bicultural Seminole Program
Address:	Ada, OK 74820

OREGON

Institution:	**Eastern Oregon State College**
Institution Type:	Public, 4 year + graduate
Unit:	Native American Program
Contact Person:	Jackie Grant, Director
Address:	1410 "L" Avenue
	La Grande, OR 97850-2899
Phone:	(503) 962-3741
Fax:	(503) 962-3849
Unit Offers:	Classes
Established:	1969
Special Features:	The Native American Program is a student support service program and works to assist American Indian and Alaskan students as they pursue their educational goals. Native American Program faculty and staff conduct workshops and student-centered classes that promote successful completion of an undergraduate degree.

PENNSYLVANIA

Institution:	**Pennsylvania State University**
Institution Type:	Public, 4 year + graduate
Unit:	Center, American Indian Education Policy
Contact Person:	Linda Sue Warner, Director
Address:	320 Rackley Building
	University Park, PA 16803
Phone:	(814) 865-1489

Fax:	(814) 863-7532
Unit Offers:	Major
Degrees Offered:	M.Ed. Education Administration; Ph.D. Education Administration; M.Ed. Special Education
Established:	1970
Special Features:	This is currently the longest-running graduate program of its type for American Indian/Alaskan Native students in this country, with a 90 percent completion rate.

SOUTH DAKOTA

Institution:	**South Dakota State University**
Institution Type:	Public, 4 year + graduate
Unit:	American Indian Studies Program
Contact Person:	D. J. Hess, Coordinator
Address:	Sociology Department
	Scobey Hall
	Brookings, SD 57007
Phone:	(605) 688-4892
Unit Offers:	Minor, classes
Degrees Offered:	Minor in American Indian Studies
Minors Per Year:	5–6
Faculty:	12
Established:	1975
Special Features:	The American Indian Studies Program offers an interdisciplinary approach to the study of American Indian life and cultures. Course work in various departments of the university provides a broad base for understanding the past, present, and future of American Indian people.

Institution:	**University of South Dakota**
Institution Type:	Public, 4 year + graduate
Unit:	Institute of American Indian Studies
Unit Type:	Institute, program, department, center
Contact Person:	Leonard R. Bruguier, Director
Address:	414 East Clark Street
	Vermillion, SD 57069-2390

Phone:	(605) 677-5209
Fax:	(605) 677-5073
Unit Offers:	Major, minor, classes
Degrees Offered:	Minors in Indian Studies are offered and supervised by the Department of History and the Institute of American Indian Studies; Master of Selected Studies in Indian Studies is also offered; Doctorate in Regional Studies is pending
Majors Per Year:	4
Minors:	10
Faculty:	6
Established:	1955
Special Features:	This academic department supports multicultural/interdisciplinary studies in areas of anthropology, history, Native language and culture, political and governmental structure, literature, and special directed studies topics. The institute administers the South Dakota Oral History Center of Indian and non-Indian interviews, and maintains the Joseph Harper Cash Memorial Library of frontier, Western, Indian, and mining history.

Institution:	**Sioux Falls College**
Unit:	Native American Studies
Address:	1501 South Prairie Avenue
	Sioux Falls, SD 57105

Institution:	**Sisseton Wahpeton Community College**
Institution Type:	Tribal, 2 year
Unit:	Institute for Dakota Studies
Contact Person:	Jim Green, Director
Address:	Old Agency Box 689
	Sisseton, SD 57262
Phone:	(605) 698-7879
Fax:	(605) 698-3132
Unit Offers:	Major, classes
Degrees Offered:	A.A. Dakota Studies
Minors Per Year:	4
Faculty:	4
Established:	1990

Special Features:	The institute offers a Special Training Program for the teaching of Native languages; it offers training in the "silent" or "discovery way" of teaching languages. The approach is designed to get students speaking, rather than allowing the teacher to do the talking.

Institution:	**Dakota Wesleyan University**
Institution Type:	Private, 4 year
Unit:	American Indian Studies Program
Contact Person:	Aaron L. Hozid, Director
Address:	1200 W. University
	Mitchell, SD 57301
Phone:	(605) 995-2637
Fax:	(605) 995-2699
Unit Offers:	Minor, classes
Minors Per Year:	2–4
Faculty:	1
Established:	1970
Special Features:	The program features an American Indian Club, which includes Indian and non-Indian students. The club and the program sponsor a number of educational and cultural events. The program also provides an additional support program for Native American students and provides a focus for dealing with issues and concerns in regard to the college and the community.

Institution:	**Northern State College**
Unit:	American Indian Studies
Address:	Aberdeen, SD 57401

Institution:	**Sinte Gleska College**
Unit:	Lakota Studies
Contact Person:	Victor Douville
Address:	P.O. Box 8
	Mission, SD 57555

Institution:	**Cheyenne River Community College**
Contact Person:	Arlouine Gay Kingman

Address:	P.O. Box 220-N. Elm Street
	Eagle Butte, SD 57625
Phone:	(605) 964-8635

Institution:	**Oglala Lakota College**
Contact Person:	Lowell Amiotte
Address:	P.O. Box 490
	Kyle, SD 57752
Phone:	(605) 455-2321

Institution:	**Oglala Sioux Community College**
Address:	Pine Ridge, SD 57770

Institution:	**Black Hills State University**
Institution Type:	Public, 4 year + graduate
Unit:	Center for Indian Studies
Contact Person:	Frank McLeod, Director
Address:	1200 University
	College Station Box 9044
	Spearfish, SD 57799-9044
Phone:	(605) 642-6285
Fax:	(605) 642-6214
Unit Offers:	Minor, classes
Special Features:	The Indian Studies minor provides courses in Native American language, history, and culture, especially for use in teacher education.

TEXAS

Institution:	**Incarnate Word College**
Unit:	Native American Studies
Address:	4301 Broadway
	San Antonio, TX 78209
Phone:	(512) 828-1261 (ext. 247)

Institution:	**Texas Tech University**
Contact Person:	James A. Goss
Address:	Lubbock, TX 79409
Phone:	(806) 742-2228

UTAH

Institution:	**University of Utah**
Unit:	Native American Studies Department
Contact Person:	Dan Edwards, Director
Address:	Salt Lake City, UT 84112
Phone:	(801) 581-5206

Institution:	**Weber State College**
Unit:	Native American Program
Contact Person:	Craig Brandow
Address:	Ogden, UT 84408

WASHINGTON

Institution:	**Northwest Indian College**
Institution Type:	Tribal, 2 year
Contact Person:	Barbara Roberts, Dean
Address:	2522 Kwina Road
	Bellingham, WA 48226
Phone:	(206) 676-2772/2773
Fax:	(206) 758-0136
Unit Offers:	Certificate
Degrees Offered:	ATA Northwest Coastal Indian Studies in Art
Majors Per Year:	1
Faculty:	2.5
Established:	1988

Institution:	**University of Washington**
Institution Type:	Public, 4 year + graduate
Unit:	American Indian Studies Center
Contact Person:	James Nason, Director
Address:	Seattle, WA 98195
Phone:	(206) 543-9082
Fax:	(206) 543-3285
E-mail:	jnason@u.washington.edu
Unit Offers:	Major, minor, classes
Degrees Offered:	B.A. via General and Interdisciplinary Studies Program

Majors Per Year:	1–2
Faculty:	12
Established:	1970
Special Features:	This program offers a broad range of national and regionally focused coursework on Native American cultural, social, legal, historical, and artistic issues, with special attention to Northwest Coast art and culture.

Institution:	**Evergreen State College**
Unit:	Native American Studies
Address:	Olympia, WA 98505

Institution:	**Central Washington University**
Unit:	American Indian Studies
Address:	Ellensburg, WA 98926

Institution:	**Eastern Washington University**
Unit:	Indian Education Program
Contact Person:	Cecil Jose, Director
Address:	Cheney, WA 99004
Phone:	(509) 359-2401

Institution:	**Washington State University**
Unit:	Comparative American Cultures Program
Contact Person:	William Willard, Director
Address:	Wilson 111
	Pullman, WA 99164
Phone:	(509) 335-2605
Unit Offers:	Major, minor
Degrees Offered:	B.A. in Comparative Cultures; minor in Native American Studies
Special Features:	Courses offered include: Native American Studies; Native Music of North America; Inter-American Native Communities of North America; Native American Literature; North American History, Prehistory to Present; America before Columbus; Contemporary Native Peoples of the Americas, Topics in Canadian Studies; Indians of

the Northwest; Indians of the Southwest; Native
Peoples of Canada; and Historical Perspectives.

Institution:	**Fort Wright College**
Unit:	Indian Studies
Address:	West 4000 Randolph Road
	Spokane, WA 99204

WISCONSIN

Institution:	**University of Wisconsin-Milwaukee**
Unit:	American Indian Studies Program
Contact Person:	John Boatman, Coordinator
Address:	College of Letters and Sciences
	P.O. Box 413
	Milwaukee, WI 53201
Phone:	(414) 229-6686
Special Features:	This program offers courses in several academic departments, does research in American Indian Studies, and publishes texts in American Indian Studies.

Institution:	**Milwaukee Area Technical College**
Institution Type:	Public, 2 year
Unit:	Department of Multicultural Affairs/ American Indian Office
Contact Person:	Pat Logan, Student Services Specialist
Address:	700 W. State Street
	Milwaukee, WI 53215
Phone:	(414) 278-6800
Fax:	(414) 271-2195
Unit Offers:	Major, certificate, classes
Degrees Offered:	A.A.
Established:	1918

Institution:	**University of Wisconsin-Madison**
Institution Type:	Public, 4 year + graduate
Unit:	American Indian Studies Program
Contact Person:	C. Matthew Snipp, Director

Address:	1188 Educational Sciences Building
	1025 West Johnson Street
	Madison, WI 53706
Phone:	(608) 253-5569 / 262-9528
Fax:	(608) 263-6448
Unit Offers:	Certificate in process
Faculty:	12
Established:	1972

Institution:	**University of Wisconsin-Green Bay**
Unit:	Native American Studies
Address:	Green Bay, WI 54311

Institution:	**University of Wisconsin-Stevens Point**
Institution Type:	Public
Unit:	Native American Center
Contact Person:	Ben Ramirez-shkwegnaabi, Acting Assistant Vice Chancellor for Advancement of Cultural Diversity
Address:	209 Student Services Building
	Stevens Point, WI 54481-3897
Phone:	(715) 346-4211
Special Features:	This is a statewide Native American Center. It provides managerial/technical education to Native American people across the state.

Institution:	**Nicolet Area Technical College**
Institution Type:	Public, 2 year
Unit:	Native American Center
Contact Person:	Michele LaRock, Director
Address:	Box 518
	Rhinelander, WI 54501
Phone:	(715) 365-4434
Unit Offers:	Classes
Established:	1970
Special Features:	Nicolet Area Technical College is a two-year institution with a variety of certificate programs and transfer courses. It offers some Native American courses. Nicolet has several outreach centers and a second Lakeland campus in Minocqua, Wisconsin. It serves mostly the three area reservations:

Mole Lake Sokaogon Chippewa, Lac du Flambeau Chippewa, and Forest Co. Potawatomi.

Institution:	**University of Wisconsin-Eau Claire**
Institution Type:	Public, 4 year + graduate
Unit:	American Indian Studies Program
Contact Person:	Richard St. Germaine, Chair
Address:	Foundations of Education
	Eau Claire, WI 54702-4004
Phone:	(715) 836-4379
Fax:	(715) 836-2380
Unit Offers:	Minor
Minors Per Year:	10
Faculty:	15
Special Features:	This program draws from many departments for a broad spectrum approach to American Indian Studies, making extensive use of area elders and leaders for special course offerings.

Institution:	**Northland College**
Unit:	Native American Studies
Address:	Ashland, WI 54806

Institution:	**Mount Senario College**
Unit:	American Indian Program
Contact Person:	Phyllis Frederick
Address:	Ladysmith, WI 54848

WYOMING

Institution:	**Central Wyoming College**
Institution Type:	Public, 2 year
Unit:	Native American Studies Program
Contact Person:	Jeff Anderson, Coordinator
Address:	2660 Peck Avenue
	Riverton, WY 82520
Phone:	(307) 856-9291 (ext. 193)
Unit Offers:	Major, classes
Degrees Offered:	A.A. Native American Studies

Majors Per Year:	2
Faculty:	4 adjunct faculty
Established:	1993–94
Special Features:	The program of study combines general issues and topics in Native American Studies with a local specific focus on Northern Arapaho and Eastern Shoshone history, language, and culture.

Ethnic Studies

CALIFORNIA

Institution:	Los Angeles City College
Institution Type:	Public, 2 year
Unit:	American Cultures Department
Contact Person:	Mary T. Crockett, Chair
Address:	855 North Vermont Avenue
	Los Angeles, CA 90029
Phone:	(213) 953-4364
Unit Offers:	Major, minor, classes
Degrees Offered:	A.A. African American Studies; A.A. Chicano Studies; A.A. Asian American Studies
Majors Per Year:	2–5
Faculty:	3
Established:	1969
Special Features:	The American Cultures Department believes course content relating to the life and history of Asians, blacks, and Chicanos is a valid and necessary part of the curricula of institutions of higher education. The department uses an interdisciplinary approach in offering courses that are relevant to the experience of Asians, blacks, Chicanos, and others in America. The background of the instructors enables them to provide a stimulating experience. The courses provide the student with a knowledge of the contributions of minorities to the past and present development of the United States. The courses also help the stu-

dent to become aware of the problems of minority communities and to assist him/her in seeking solutions to be better prepared to assist the community in solving these problems.

Institution:	**University of Southern California**
Unit:	Ethnic Studies Program
Contact Person:	James Diego Vigil, Director
Address:	Los Angeles, CA 90089
Phone:	(213) 743-2084

Institution:	**El Camino College**
Institution Type:	Public, 2 year
Unit:	American Studies and Ethnic Studies Program
Contact Person:	G. E. Miranda, Dean of Behavioral and Social Sciences
Address:	16007 Crenshaw Boulevard
	Torrance, CA 90506
Phone:	(310) 715-7735
Fax:	(310) 715-7818
Unit Offers:	Major, classes
Degrees Offered:	A.A.
Majors Per Year:	2–5
Faculty:	2
Established:	1970
Special Features:	The division offers courses on African Americans, Native Americans, women, and the immigrant experience.

Institution:	**Cerritos Community College**
Institution Type:	Public, 2 year
Unit:	Multicultural Studies Program
Contact Person:	Ceci Medina, Dean
Address:	11110 Alondra Boulevard
	Norwalk, CA 90650
Phone:	(310) 860-2451 (ext. 783)
Fax:	(310) 402-5893
Unit Offers:	Classes
Special Features:	The program offers several ethnic courses: Introduction to Chicano Culture, Introduction to

Mexican American Art, Philipino American Experiences, African American History, Mexican Literature in Translation, ESL Introduction, and vocational education courses presented in a bilingual mode.

Institution:	**Pasadena City College**
Institution Type:	Public, 2 year
Unit:	Social Sciences Department
Contact Person:	Susie Ling
	or Paul C. Price
Address:	1570 E. Colorado Boulevard
	Pasadena, CA 91106
Phone:	(818) 585-7248/7748
Unit Offers:	Classes
Degrees Offered:	A.A., A.S.
Faculty:	7
Special Features:	This community college has a 75 percent non-white population and offers courses such as Introduction to Ethnic Studies: African American history, sociology and psychology; Chicano history, sociology and psychology; and Asian American history, sociology and psychology.

Institution:	**California State Polytechnic University-Pomona**
Institution Type:	Public, 4 year
Unit:	Ethnic and Women's Studies Department
Contact Person:	Laurie Shrage, Acting Chair
Address:	3801 West Temple Avenue
	Building 94, Room 326
	Pomona, CA 91768
Phone:	(909) 869-3593
E-mail:	ljshrage@csupomona.edu
Unit Offers:	Minor, certificate, classes (major pending)
Minors Per Year:	20
Faculty:	6
Special Features:	The department offers courses that simultaneously address issues of ethnicity, gender, and multiculturalism. Students may minor in African American, American Indian/Native American,

Chicano/Latino, or Asian American Studies as well as Women's Studies. The department emphasizes an interdisciplinary and cross-cultural approach to all of its classes. The curriculum is designed to help students think critically and analytically about the complexities of modern society, but course content also strengthens the curricula of students' major discipline.

Institution:	**Palomar Community College**
Institution Type:	Public, 2 year
Unit:	Multicultural Studies Program
Contact Person:	José C. Rangel, Director
Address:	1140 West Mission Road
	San Marcos, CA 92069
Phone:	(619) 744-1150
Unit Offers:	Classes, certificate
Faculty:	4 full-time, 5 hourly
Established:	1969
Special Features:	There is a certificate program in Afrikana Studies. Classes in Chicano Studies, Judaic Studies, and Pan-Asian Studies are also offered.

Institution:	**University of California-San Diego**
Institution Type:	Public, 4 year
Unit:	Ethnic Studies Department
Contact Person:	Barbara Reyes, Undergraduate Coordinator
Address:	9500 Gilman Drive, Department 0414
	La Jolla, CA 92093-0414
Phone:	(619) 534-3276
Fax:	(619) 534-8194
Unit Offers:	Major, minor, classes
Degrees Offered:	B.A. Ethnic Studies
Majors Per Year:	50
Minors:	35
Faculty:	7
Established:	1990
Special Features:	The curriculum of the Department of Ethnic Studies is designed to: (1) study intensively the particular histories of different ethnic and racial groups

in the United States, especially intragroup stratification; (2) to draw larger theoretical lessons from comparison among these groups; (3) to articulate general principals that shape racial and ethnic relations both currently and historically; and (4) to explore how ethnic identity is constructed and reconstructed over time both internally and externally.

Institution:	**California State University-San Bernardino**
Institution Type:	Public, 4 year + graduate
Unit:	Ethnic Studies Program
Contact Person:	Brij Khare, Coordinator
Address:	5500 University Parkway
	San Bernardino, CA 92407
Phone:	(909) 880-5476
Fax:	(909) 880-7018
E-mail:	bkhare@wiley.csusb.edu
Unit Offers:	Minor
Minors Per Year:	25
Faculty:	5

Institution:	**Riverside Community College**
Institution Type:	Public, 2 year
Unit:	Ethnic Studies Department
Contact Person:	Dwight Lomayesva
Address:	4800 Magnolia Avenue
	Riverside, CA 92504
Phone:	(909) 684-3240
Unit Offers:	Classes, A.A.
Faculty:	3 part-time
Established:	1970

Institution:	**University of California-Riverside**
Institution Type:	Public, 4 year + graduate
Unit:	Department of Ethnic Studies
Contact Person:	Clifford Trafzer, Chair
Address:	101 University Office Building
	Riverside, CA 92521
Phone:	(909) 787-4577

Fax:	(909) 787-4341
Unit Offers:	Major, minor, classes
Degrees Offered:	B.A.
Majors Per Year:	40
Minors:	25
Faculty:	9
Established:	1987
Special Features:	The department's areas of emphasis are Chicano Studies, Asian American Studies, African American Studies, and Native American Studies. Graduate degrees are not offered yet but may be obtained via history, anthropology, and sociology.

Institution:	**Rancho Santiago College**
Institution Type:	Public, 2 year
Unit:	Ethnic Studies Department
Unit Type:	Institute
Contact Person:	Harold Forsythe, Chair
Address:	1530 West 17th Street
	Santa Ana, CA 92706
Phone:	(714) 564-6500
Unit Offers:	Major, minor
Degrees Offered:	A.S. Ethnic Studies; A.S. Chicano Studies; A.S. Black Studies
Majors Per Year:	10
Faculty:	12
Established:	1989 (Black and Chicano Studies date from 1970)

Institution:	**Santa Barbara City College**
Institution Type:	Public, 2 year
Unit:	American Ethnic Studies Department
Contact Person:	David N. Lawyer, Jr., Chair
Address:	721 Cliff Drive
	Santa Barbara, CA 93109
Phone:	(805) 965-0581
Fax:	(805) 963-7222
Unit Offers:	Major, classes
Degrees Offered:	A.A. Black Studies; A.A. Chicano Studies; A.A. Native American Studies; A.A. Ethnic Studies
Faculty:	7 full-time, 4 part-time

Established:	1972

Institution:	**California State University-Fresno**
Institution Type:	Public, 4 year + graduate
Unit:	Ethnic Studies Program
Contact Person:	Lily B. Small, Chair
Address:	Fresno, CA 93740-0100
Phone:	(209) 278-2832
Fax:	(209) 278-7664
Unit Offers:	Minor
Minors Per Year:	10
Faculty:	5 full-time
Established:	1968
Special Features:	The Ethnic Studies Program at CSU-Fresno is an interdisciplinary program consisting of the African American Studies and the American Indian Studies Programs. There are two minors—Ethnic Studies and African American Studies.

Institution:	**Monterey Peninsula College**
Institution Type:	Public, 2 year
Unit:	Ethnic Studies Department
Contact Person:	Henry Royal, Chair
Address:	980 Fremont Boulevard
	Monterey, CA 93940
Phone:	(408) 646-4158/4160
Unit Offers:	Classes
Faculty:	1
Established:	1970
Special Features:	Courses offered in this department include: (1) Afro-American History; (2) Afro-American Political Science; (3) Afro-American Arts/Jazz; (4) Afro-American Women History in the United States; and (5) Afro-American Sociology.

Institution:	**Canada College**
Institution Type:	Public, 2 year
Unit:	Ethnic Studies requirement to receive A.A./A.S. degree
Unit Type:	Student Services

Contact Person:	Olivia Martinez, Vice President of Student Services
Address:	4200 Farm Hill Boulevard
	Redwood City, CA 94061
Phone:	(415) 306-3234
Fax:	(415) 306-3457
E-mail:	martinez@smcccd.cc.ca.us
Unit Offers:	Classes

Institution:	**San Francisco State University**
Institution Type:	Public, 4 year + graduate
Unit:	School of Ethnic Studies
Contact Person:	D. Phillip McGee, Dean
Address:	San Francisco, CA 94132
Phone:	(415) 338-1693
Unit Offers:	Major, minor, classes
Degrees Offered:	B.A. Black Studies; B.A. La Raza Studies; M.A. Ethnic Studies
Faculty:	85
Established:	1969
Special Features:	The school has four departments: American Indian Studies, Asian American Studies, Black Studies, and La Raza Studies. It is the first and only school of Ethnic Studies in the nation offering approximately 150 classes per semester to over 500 students. The school also offers the only M.A. in Ethnic Studies in the nation.

Institution:	**Diablo Valley College**
Unit:	Special Programs
Contact Person:	Lawrence P. Crouchett, Director
Address:	Pleasant Hill, CA 94523

Institution:	**California State University-Hayward**
Institution Type:	4 year + graduate
Unit:	Ethnic Studies Department
Contact Person:	Michael Clark, Chair
Address:	Hayward, CA 94542
Phone:	(510) 881-3255
Fax:	(510) 888-4176
Unit Offers:	Major, minor

Degrees Offered:	B.A. Ethnic Studies
Majors Per Year:	36
Minors:	62
Faculty:	8

Institution:	**Chabot College**
Unit:	Readiness and Ethnic Studies Program
Contact Person:	Debra Wilkerson, Dean
Address:	Hayward, CA 94545

Institution:	**Solano Community College**
Institution Type:	Public, 2 year
Unit:	Ethnic Studies Program
Contact Person:	Sanford Wright, Coordinator
Address:	4000 Suisun Valley Road
	Suisun City, CA 94585
Phone:	(707) 864-0361 (ext. 429)
Fax:	(707) 864-0361
Unit Offers:	Major
Degrees Offered:	A.A. African American Studies; Mexican American Studies; Ethnic Studies

Institution:	**Mills College**
Institution Type:	Private, 4 year + graduate
Unit:	Ethnic Studies Department
Contact Person:	Dorothy Tsuruta, Head
Address:	5000 MacArthur Boulevard
	Oakland, CA 94613
Phone:	(510) 430-3163
Fax:	(510) 430-3314
Unit Offers:	Major, minor, classes
Majors Per Year:	30
Minors:	60
Faculty:	4
Established:	1968
Special Features:	This department has comparative and ethnic specific courses, as well as a Womanist area of emphasis. It also has concentrations in mixed race identity, autobiography, and migration to the United States.

Institution:	**Merritt College**
Institution Type:	Public, 2 year
Unit:	Ethnic Studies Department
Contact Person:	F. Lozada, Instructor
Address:	12500 Campus Drive
	Oakland, CA 94619
Phone:	(510) 531-4911
Unit Offers:	Major
Degrees Offered:	A.A. Mexican/Latino Studies; A.A. African American Studies
Established:	1969

Institution:	**University of California-Berkeley**
Institution Type:	Public, 4 year + graduate
Unit:	Department of Ethnic Studies
Contact Person:	Barbara Quan, Ethnic Studies Graduate Group
Address:	3407 Dwinelle Hall
	Berkeley, CA 94720-2570
Phone:	(510) 642-0240
Fax:	(510) 642-4564
Unit Offers:	Major, minor
Degrees Offered:	B.A. Ethnic Studies, Asian American Studies, Chicano Studies, Native American Studies; M.A. Ethnic Studies; Ph.D. Ethnic Studies
Majors Per Year:	95
Minors:	15
Faculty:	18
Established:	1969
Special Features:	The Ethnic Studies Program at UC Berkeley offers a comparative approach to the histories, culture, and communities of racial minorities in the United States. It seeks to analyze how the experience of various racial minorities were similar to and different from each other, how developments such as slavery and racial discrimination set apart Americans of color from Americans of European ancestry, and how race and class intersected in American society. Multidisciplinary in approach, it uses a broad range of social sciences and humanities methods to examine the critical area of race in American life.

Institution:	**New College of California**
Institution Type:	Private, 4 year + graduate
Unit:	World College Institute Program
Contact Person:	Jeni Strube-Callihan, Coordinator
Address:	1211 Second Street
	San Rafael, CA 94901
Phone:	(415) 455-9300
Fax:	(415) 455-9027
Unit Offers:	Major
Degrees Offered:	B.A. Humanities
Faculty:	4 and adjuncts
Established:	1992
Special Features:	New College offers an interdisciplinary Global Studies Program. Students are encouraged to direct their own education and participate in the college governance system. Students are required to study for one or two semesters in a culture very different from their own.

Institution:	**Cabrillo College**
Unit:	Bilingual-Bicultural Studies
Contact Person:	Consuelo España
Address:	6500 Soquel Drive
	Aptos, CA 95003
Phone:	(408) 479-6515

Institution:	**De Anza College**
Institution Type:	Public, 2 year
Unit:	Intercultural/International Studies Division
Contact Person:	Duane Kubo, Dean
Address:	21250 Stevens Creek Boulevard
	Cupertino, CA 95014
Phone:	(408) 864-8769
Unit Offers:	Major, classes
Degrees Offered:	A.A. Intercultural Studies
Majors Per Year:	10–12
Faculty:	11 full-time, 1 part-time
Established:	1969
Special Features:	This program offers Intercultural/International Studies classes. Departments under Intercultural

Studies are Chicano, Asian American, African American, Latin American, Intercultural, and Native American. Departments under International Studies are African, Asian, Latin American, and International.

Institution:	**Santa Clara University**
Institution Type:	Private, 4 year + graduate
Unit:	Ethnic Studies Program
Contact Person:	Stephen S. Fugita, Director
Address:	Santa Clara, CA 95053
Phone:	(408) 554-4472
Fax:	(408) 554-6880
E-mail:	sfugita@scuacc.scu.edu
Unit Offers:	Minor, classes
Minors Per Year:	8
Faculty:	4
Established:	1969
Special Features:	The focus of the program is on African Americans, Asian/Pacific Islander Americans, Chicanos, Native Americans, and their roles in the development of the United States.

Institution:	**San Joaquin Delta College**
Institution Type:	2 year
Unit:	Social Science Division
Contact Person:	William Dofflemyer, Chair
Address:	5151 Pacific Avenue
	Stockton, CA 95203
Phone:	(209) 474-5262
Unit Offers:	Classes
Degrees Offered:	A.A.
Established:	1967
Special Features:	The division offers courses in the areas of African American, Native American, and gender.

Institution:	**California State University-Stanislaus**
Institution Type:	Public, 4 year
Unit:	Ethnic and Women's Studies Department
Contact Person:	Richard L. Luevano, Chair

Address:	801 West Monte Vista Avenue
	Turlock, CA 95382
Phone:	(209) 667-3238/3341
Unit Offers:	Minor, classes
Minors Per Year:	27
Faculty:	3 full-time, 1 part-time
Established:	1971
Special Features:	The department offers minors in Ethnic Studies, Chicano Studies, Black Studies, and Women's Studies, along with concentrations in Ethnic Studies, Chicano Studies, and Black Studies.

Institution:	**Humboldt State University**
Institution Type:	Public, 4 year + graduate
Unit:	Ethnic Studies Department
Contact Person:	Nathan Smith, Chair
Address:	4719 Herron Road
	Eureka, CA 95501
Phone:	(707) 826-3820
Unit Offers:	Major, Minor, classes
Minors Per Year:	75
Faculty:	7
Established:	1973
Special Features:	The department includes African American, Asian American, Chicano, and Native American Divisions (NAS). The NAS Division offers a major in Native American Studies as well as a minor.

Institution:	**California State University-Sacramento**
Institution Type:	Public, 4 year + graduate
Unit:	Ethnic Studies Center
Contact Person:	Otis L. Scott, Coordinator
Address:	6000 J Street
	Sacramento, CA 95819
Phone:	(916) 278-6645
Fax:	(916) 278-5787
E-mail:	scottol@ccvax.ccs.csus.edu
Unit Offers:	Major, minor, classes

Degrees Offered:	B.A. Ethnic Studies; concentrations in Asian American Studies, Chicano Studies, Native American Studies, and Pan African Studies
Majors Per Year:	30
Minors:	35
Faculty:	10
Established:	1969–70
Special Features:	Ethnic Studies at CSU-Sacramento is a degree-granting, interdisciplinary program. Course work is offered that allows students to study the cultures, institutional placement, contributions, and the myriad of issues—past and present—framing the experiences of people of color both within and outside of the United States.

Institution:	**Yuba Community College**
Institution Type:	Public, 2 year
Unit:	Fine Arts and Social Science Division
Unit Type:	Department
Contact Person:	Beverly Paget, Associate Dean
Address:	2088 N. Beale Road
	Marysville, CA 95901
Phone:	(916) 741-6764
Unit Offers:	Classes
Special Features:	Ethnic Studies courses are available in the following areas: Afro-American Studies, Native American Studies, Asian-American Studies, and La Raza Studies.

Institution:	**California State University-Chico**
Institution Type:	Public, 4 year + graduate
Unit:	Ethnic and Women's Studies Program
Contact Person:	Hassan Sisay, Coordinator
Address:	Chico, CA 95929
Phone:	(916) 898-5249
Fax:	(916) 898-6824
Unit Offers:	Major
Degrees Offered:	B.A. Ethnic and Women's Studies
Majors Per Year:	4
Minors:	65

Faculty:	5
Established:	1969
Special Features:	This program has combined Ethnic and Women's Studies into a degree program. It has minors in Black, Women, American Indian, and Chicano Studies.

COLORADO

Institution:	**University of Colorado at Denver**
Institution Type:	Public, 4 year + graduate
Unit:	Ethnic Studies Department
Contact Person:	Cecil Glenn, Chair
Address:	1380 Lawrence Street
	P.O. Box 173364
	Campus Box 134
	Denver, CO 80217
Phone:	(303) 556-2726
Fax:	(303) 556-3547
Unit Offers:	Minor
Minors Per Year:	56

Institution:	**Metropolitan State College of Denver**
Institution Type:	Public, 4 year
Unit:	Institute for Intercultural Studies and Services
Contact Person:	Akbarali Thobhani, Director
Address:	P.O. Box 173362, Campus Box 36
	Denver, CO 80217-3362
Phone:	(303) 556-4004
Fax:	(303) 556-4941
Unit Offers:	Major, minor
Degrees Offered:	B.A. African American Studies; B.A. Chicano Studies
Majors Per Year:	2–3
Minors:	5–7
Faculty:	8–10 joint and part-time
Established:	1985
Special Features:	The institute's emphasis is on historical, sociological, political, and humanities studies.

Institution:	**University of Colorado**
Institution Type:	Public, 4 year + graduate
Unit:	Center for the Study of Ethnicity and Race in America
Contact Person:	Evelyn Hu-DeHart, Director
Address:	C. B. 339
	Boulder, CO 80309-0339
Phone:	(303) 492-8852
Fax:	(303) 492-2799
Unit Offers:	Certificate, classes
Faculty:	6
Established:	1989
Special Features:	The center has four components: Chicano Studies, Native American Studies, Asian American Studies, African American Studies, which are interdepartmental and interdisciplinary

Institution:	**Colorado State University**
Institution Type:	Public, 4 year + graduate
Unit:	Center for Applied Studies in American Ethnicity (CASAE)
Contact Person:	Carolyn Fowler, Director
Address:	53 Willard O. Eddy Building
	Fort Collins, CO 80523
Phone:	(303) 491-2418
Fax:	(303) 491-2717
E-mail:	cfowler@vines.colostate.edu
Unit Offers:	Minor, certificate, classes
Minors Per Year:	20–50
Faculty:	3
Established:	1993
Special Features:	The CASAE has a threefold mission of teaching, research, and service to the community. It sponsors research across disciplines that can be put to the service of the community and the nation. The center also studies the more specific condition and culture in America of marginalized ethnicities, particularly Native Americans, African Americans, Hispanic Americans, and Asian/Pacific Americans, and the interaction culturally and so-

cially of these groups with the larger American society.

Institution:	**Fort Lewis College**
Institution Type:	Public, 4 year
Unit:	Department of Southwest Studies
Contact Person:	Mary Jean Moseley, Chair
Address:	1000 Rim Drive
	Room 22 Reid Library
	Durango, CO 81301
Phone:	(303) 247-7219
Unit Offers:	Major, minor, classes
Degrees Offered:	B.A.
Established:	Prior to 1980

CONNECTICUT

Institution:	**Trinity College**
Institution Type:	Private
Unit:	Area Studies Program
Contact Person:	Leslie Desmangles
Address:	McCook Hall
	Hartford, CT 06106
Phone:	(203) 297-2407
Fax:	(203) 297-5358
E-mail:	leslie.desmangles@mail.trincoll.edu
Unit Offers:	Major, minor
Degrees Offered:	B.A. Asian Studies, African Studies, Latin American Studies, Middle Eastern Studies, Russian and East European Studies, Caribbean Studies, Post-Colonial Studies
Majors Per Year:	50
Minors:	15
Faculty:	20
Established:	1968
Special Features:	This is an interdisciplinary program that focuses on Asia, Africa, Eastern Europe, Latin America, the Caribbean, and the people who trace their heritage from these regions. Critical languages

essential to the study of these regions are required as part of the major.

FLORIDA

Institution:	**Florida Atlantic University**
Institution Type:	Public, 4 year + graduate
Unit:	Ethnic Studies Program
Contact Person:	Arthur S. Evans, Jr., Acting Director
Address:	Department of Sociology and Social Psychology
	P.O. Box 3091
	Boca Raton, FL 33431-0991
Phone:	(407) 367-3270
Fax:	(407) 367-2744
E-mail:	evansa@acc.fau.end
Unit Offers:	Certificate, classes
Majors Per Year:	3
Faculty:	10
Established:	1992

HAWAII

Institution:	**University of Hawaii**
Institution Type:	Public, 4 year
Unit:	Ethnic Studies Program
Contact Person:	Ibrahim Aoude, Acting Director
Address:	E-W Road 4
	Room 4D
	Honolulu, HI 96822
Phone:	(808) 956-8086
Fax:	(808) 956-9494
Unit Offers:	Major, certificate, classes
Degrees Offered:	B.A. Ethnic Studies (offered through the Liberal Studies Program)
Faculty:	8
Established:	1970
Special Features:	The Ethnic Studies Program at UH offers an integrated program of instruction to students interested

in the role of ethnicity in Hawaiian and American society, history, and culture. It is designed to bring together resources at the university and in the community in a way that facilitates a thorough understanding of the historical and contemporary experiences of a multiethnic community.

IDAHO

Institution:	**Boise State University**
Institution Type:	Public, 4 year + graduate
Unit:	Bilingual Education Program
Contact Person:	Jay R. Fuhriman, Director
Address:	E-215
	Boise, ID 83725
Phone:	(208) 385-1194
Fax:	(208) 385-4365
Unit Offers:	Major, certificate
Degrees Offered:	B.A. Elementary Bilingual Education; M.A. Bilingual Education or ESL
Majors Per Year:	150
Faculty:	6
Special Features:	This program is especially designed to take advantage of the language and cultural backgrounds of Hispanic students with its combination of Spanish/English. The M.A. program is an after-hours program to permit participants to work full-time and study.

ILLINOIS

Institution:	**Illinois State University**
Institution Type:	Public, 4 year + graduate
Unit:	Interdisciplinary Studies Program
Contact Person:	Janet Claus, Academic Advisor
Address:	Academic Advisement Center
	4060 Illinois State University
	Normal, IL 61790-4060

Phone:	(309) 438-7604
Fax:	(309) 438-3787
E-mail:	advclaus@ilstu.bitnet
Unit Offers:	Minor, classes
Degrees Offered:	Minor in Ethnic and Cultural Studies; minor in Latin American Studies
Minors Per Year:	10 in Ethnic and Cultural Studies, 15 in Latin American Studies
Established:	1983
Special Features:	The Ethnic and Cultural Studies minor allows students to design a minor that focuses on one ethnic group or a minor that explores the issues of ethnicity in a more general way.

INDIANA

Institution:	**Valparaiso University**
Institution Type:	Private, 4 year
Unit:	Intercultural Studies Program
Contact Person:	Julian Kunnie, Chair
Address:	Valparaiso, IN 46383
Phone:	(219) 464-5760
Fax:	(219) 464-5496
Unit Offers:	Minor, classes
Degrees Offered:	B.A. (with an Ethnic Studies minor)
Faculty:	25
Established:	1992
Special Features:	The program is designed toward incorporating multiracial and multicultural perspectives in all course offerings and recruiting students and faculty of color; it also holds programs on racial awareness/multicultural education.

Institution:	**Indiana University Northwest**
Unit:	Minority Studies Program
Contact Person:	Earl Jones, Director
Address:	Gary, IN 46408
Phone:	(219) 980-6629

IOWA

Institution:	**Cornell College**
Institution Type:	Private, 4 year
Unit:	Ethnic Studies Program
Contact Person:	Mary Olson, Chair
Address:	600 First Street West
	Mount Vernon, IA 52314
Phone:	(319) 895-4359
Fax:	(319) 895-4492
Unit Offers:	Major, classes
Degrees Offered:	B.A. Ethnic Studies
Majors Per Year:	10
Faculty:	8
Established:	1992

KANSAS

Institution:	**Kansas State University**
Institution Type:	Public, 4 year + graduate
Unit:	American Ethnic Studies Program
Contact Person:	Harriet Ottenheimer, Director
Address:	Leisure Hall Room 3
	Manhattan, KS 66506-3505
Phone:	(913) 532-5738
Fax:	(913) 532-7004
E-mail:	mahafan@ksuvm.ksu.edu
Unit Offers:	Major, classes
Degrees Offered:	Secondary Major in American Ethnic Studies
Majors Per Year:	22
Faculty:	20
Established:	1986
Special Features:	American Ethnic Studies is concerned with increasing the understanding of ethnicity in the United States and with affirming the validity of every ethnic heritage and identity. The courses prepare students to function successfully in multiethnic, multiracial, and multicultural settings. The program focuses primarily on African

Americans, Asian Americans, Hispanic Americans, and Native Americans, but also includes courses about other U.S. ethnic groups. The secondary major, open to all students, can be taken in addition to a primary major.

Institution:	**Wichita State University**
Institution Type:	4 year + graduate
Unit:	Department of Minority Studies
Contact Person:	Anna Chandler, Chair
Address:	Hugo Wall School of Urban Studies
	Fairmont College of Liberal Arts and Sciences
	1845 Fairmont
	Wichita, KS 67260-0066
Phone:	(316) 689-3380
Fax:	(316) 689-3234
Unit Offers:	Major, minor, classes
Degrees Offered:	B.A. Minority Studies
Majors Per Year:	18
Minors:	30
Faculty:	4
Special Features:	This is a multiethnic department offering an undergraduate major in Minority Studies, and it strives to ascertain the impact of cultural diversity on cross-cultural and intercultural communication between America's ethnic groups.

KENTUCKY

Institution:	**Western Kentucky University**
Institution Type:	Public, 4 year + graduate
Unit:	Folk Studies Program
Contact Person:	Larry W. Danielson, Chair
Address:	Department of Modern Languages and Intercultural Studies
	Bowling Green, KY 42101
Phone:	(502) 745-5900
Fax:	(502) 745-5387
Unit Offers:	Major, minor, classes

Degrees Offered:	M.A. Folk Studies
Majors Per Year:	25 (M.A.)
Minors:	20 (B.A.)
Faculty:	7
Established:	1970
Special Features:	This program offers three M.A. degree tracks: thesis, applied folklore, and historic preservation. It also includes an internship program and provides substantial preparation for Ph.D. programs and for public sector vocations.

MARYLAND

Institution:	**Morgan State University**
Institution Type:	Public, 4 year + graduate
Unit:	History Department
Contact Person:	Coordinator of African American Studies
Address:	Baltimore, MD 21239
Phone:	(410) 319-3190/3400
Unit Offers:	Major, minor, classes
Degrees Offered:	B.A. African American History; M.A. African Diaspora History
Majors Per Year:	25 (10 undergraduate, 15 graduate)
Established:	1968 (undergraduate); 1989 (graduate)

MASSACHUSETTS

Institution:	**Hampshire College**
Institution Type:	Private, 4 year
Unit:	Third World Studies Program
Contact Person:	Mitzi Sawada, Dean of Multicultural Affairs
Address:	School of Social Science
	Amherst, MA 01002
Phone:	(413) 549-4610
Fax:	(413) 582-5620
Faculty:	27
Established:	1980
Special Features:	This program combines domestic and interna-

tional Third World Studies because many of the faculty teach both and because they are interested in the relationships between the two. Hampshire does not have a department and major structure. It has four schools, and this program crosses all four schools.

Institution:	**Radcliffe College-Harvard University**
Institution Type:	Private, 4 year + graduate
Unit:	Education for Action (E4A) Program
Contact Person:	Faith Adiele, Coordinator
Address:	10 Garden Street
	Cambridge, MA 02138
Phone:	(617) 495-8604
Fax:	(617) 496-4640
E-mail:	f-adiele@harvard.edu
Special Features:	This program offers noncredit study groups and extracurricular projects for undergraduates interested in social justice, the global effects of race, class, and gender, and working in a multicultural collective.

MINNESOTA

Institution:	**Saint Olaf College**
Institution Type:	Private, 4 year
Unit:	American Racial and Multicultural Studies Department
Contact Person:	Michael Fitzgerald, Director
Address:	History Department
	Northfield, MN 55057
Phone:	(507) 663-6041
E-mail:	fitz@stolaf.edu
Unit Offers:	Major, minor, classes
Minors:	10–20
Faculty:	15

Institution:	**Mankato State University**
Institution Type:	Public, 4 year + graduate

Unit:	Department of Ethnic Studies
Contact Person:	Charles Grose
Address:	Box 62
	Mankato, MN 56002
Phone:	(507) 389-2798
Fax:	(507) 389-2980
Unit Offers:	Major, minor
Degrees Offered:	B.A., B.S., M.S. Interdisciplinary Studies with emphasis in Ethnic Studies
Majors Per Year:	5
Minors:	10
Faculty:	4
Established:	1978
Special Features:	The Department of Ethnic Studies at Mankato State University is racially balanced and offers both graduate and undergraduate degrees. The program is interdisciplinary, and the faculty is trained in different social science fields.

Institution:	**St. Cloud State University**
Institution Type:	Public, 4 year + graduate
Unit:	Minority Studies
Contact Person:	Robert C. Johnson, Director
Address:	Education Building, Room B120
	720 4th Avenue South
	St. Cloud, MN 56301-4498
Phone:	(612) 255-4928
Fax:	(612) 255-4237
Unit Offers:	Minor, classes
Minors Per Year:	3
Faculty:	6
Established:	1974

Institution:	**Moorhead State University**
Institution Type:	Public, 4 year
Unit:	Department of Humanities and Multicultural Studies
Contact Person:	Dieter Berninger, Chair
Address:	Moorhead, MN 56563
Phone:	(218) 236-2196

Unit Offers:	Minor, classes
Degrees Offered:	Individualized major available
Minors Per Year:	25
Faculty:	4
Established:	1985
Special Features:	The department offers minors in American Indian, Chicano, African-American and more general Multicultural Studies. A major in American Studies offers significant Multicultural Studies courses/content.

MISSOURI

Institution:	**Harris-Stowe State College**
Unit:	Multicultural Studies Program
Contact Person:	Lores Wells, Director
Address:	St. Louis, MO 63103
Phone:	(314) 340-3517

Institution:	**Penn Valley Community College**
Institution Type:	2 year
Unit:	Social Science Division
Unit Type:	Department within Social Science Division
Contact Person:	Harold Koch, Chair
Address:	3201 S.W. Trafficway
	Kansas City, MO 64111
Phone:	(816) 759-4284
Fax:	(816) 759-4161
Unit Offers:	Classes
Faculty:	2
Special Features:	The classes offered are Survey of African-American History, Hispanic Studies, and Survey of Afro-American Psychology Development.

NEBRASKA

Institution:	**University of Nebraska-Lincoln**
Institution Type:	Public, 4 year

Unit:	Institute for Ethnic Studies
Contact Person:	Charles Ballard, Coordinator
Address:	301 Burnett Hall
	Lincoln, NE 68588-0335
Phone:	(402) 472-1663
Unit Offers:	Minor
Minors Per Year:	13
Faculty:	8
Established:	1967
Special Features:	The institute is in the process of upgrading its minor to a major and is also hiring two new faculty members.

NEW JERSEY

Institution:	**Seton Hall University**
Unit:	Bilingual-Bicultural Program
Contact Person:	Juan Cobarrubias, Director
Address:	South Orange, NJ 07079

NEW YORK

Institution:	**The Borough of Manhattan Community College**
Institution Type:	Public, 2 year
Unit:	The Center for Ethnic Studies
Contact Person:	William Coleman, Director
	or Salvador Ocasio, Deputy Director
Address:	199 Chambers Street
	New York, NY 10007
Phone:	(212) 346-8251/8252
Fax:	(212) 346-8624
Unit Offers:	Classes
Degrees Offered:	A.A., A.S., A.A.S.; the center's courses satisfy requirements within the liberal arts distribution for each degree; the A.A. curricula are articulated with the four-year colleges in CUNY and elsewhere in the metropolitan area
Faculty:	6 full-time, 4–6 adjuncts

Established:	1970
Special Features:	Disciplines include art (African and African American), political economy, history, literature, and sociology. Categories include African, African American, Asian American, Caribbean, Dominican, Haitian, and Puerto Rican history. African American, Asian American, Caribbean, and literature courses are conducted in Spanish. Courses in the sociology area—The Family, Contemporary Black Woman, Contemporary Black Male, Politics of Puerto Rico—are designed for implementation in such courses as early childhood education and human services.

Institution:	**State University of New York-Plattsburgh**
Institution Type:	Public, 4 year
Unit:	College of Arts and Sciences
Unit Type:	Program
Contact Person:	Charles Herod, Coordinator
Address:	Hawkins Hall 112F
	Plattsburgh, NY 12901
Phone:	(518) 564-4445
Unit Offers:	Minor

Institution:	**Utica College**
Institution Type:	Private, 4 year
Unit:	Ethnic Heritage Studies Center
Contact Person:	Eugene Nassar, Director
Address:	Burrstone Road
	Utica, NY 13502
Phone:	(315) 792-3080
Fax:	(315) 792-3292
Unit Offers:	Classes
Established:	1981

NORTH CAROLINA

Institution:	**East Carolina University**
Institution Type:	4 year + graduate

Unit:	Ethnic Studies Program
Contact Person:	Michael F. Bassman, Director
Address:	General Classroom Building 3323
	Greenville, NC 27858-4353
Phone:	(919) 328-6032
Fax:	(919) 328-6233
E-mail:	flbassma@ecuvm.cisecu.edu
Unit Offers:	Minor, classes
Minors Per Year:	15–20
Faculty:	10
Established:	1990
Special Features:	The program consists of a minor in Ethnic Studies; guest lectures/performances by nationally recognized speakers, artists, musicians, and authors; and programs to raise the consciousness of the university community and encourage exploration of issues related to cultural diversity. The courses explore the cultural, economic, historical, political, and social aspects of each group's experience in America. The cultural and social sources of bias and discrimination are examined in courses in literature, philosophy, social sciences, and visual and performing arts. In addition, courses focused on selected topics are offered each semester.

OHIO

Institution:	**Capital University**
Institution Type:	Private
Unit:	Ethnic Studies Program
Contact Person:	T. Maroukis, Coordinator
Address:	145 Renner Hall
	Columbus, OH 43209
Phone:	(614) 236-6447
Unit Offers:	Minor
Minors Per Year:	5–6
Established:	1976
Special Features:	This program requires an internship in a minority firm, organization, or agency.

Institution:	**Bowling Green State University**
Institution Type:	Public, 4 year + graduate
Unit:	Ethnic Studies Department
Contact Person:	Robert L. Perry, Chair
Address:	228 Shatzel Hall
	Bowling Green, OH 43403
Phone:	(419) 372-2797
Fax:	(419) 372-2300
Unit Offers:	Major, minor, classes
Degrees Offered:	B.A. Black Studies, Native American, Latino, and Asian American Studies
Majors Per Year:	20
Minors:	17
Faculty:	9
Established:	1970
Special Features:	This department hosts an annual Ethnic Studies Conference and is involved in a Summer in Mexico Program through the International Studies Office. The Cultural Diversity Curriculum on campus has a director from this department.

Institution:	**Kent State University**
Institution Type:	Public, 4 year + graduate
Unit:	Ethnic Heritage Program
Contact Person:	Herbert Hochhauser, Director
Address:	314 Satterfield Hall
	Kent, OH 44242
Phone:	(216) 672-2389
Fax:	(216) 672-3152
Unit Offers:	Major, minor, certificate, classes
Degrees Offered:	Certificate in Jewish Studies; B.A. Ethnic Heritage Studies
Majors Per Year:	5
Minors:	10
Faculty:	10
Established:	1976

Institution:	**The Union Institute**
Unit:	Graduate School
Contact Person:	Sandra Hurlong

Address:	440 E. McMillon St.
	Cincinnati, OH 45206
Phone:	(513) 861-6400
Fax:	(513) 861-0779
Unit Offers:	Major, minor
Degrees Offered:	Ph.D.

OKLAHOMA

Institution:	**Northeastern Oklahoma State University**
Unit:	Ethnic Studies Program
Contact Person:	R. Halliburton, Jr., Director
Address:	Tahlequah, OK 74464
Phone:	(918) 456-5511 (ext. 3521)

OREGON

Institution:	**University of Oregon**
Institution Type:	Public, 4 year + graduate
Unit:	Folklore and Ethnic Studies Program
Contact Person:	Letty Fotta, Program Secretary
Address:	466 PLC
	Eugene, OR 97403
Phone:	(503) 346-3539
Fax:	(503) 346-5026
Unit Offers:	Minor, certificate, classes
Minors Per Year:	20
Faculty:	8
Established:	1981

Institution:	**Eastern Oregon State College**
Institution Type:	4 year
Unit:	Bilingual and Hispanic Studies/School of Education Program
Contact Person:	Felipe Veloz, Director
Address:	1410 L Avenue
	School of Education
	La Granda, OR 97850

Phone:	(503) 962-3312
Fax:	(503) 962-3701
Unit Offers:	Minor
Degrees Offered:	B.A., M.A.
Special Features:	Language proficiency (Spanish) is required for program participation.

PENNSYLVANIA

Institution:	**University of Pittsburgh**
Institution Type:	4 year + graduate
Unit:	Pennsylvania Ethnic Heritage Studies Center
Contact Person:	Joseph T. Makarewicz, Director
Address:	406 Bellefield Hall
	Pittsburgh, PA 15260
Phone:	(412) 648-7420
Fax:	(412) 648-1168
Special Features:	Some responsibilities include teacher education, curriculum development, research, and archival functions.

Institution:	**West Chester University**
Institution Type:	Public, 4 year
Unit:	Ethnic Studies Institute
Contact Person:	Bonita Freeman-Witthoft, Director
Address:	West Chester, PA 19383
Phone:	(215) 436-2725
Fax:	(215) 436-3150
Unit Offers:	Minor, certificate, classes
Degrees Offered:	Ethnic Studies minor with concentrations in Afro-American Studies, Hispanic American Studies, Jewish American Studies, Native American Studies, and a General Ethnic Studies minor; a Holocaust minor is also available
Minors Per Year:	30
Faculty:	20
Established:	1974
Special Features:	The Ethnic Studies Program offers an interdisciplinary minor. Students expecting to work with

minority populations or those wishing to learn more about their heritage often choose the Ethnic Studies minor. Anthropology, sociology, social work, psychology, history, and public administration majors comprise most of the Ethnic Studies minors.

RHODE ISLAND

Institution:	**Rhode Island College**
Institution Type:	Public, 4 year + graduate
Unit:	Bilingual Education Program
Contact Person:	Joao P. Botelho, Director
Address:	600 Mount Pleasant Avenue
	Providence, RI 02908
Phone:	(401) 456-8173
Unit Offers:	Certificate, classes
Degrees Offered:	This program offers Elementary/Secondary Education Bilingual Education Teacher Certifications; M. Ed in Bilingual Education; and Administration with Bilingual Certification

Institution:	**Brown University**
Unit:	Center for Study of Race and Ethnicity in America
Contact Person:	Rhett S. Jones, Director
Address:	Box 1886
	Providence, RI 02912
Phone:	(401) 863-3080
Fax:	(401) 863-7589

TEXAS

Institution:	**Southern Methodist University**
Institution Type:	Private
Unit:	Ethnic Studies Department
Contact Person:	Kenneth M. Hamilton, Director
Address:	222 Dallas Hall
	Dallas, TX 75275-0322

Phone:	(214) 768-3598
Fax:	(214) 768-4129
Unit Offers:	Major, minor
Degrees Offered:	B.A., B.S. Ethnic Studies with concentration in African American Studies or concentration in Mexican American Studies; minors in Mexican and African American Studies
Majors Per Year:	5
Minors:	5
Established:	1989

Institution:	**University of Texas at Arlington**
Institution Type:	Public, 4 year
Unit:	Office of Multicultural Services
Contact Person:	Richard Massie, Director
Address:	P.O. Box 19350
	Arlington, TX 76019
Special Features:	The office offers student support services.

Institution:	**Incarnate Word College**
Institution Type:	Private
Unit:	Division of Humanities and Fine Arts
Contact Person:	Gilberto M. Hinojosa, Dean
Address:	4301 Broadway
	San Antonio, TX 78209
Phone:	(210) 829-6022
Fax:	(210) 829-3880
Unit Offers:	Major
Degrees Offered:	B.A. Native American Studies
Majors Per Year:	2
Minors:	2
Faculty:	4
Established:	1988
Special Features:	This program is multidisciplinary (anthropology, literature, and art).

Institution:	**Texas Tech University**
Institution Type:	Public, 4 year + graduate
Unit:	Ethnic Studies Program
Contact Person:	Alwyn Barr, Director

Address:	Department of History
	Lubbock, TX 79409-1013
Phone:	(806) 742-3744
Fax:	(806) 742-1060
Unit Offers:	Minor, classes
Degrees Offered:	A minor is offered in the College of Arts and Sciences; students may emphasize African American Studies, Mexican American Studies, or Native American Studies
Minors Per Year:	3–4
Faculty:	12 (in 7 different departments)
Established:	1971
Special Features:	The Ethnic Studies Program at Texas Tech is interdisciplinary and leads to an eighteen-hour minor. Its goals are increased student understanding of the nature and development of race relations, stimulation of a greater sense of dignity for minority students, and expanded student knowledge of problem solving in this area of life.

Institution:	**University of Texas-El Paso**
Institution Type:	Public, 4 year + graduate
Unit:	Center for Multicultural and International Education
Contact Person:	Dennis Bixler-Márquez, Director
Address:	College of Education, Room 400
	El Paso, TX 79902
Phone:	(915) 747-7667
Fax:	(915) 747-6801
Unit Offers:	Classes
Faculty:	4
Established:	1979
Special Features:	The center offers courses in multicultural, social studies, and international education with an emphasis on the United States/Mexico border region.

Institution:	University of Utah
Institution Type:	Public, 4 year + graduate
Unit:	Ethnic Studies Program
Contact Person:	Wilfred D. Samuels, Coordinator
Address:	112 Carlson Hall
	Salt Lake City, UT 84112
Phone:	(801) 581-5206
Fax:	(801) 581-8437
Unit Offers:	Minor, classes
Minors Per Year:	10–15
Faculty:	15
Established:	1976
Special Features:	Ethnic Studies is the scholarly study of the distinctive social, political, cultural, and historical experiences of nonwhite racial groups in the United States. The Ethnic Studies Program provides students of all backgrounds with an opportunity to broaden their knowledge of minority groups in the United States.

Institution:	Weber State University
Institution Type:	Public, 4 year
Unit:	Ethnic Studies Program
Contact Person:	Daily E. Oliver, Director
Address:	3750 Harrison Boulevard
	Ogden, UT 84408-2904
Phone:	(801) 626-6360
Fax:	(801) 626-7568
Unit Offers:	Minor, classes
Degrees Offered:	Bachelor of Integrated Studies
Minors Per Year:	50
Faculty:	20
Established:	1968
Special Features:	The Ethnic Studies Program is unique because it forces students to integrate three academic disciplines that relate to educational and career goals.

Institution:	Southern Utah University
Institution Type:	Public, 4 year
Unit:	Multicultural Center
Contact Person:	Lynne J. Finton, Director
Address:	Box 9379
	Cedar City, UT 84720
Phone:	(801) 586-7771
Fax:	(801) 586-7934
Unit Offers:	Classes
Faculty:	1
Established:	1978
Special Features:	Through the Multicultural Center and History Department, three "focus" weeks are offered each year for one credit per week. These include a Black History Week, Native American Week, and Polynesian Week. These programs are primarily enrichment academic offerings rather than a more in-depth study students would receive over a full quarter.

WASHINGTON

Institution:	**Shoreline Community College**
Institution Type:	Public, 2 year
Unit:	Intra-American Studies (American Ethnic Studies) Department
Contact Person:	Andrea M. Rye, Dean
Address:	16101 Greenwood Avenue North
	Seattle, WA 98133
Phone:	(206) 546-4676
Fax:	(206) 546-5826
Unit Offers:	Classes
Special Features:	S.C.C. plans an academic transfer degree in Multicultural Studies and a one-year certificate for teachers in K–12, which will give them an endorsement to teach multicultural education courses.

Institution:	University of Washington
Institution Type:	Public, 4 year + graduate
Unit:	American Ethnic Studies Department
Contact Person:	John C. Walter, Chair
Address:	B510 Padelford Hall, GN-80
	Seattle, WA 98195
Phone:	(206) 543-5401/5309
Fax:	(206) 685-4083
Unit Offers:	Major, classes
Degrees Offered:	Major in American Ethnic Studies with concentrations in one of the following groups: Afro-American Studies, Asian American Studies, or Chicano Studies.
Majors Per Year:	200
Faculty:	12
Established:	1985

Institution:	Western Washington University
Institution Type:	Public, 4 year + graduate
Unit:	American Cultural Studies Program
Contact Person:	Larry J. Estrada, Vice Provost and Director
Address:	Old Main 450
	Bellingham, WA 98225-9000
Phone:	(206) 650-3480
Fax:	(206) 650-6141
E-mail:	uis!lestrada@henson.cc.wwu.edu
Unit Offers:	Major, minor, classes
Degrees Offered:	B.A. American Cultural Studies; minors in American Cultural Studies and Native American Studies
Majors Per Year:	15
Minors:	35
Faculty:	9
Established:	1978
Special Features:	The program offers a Native American Studies minor with curricula and faculty both at Western Washington University and the Northwest Indian College located on the Lummi Reservation. The ACS Program also offers curricula in Euro-American and Gay, Lesbian, and Bisexual Studies.

Institution:	**Skayit Valley College**
Institution Type:	Public, 2 year
Unit:	Department of Sociology
Contact Person:	David Muga
Address:	2405 College Way
	Mount Vernon, WA 98273
Phone:	(206) 428-1157
E-mail:	dmuga@ctc.ctc.edu
Unit Offers:	Classes
Faculty:	1
Established:	1985

Institution:	**Yakima Valley Community College**
Institution Type:	Public, 2 year
Unit:	Ethnic Studies Program
Contact Person:	Francisco F. Ivarra, Chair
Address:	16 Avenue and Nob Hill Boulevard
	Yakima, WA 98907
Phone:	(509) 575-2415
Unit Offers:	Classes
Faculty:	3
Established:	1970

Institution:	**Central Washington University**
Institution Type:	Public, 4 year
Unit:	Ethnic Studies Program
Contact Person:	Jimmie J. John, Director
Address:	Sociology Department
	Ellensburg, WA 98926
Phone:	(509) 963-1348
Fax:	(509) 963-3215
Unit Offers:	Minor
Minors Per Year:	45
Faculty:	1–4
Established:	1989
Special Features:	This is an interdisciplinary program, currently offering course work at four levels and specialized studies in numerous disciplines.

Institution:	**Washington State University**
Institution Type:	Public, 4 year + graduate
Unit:	Department of Comparative American Cultures
Contact Person:	Paul Wong, Chair
Address:	Pullman, WA 99164
Phone:	(509) 335-2605
Fax:	(509) 335-8338
Unit Offers:	Major, minor
Degrees Offered:	B.A. Comparative American Cultures; concentrations in Asian American, Black, Hispanic/Chicano, and American Indian Studies; M.A., Ph.D. in individual interdisciplinary studies in Comparative American Cultures
Majors Per Year:	5
Minors:	10
Faculty:	12 full-time, 5 part-time
Established:	1980
Special Features:	The department's focus includes emphasis on Comparative Studies on American Ethnic Cultures; humanistic and social scientific approaches to American ethnic literatures; and interaction between culture, technology, and the environment.

WISCONSIN

Institution:	**University of Wisconsin-Parkside**
Institution Type:	Public, 4 year + graduate
Unit:	Ethnic Studies Center
Contact Person:	Surinder Datta, Director
Address:	Box 2000
	900 Wood Road
	Kenosha, WI 53141-2000
Phone:	(414) 595-2177
Fax:	(414) 595-2265
E-mail:	dattas@cs.uwp.edu
Unit Offers:	Minor, classes
Minors Per Year:	10
Faculty:	12

Established: 1989
Special Features: The core curriculum for the twenty-four credit
                      minor emphasizes a comparative approach to is-
                      sues of race and ethnicity in the United States.
                      Electives focus on particular ethnic groups.

Institution: **University of Wisconsin-Whitewater**
Institution Type: Public, 4 year
Unit: Race and Ethnic Cultures Department
Contact Person: Carlos de Onis, Chair
Address: 240 Baker Hall
                      College of Letters and Sciences
                      Whitewater, WI 53190
Phone: (414) 472-1553
Unit Offers: Minor, classes
Degrees Offered: Minor in Race and Ethnic Cultures
Minors Per Year: 25
Faculty: 4.5
Established: 1973 (program); 1988 (department)
Special Features: The department includes sections on Afro-Ameri-
                      can Studies, American Indian Studies, and
                      Chicano Studies.

Institution: **University of Wisconsin-Milwaukee**
Institution Type: Public, 4 year + graduate
Unit: Ethnic Studies Certificate Program
Contact Person: Karel Bayer, Coordinator and Chair
Address: Department of Geography
                      Sabin Hall
                      P.O. Box 413
                      Milwaukee, WI 53201
Phone: (414) 229-4861/4866
Fax: (414) 229-3981
Unit Offers: Certificate, classes
Degrees Offered: Certificate in Ethnic Studies
Faculty: 2
Established: 1980

Institution: **University of Wisconsin-River Falls**
Institution Type: Public, 4 year + graduate

Unit:	Ethnic Studies Minor Program
Contact Person:	Marshall Toman, Coordinator
Address:	Department of English
	River Falls, WI 54022
Phone:	(715) 425-3124
Unit Offers:	Minor, classes
Minors Per Year:	5
Faculty:	20
Established:	1989

ETHNIC STUDIES ASSOCIATIONS

American Indian Science and Engineering Society (AISES)
Norbert S. Hill, Jr., Executive Director
1630 30th Street
Suite 301
Boulder, CO 80301-1014
Phone: (303) 492-8658
Fax: (303) 492-3400
E-mail: aiseshq@spot.colorado.edu

American Society for Ethnohistory, The
William O. Autry, Secretary/Treasurer
P.O. Box 917
Goshen, IN 46527-0917
E-mail: woautry@mcimail.com

Asian American Psychological Association
Graduate School of Education
University of California
Santa Barbara, CA 93106
Phone: (805) 893-8564
Fax: (805) 893-3324

Association for Asian American Studies
Elaine Kim, President
Asian American Studies
3407 Dwinelle Hall
University of California-Berkeley
Berkeley, CA 94720

Association for Latina/o Sociology
Nelson Pichardo, Chair
Department of Sociology
University of Albany, SUNY
Albany, NY 12222

Association for the Study of Afro-American Life and History
Janette Hoston Harris, President
ASALH
1407 Fourteenth Street, N.W.
Washington, DC 20005-3704
Phone: (202) 667-2822
Fax: (202) 387-9802

The Association for the Study of Afro-American Life and History, Inc. (ASALH), is a nonprofit corporation organized on September 8, 1915. The purpose of the ASALH is to provide needed reconstruction of thought based on historical truths about the African heritage of black people, ancient history, and worthwhile contributions to the founding and the continuance of the United States of America.

Association for the Study of American Indian Literatures (ASAIL)
Kathryn Shanley, President
Department of English
Goldwin Smith
Cornell University
Ithaca, NY 14853
Phone: (607) 255-3411

An allied organization of the Modern Language Association and the American Literature Association. In addition to sponsoring MLA and ALA conference sessions, ASAIL supports two publications: *Studies in American Indian Literature (SAIL),* a scholarly journal, and *ASAIL Notes,* a quarterly newsletter.

Association of Black Psychologists
Timothy R. Moragne, President
Director of Minority Affairs
Nova University
School of Psychology
3301 College Avenue
Fort Lauderdale, FL 33314
Phone: (305) 475-7550 or 7018
Fax: (305) 475-7090

Canadian Ethnic Studies Association
Natalia Aponiuk, President
c/o The Centre for Ukranian Canadian Studies
St. Andrew's College
The University of Manitoba
Winnipeg, Manitoba R3T 2N2
CANADA
Phone: (204) 474-8906
Fax: (204) 275-0803

The Canadian Ethnic Studies Association is a nonprofit interdisciplinary organization devoted to the study of ethnicity, multiculturalism, immigration, intergroup relations, and the cultural life of ethnic groups in Canada.

Hispanic Association of Colleges and Universities (HACU)
Laudelina Martinez, President
4202 Gardendale Street
Suite 216
San Antonio, TX 78229
Phone: (512) 692-3805
Fax: (512) 692-0823

Immigration History Society
John Bodnar, President
Department of History
Indiana University
Bloomington, IN 47405

The society promotes the historical study of immigration to the United States and Canada from all parts of the world, and the study of ethnic groups that developed as a result of this immigration.

Inter-University Program for Latino Research
Centro de Estudios Puertorriqueños
Hunter College, CUNY
695 Park Avenue
New York, NY 10021

Minorities in Agriculture, Natural Resources, and Related Sciences
Executive Manager
MANRRS National Headquarters
P.O. Box 24083
Lansing, MI 48909-4083
Phone: (517) 355-6580

Minorities in Agriculture, Natural Resources, and Related Sciences
(MANRRS) promotes regional workshops for students and young professionals to develop leadership and communication skills. To help students
acquire professional experiences, career fairs have been a part of the national
conferences held each April.

National Association for Chicano Studies
Luis Torres, General Coordinator
English and Chicano Studies
University of Southern Colorado
Pueblo, CO 81001-4901
Phone: (719) 549-2082
Fax: (719) 549-2705
Carlos S. Maldonado, Director
NACS National Office
Chicano Education Program
Eastern Washington University
MS170
Cheney, WA 99004
Phone: (509) 359-2404
Fax: (509) 359-6927

National Association of Black Geologists and Geophysicists
P.O. Box 720157
Houston, TX 77272

National Association for Ethnic Studies
Jesse Vasquez, President
NAES National Office
Department of English
Arizona State University
Tempe, AZ 85287-0302
Phone: (602) 965-2197
Fax: (602) 965-3451
E-mail: naesi@asuvm.inre.asu.edu

The National Association for Ethnic Studies has as its basic purpose the promotion of activities and scholarship in the field of ethnic studies. The association is open to any person or institution. The association serves as a forum to its members for promoting research, study, curriculum design, and publications of interest. The association sponsors an annual conference on ethnic studies.

National Conference of Black Political Scientists

Lois Hollis, Executive Director
Department of Political Science
Albany State College
Albany, GA 31703

National Council for Black Studies, Inc.

Jacqueline E. Wade, Executive Director
The Ohio State University
208 Mount Hall
1050 Carmack Road
Columbus, OH 43210
Phone: (614) 292-1035
Fax: (614) 292-7363

The National Council for Black Studies, Inc. (NCBS), came into existence in 1975 out of the need for a stabilizing force in the developing discipline. That recognition came only seven years after the establishment of the first Black Studies program in the United States. Today the purposes of NCBS are numerous. As a professional organization that subscribes to the philosophy that education should engender academic excellence and social responsibility, the council is steadfastly working to establish standards of excellence and provide development guidance for Black Studies programs in institutions of higher education; facilitate the recruitment of black scholars at all levels; assist in the creation of multicultural education programs and materials for K–12 schools; promote scholarly research on all aspects of the African world experience; increase and improve the informational resources available to the general public on that experience, and provide professional advice to policy makers in education, government, and community development.

National Hispanic Psychological Association
Mary DeFerreire, President
Texas Department of Mental Health and Mental Retardation
4110 Guadalupe
Austin, TX 78751-4296
Phone: (512) 462-0381 (ext. 4802)
Fax: (512) 478-2044

Puerto Rican Studies Association
Virginia Sánchez-Korrol, President
Puerto Rican Studies Association
Brooklyn College, CUNY
Bedford Avenue and Avenue H
New York, NY 11210
Phone: (718) 951-5561
Fax: (718) 951-4872

The Puerto Rican Studies Association is a nonprofit organization that has as its fundamental objective the promotion and integration of interdisciplinary research, praxis, and community empowerment of Puerto Ricans in Puerto Rico, the United States, and elsewhere. It serves as an international forum for members engaged in diverse forms of scholarship through teaching, study, research, and community development. The association encourages interaction between individuals and groups from diverse regions, educational institutions, research organizations, community agencies, and individuals engaged in independent scholarly pursuits.

Society for Advancement of Chicanos and Native Americans in Science
George Castro, President
Sinsheimer Labs
University of California
Santa Cruz, CA 95064
Phone: (408) 459-3558
E-mail: sacnas@eats.ucsc.edu

Society for Ethnomusicology, The
Shelly Kennedy, Office Administrator
Morrison Hall 005
Indiana University
Bloomington, IN 47405-2501
Phone: (812) 855-6672
Fax: (812) 855-6673
E-mail: kennedys@ucs.indiana.edu

The Society for Ethnomusicology (SEM) was founded in 1956 to promote the research, study, and performance of music in all historical periods and cultural contexts. Through its publications and its national and regional meetings, the society provides a forum for discussion of current scholarly research. The society also fosters the promotion and development of a variety of traditional art forms. Performing members of SEM have access to informed audiences and new musical contacts.

Society of Indian Psychologists
Paul Dauphinais, President
DOP, C-249
University of Colorado
Health and Science Center
4200 E. Ninth Avenue
Denver, CO 80262
Phone: (303) 270-4600
Fax: (303) 270-5969

ETHNIC STUDIES JOURNALS

Afrocentric Scholar, The
William Little, Editor
Center for Black Culture and Research
West Virginia University
590 Spruce Street
P.O. Box 6417
Morgantown, WV 26505-6417
Phone: (304) 293-7029
Fax: (304) 293-2967

Akwe:kon Journal (formerly Indian Studies Quarterly)
Susan Dixon, Managing Editor
300 Caldwell Hall
Cornell University
Ithaca, NY 14853
Phone: (607) 255-4308
Fax: (607) 255-0185
E-mail: susan_dixon@qmcampl.mail.cornell.edu

Akwesasne Notes
Mark Narsisian, Publisher
P.O. Box 196
Mohawk Nation
Rooseveltown, NY 13655
Phone: (518) 358-9531

Amerasia Journal
Glenn Omatsu, Associate Editor
Asian American Studies Center Publications
3230 Campbell Hall
405 Hilgard Avenue
University of California-Los Angeles
Los Angeles, CA 90024-1546
Phone: (310) 825-2974
Fax: (310) 206-2974

American Indian Culture and Research Journal
Duane Champagne, Editor
American Indian Studies Center
3220 Campbell Hall
405 Hilgard Avenue
University of California-Los Angeles
Los Angeles, CA 90024-1548
Phone: (310) 825-7315
Fax: (310) 206-7060

American Indian Journal
Kirk Kickingbird, Editor
Institute of the Development of Indian Law
Oklahoma City University-School of Law
2501 N. Blackwelder
Oklahoma City, OK 73106
Phone: (405) 531-5337

American Indian Law Review
Sandra Lee Nowack, Editor
University of Oklahoma
College of Law
300 Timberdell Road
Norman, OK 73019-0701
Phone: (405) 325-2840/5191
Fax: (405) 325-6282

American Indian Quarterly
Morris W. Foster, Editor
Department of Anthropology
455 West Lindsey
Room 521
University of Oklahoma
Norman, OK 73019-1535
Phone: (405) 325-2491

Americas Review, The (formerly **Revista Chicano-Riqueña**)
Nicolás Kanellos, Publisher
Arte Público Press
University of Houston
4800 Calhoun-429 AH
Houston, TX 77004
Phone: (713) 743-2849
Fax: (713) 743-2847

Aztlán—A Journal of Chicano Studies
Candelyn Cadelaria, Managing Editor
Chicano Studies Research Center
University of California-Los Angeles
405 Hilgard Avenue
Los Angeles, CA 90024
Phone: (310) 825-2642
Fax: (310) 206-1784

The Bilingual Review/La Revista Bilingue
Gary D. Keller, Editor
Hispanic Research Center
Arizona State University
Box 872702
Tempe, AZ 85287-2702
Phone: (602) 965-3867
Fax: (602) 965-8309

Black Scholar, The
Robert Chrisman, Editor
P.O. Box 2869
485 65th Street
Oakland, CA 94609
Phone: (510) 547-6633

Callaloo
Charles H. Rowell, Editor
Department of English
Wilson Hall
University of Virginia
Charlottesville, VA 22903
Phone: (410) 516-6988
Fax: (410) 516-6998
Distributed by:
Ms. Stasia Macsherry
The Johns Hopkins University Press
Journals Publishing Division
2715 North Charles Street
Baltimore, MD 21218-4319

Canadian Ethnic Studies/Études éthniques au Canada
Anthony Rasporich and James Frideres, Co-editors
c/o Research Unit for Canadian Ethnic Studies
Office of the Dean
Faculty of Social Science
University of Calgary
2500 University Drive N.W.
Calgary, Alberta T2N 1N4
CANADA
Phone: (403) 220-7257
Fax: (403) 282-8606
E-mail: frideres@aes.calgary.ca

Centro Bulletin
Blanca Vazquez, Editor
Centro de Estudios Puertorriqueños
Hunter College
City University of New York
695 Park Avenue
New York, NY 10021
Phone: (212) 772-5689
Fax: (212) 650-3673

Diálogo
Felix Masud-Piloto, Editor
Center for Latino Research
Department of History
DePaul University
2323 N. Seminary
Chicago, IL 60614
Phone: (312) 362-5607
Fax: (312) 362-5481

East/West News
838 Grant Avenue
San Francisco, CA 94108
Phone: (415) 781-3194

Ethnic Forum—Journal of Ethnic Studies and Ethnic Bibliography
Lubomyr R. Wynar, Editor
Center for the Study of Ethnic Publications and Cultural Institutions
Room 318
University Library
Kent State University
P.O. Box 5190
Kent, OH 44242-0001
Phone: (216) 672-2782
Fax: (216) 672-7965
E-mail: wynar@lsci.kent.edu

Ethnohistory
Ross Hassig, Editor
University of Oklahoma
American Society for Ethnohistory
Duke University Press
Box 90660
Durham, NC 27708-0660
Phone: (405) 325-3271
Fax: (405) 325-3261

Ethnomusicology
P.O. Box 2984
Ann Arbor, MI 48106
Phone: (313) 665-9400

Études/Inuit/Studies
Francois Therien, Editor
Pavillon Jean-Durand
Université Laval
Quebec G1K 7P4
CANADA
Phone: (418) 656-2353
Fax: (418) 656-3023

European Review of Native American Studies
Christian F. Feest, Editor/Publisher
Fasanenweg 4A
D-63674 Altenstadt
GERMANY
Phone: +49-06047-67566

Explorations in Ethnic Studies
Miguel Carranza, Editor
Institute for Ethnic Studies
University of Nebraska-Lincoln
Lincoln, NE 68588-0335
Phone: (402) 472-3080
Fax: (402) 472-1123

Explorations in Sights and Sounds
Miguel Carranza, Editor
Institute for Ethnic Studies
University of Nebraska-Lincoln
Lincoln, NE 68588-0335
Phone: (402) 472-3080
Fax: (402) 472-1123

Hispanic Journal of Behavioral Sciences
Amado M. Padilla, Editor
Center for Educational Research at Stanford
Stanford University
Stanford, CA 94305

Identities: Global Studies in Culture and Power (formerly **Ethnic Groups**)
Nina Glick Schiller, Editor
Gordon and Breach Publishers
P.O. Box 786
Cooper Station
New York, NY 10276

International Journal of African Dance
Karianne Welsh-Asante, Director
Institute for Africa Dance Research and Performance
814 Gladfelter Hall
12th and Berks Streets
Temple University
Philadelphia, PA 19122-1199
Phone: (215) 204-8480/8626
Fax: (215) 204-5953

International Migration Review
Lydio F. Tomasi, Managing Editor
Center for Migration Studies
209 Flagg Place
Staten Island, NY 10304-1199
Phone: (718) 351-8800
Fax: (718) 667-4598

Journal of Alaska Native Arts
Jan Steinbright, Editor
Institute of Alaska Native Arts
P.O. Box 70769
Fairbanks, AK 99707
Phone: (907) 456-7491
Fax: (907) 451-7268
E-mail: iana@tmn.com

Journal of Afro-Latin American Studies and Literatures
Rosangela Maria Vieira, Editor
Department of Languages and Modern Literatures
Howard University
2400 6th Street N.W.
Locke Hall
Washington, DC 20059

Journal of American Ethnic History
Ronald H. Bayor, Editor
Immigration History Society
School of History
Technology and Society
Georgia Institute of Technology
Atlanta, GA 30332-0345
Phone: (404) 894-6834
Fax: (404) 853-0535
E-mail: rb2@rprism.gatech.edu
Distributed by: Transaction Periodicals Consortium
Department 8110
Rutgers University
New Brunswick, NJ 08903

Journal of American Indian Education

Karen Swisher, Editor
Center for Indian Education
College of Education
Arizona State University
Box 871311
Tempe, AZ 85287-1311
Phone: (602) 965-6292
Fax: (602) 965-8115

Journal of American Indian Family Research

Larry S. Watson, Editor
Histree
803 S. 5th Avenue
Yuma, AZ 85364
Phone: (602) 343-2755

Journal of Black Psychology, The

Ann Kathleen Burlew, Editor
Department of Psychology
Mail Location #376
University of Cincinnati
Cincinnati, OH 45221
Phone: (513) 556-5541

Journal of Black Studies

Molefi Kete Asante, Editor
Department of African-American Studies
Temple University
Philadelphia, PA 19122
Phone: (215) 204-4322
Fax: (215) 204-5953

Journal of Blacks in Higher Education, The

Robert Bruce Slater, Managing Editor
200 West 57th Street/15th Floor
New York, NY 10019
Phone: (212) 399-1084 or 245-1973

Journal of Cherokee Studies
Duane King, Editor
Museum of the Cherokee Indian
P.O. Box 1599
Cherokee, NC 28719
Phone: (704) 497-3481
Fax: (704) 497-4985

Journal of Multicultural Counseling and Development
Frederick D. Harper, Editor
American Counseling Association
5999 Stevenson Avenue
Alexandria, VA 22304-3300
Phone: (800) 347-6647

Journal of Multicultural Social Work
Paul R. Keys, Editor
Hunter College, CUNY
School of Social Work
129 East 79th Street
New York, NY 10021

Journal of Multilingual and Multicultural Development
John Edwards, Editor
c/o Multilingual Matters
Frankfurt Lodge
Clevedon Hall
Victoria Road
Clevedon, ENGLAND BS21 7SJ

Journal of Negro History
Alton Hornsby, Editor
ASALH
Department of History
Morehouse College
Box 20
Atlanta, GA 30314
Phone: (404) 215-2620
Fax: (404) 215-2715

Latino Studies Journal
Felix M. Padilla, Editor
Center for Latino Research
Department of Sociology and Anthropology
Northeastern University
521 Holmes Hall
Boston, MA 02155

MELUS
Joseph T. Skerrett, Jr., Editor
Department of English
272 Bartlett Hall
University of Massachusetts
Amherst, MA 01003
Phone: (413) 545-3166
Fax: (413) 545-3880

MultiCultural Review
Meg Fergusson, Production Editor
Greenwood Publishing Group, Inc.
88 Post Road West
P.O. Box 5007
Westport, CT 06881-5007
Phone: (203) 226-3571
Fax: (203) 222-1502

Native Peoples
Gary Avey, Editor
5333 N. Seventh Street
Suite C-224
Phoenix, AZ 85014
Phone: (602) 252-2236
Fax: (602) 265-3113

Native Press Research Journal
D. F. Littlefield and J. W. Parins, Editors
University of Arkansas
Little Rock, AR 72204
Phone: (501) 569-3160

New Asia Review
James Borton, Editor
Greenwood Publishing Group, Inc.
88 Post Road West
P.O. Box 5007
Westport, CT 06881-5007
Phone: (203) 226-3571
Fax: (203) 222-1502

News from Native California
P.O. Box 9145
Berkeley, CA 94709
Phone: (510) 549-3564
Fax: (510) 549-1889

Phylon—The Clark Atlanta University Review of Race and Culture
Lucy C. Grigsby, Interim Editor
Clark Atlanta University
James P. Brawley at Fair Street, S.W.
Atlanta, GA 30314

Race, Sex and Class
Jean Belkhir, Editor
Institute for Teaching and Research on Women
Towson State University
Towson, MD 21204-7097
Phone: (410) 830-2580
Fax: (410) 830-3469
E-mail: e7w8cct.toe.towson.edu

Research in African Literatures
Abiola Irele, Editor
Africa Literature Assoc. and the African Lits. Div. of the MLA
The Ohio State University
P.O. Box 3509
Columbus, OH 43210-0509
Phone: (614) 292-9735
Fax: (614) 292-3927
E-mail: ral@magnus.acs.ohio-state.edu
Distributed by: Indiana University Press
601 N. Morton Street
Bloomington, IN 47404

Saguaro
Mexican American Studies and Research Center
University of Arizona
315 Douglass Building
Tucson, AZ 85721
Phone: (602) 621-7551

SAIL: Studies in American Indian Literatures
Rodney Simard, General Editor
Department of English
California State University-San Bernardino
5500 University Parkway
San Bernardino, CA 92407-2397
Phone: (909) 880-5926
Robert M. Nelson, Managing Editor
Department of English
Box 112
University of Richmond
Richmond, VA 23173

Spectrum
Joel Wurl, Managing Editor
University of Minnesota
Immigration History Research Center
826 Berry Street
St. Paul, MN 55114
Phone: (612) 627-4208
Fax: (612) 627-4190
E-mail: wurlx001@maroon.tc.umn.edu

Torre De Papel
Adrian Pablo Massei, Editor
211 Schaffer Hall
University of Iowa
Iowa City, IA 52242

Wanbli Ho: A Literary Arts Journal
Victor Douville, Editor
Lakota Studies/Creative Writing Program
Sinte Gleska College
P.O. Box 8
Mission, SD 57555

Western Journal of Black Studies
Talmadge Anderson, Editor
Heritage House
Black Studies Program
Washington State University
Pullman, WA 99164-3310
Phone: (509) 335-8681

Wicazo Sa Review
Indian Studies
Eastern Washington University
Cheney, WA 99004

Ethnic Studies Newsletters

AAAS Newsletter
Gary Y. Okihiro, Editor
Association for Asian American Studies
Caldwell Hall 492
Cornell University
Ithaca, NY 14853
Phone: (607) 255-3320
Fax: (607) 255-3320
E-mail: apai@cornell.edu

African-American Family History Association Newsletter
African/American Family History Association
Box 115268
Atlanta, GA 30310
Phone: (404) 344-7405
Fax: (404) 523-4672

Alambraso
Jim Escalante, Acting Director
Chicano Studies Program
University of Wisconsin-Madison
175 Science Hall
550 North Park Street
Madison, WI 53706
Phone: (608) 263-4486

American Indian Culture and Research Center Newsletter
American Indian Culture and Research Center
Marvin, SD 57251

American Indian Law Students Association Newsletter
American Indian Law Center
University of New Mexico-School of Law
117 Stanford Drive, NE
Albuquerque, NM 87196
Phone: (505) 277-5462

American Indian Libraries Newsletter
Lutsee Patterson, Editor
American Indian Library Association
Office of Library Outreach Services (OLOS)
c/o American Library Association
50 Huron Street
Chicago, IL 60611
Phone: (312) 944-6780

American Indian News
Office of Native American Programs
P.O. Box 217
Fort Washakie, WY 82514

American Indian Program Newsletter
Native American Student Center
Multicultural Center 107
Washington State University
Pullman, WA 99164-2314
Phone: (509) 335-8676
Fax: (509) 335-8368

American Indian Rehabilitation
Sheri R. Nolen, Administrative Assistant
American Indian Rehabilitation Research and Training Center
Northern Arizona University
CU Box 5630
Flagstaff, AZ 86011
Phone: (602) 523-4791
Fax: (602) 523-1927
E-mail: srn@nauvax.nau.edu

Americans Before Columbus
National Indian Youth Council
318 Elm Street S.E.
Albuquerque, NM 87102

ASAIL Notes
John Purdy, Editor
Association for Study of American Indian Literatures
Department of English
Western Washington University
Bellingham, WA 98225-9055
Phone: (206) 650-3243
Fax: (206) 650-4837
E-mail: purdy@henson.cc.wwu.edu

ATUMPAN
Audrey Thomas McCluskey, Editor
Indiana University Alumni Association
Fountain Square
Suite 219
P.O. Box 4822
Bloomington, IN 47402-4822
Phone: (812) 855-2082
Fax: (812) 855-4869
E-mail: mcclusk@iubacs.indiana.edu

Bridges Newsletter
Robert F. Gish, Director
Ethnic Studies Program
Room 201, Building 22
California Polytechnic State University-San Luis Obispo
San Luis Obispo, CA 93407
Phone: (805) 756-1707
Fax: (805) 756-5748
E-mail: di597@oasis.calpoly.edu

CAA Newsletter
Mimi Kuo, Editor
Chinese for Affirmative Action
The Kuo Building
17 Walter U. Lum Place
San Francisco, CA 94108
Phone: (415) 274-6750
Fax: (415) 397-8770

CAAS Report
Cherie Francis, Assistant to the Director
Center for Afro-American Studies
University of California-Los Angeles
160 Haines Hall
405 Hilgard Avenue
Los Angeles, CA 90024-1545
Phone: (310) 825-7403
Fax: (310) 206-3421

Carta Abierta
Juan Rodriguez, Editor-Publisher
Texas Lutheran College
1000 W. Court Street
Seguin, TX 78155
Phone: (210) 372-6059

CASAE
Rachel San Pedro Davis, Editor
Center for Applied Studies in American Ethnicity
Colorado State University
Education Building
Fort Collins, CO 80523
Phone: (303) 491-2730
Fax: (303) 491-2717

Center for Western Studies Newsletter, The
Augustana College
P.O. Box 727
Sioux Falls, SD 57197
Phone: (605) 336-4007

CESA Bulletin, The
Natalia Aponiuk, President
c/o The Centre for Ukrainian Canadian Studies
St. Andrew's College
University of Manitoba
Winnipeg, Manitoba R3T 2N2
CANADA
Phone: (204) 474-8906
Fax: (204) 275-0803

Comunica Horizons
Marla E. K. Moon, Editor
Mexico-United States Consortium for Academic Cooperation
Julian Samora Research Institute
Michigan State University
216 Erickson Hall
East Lansing, MI 48824-1034
Phone: (517) 336-1317
Fax: (517) 336-2221

COSSMHO Reporter, The
Brent Wilkes, Editor
1501 16th Street, NW
Washington, DC 20036
Phone: (202) 387-5000

CSERA News
Steven E. Medina, Editor
Center for Studies of Ethnicity and Race in America
University of Colorado at Boulder
Ketchum 30
Campus Box 339
Boulder, CO 80309-0339
Phone: (303) 492-8852
Fax: (303) 492-7799
E-mail: medina@spot.colorado.edu

El Puente
Mary Montano, Co-Editor
P.O. Box 7279
Albuquerque, NM 87194
Phone: (505) 831-8360
Fax: (505) 831-8365

Enfoque
Graciela Platero, Program Officer
Center for U.S.-Mexican Studies
University of California-San Diego
9500 Gilman Drive Dept. 0510
La Jolla, CA 92093-0510
Phone: (619) 534-4503
Fax: (619) 534-6447
E-mail: gplatero@weber.ucsd.edu

ERIC/CRESS Bulletin
Patricia Cahape, Editor
Appalachia Educational Laboratory
P.O. Box 1348
Charleston, WV 25325-1348
Phone: (800) 624-9120
Fax: (304) 347-0487

Ethnic Reporter, The
Miguel A. Carranza, Editor
National Association for Ethnic Studies
NAES Publications
Department of English
Arizona State University
Tempe, AZ 85287-0302
Phone: (602) 965-2197
Fax: (602) 965-3451
E-mail: naesi@asuvm.inre.asu.edu

Fourth World Bulletin
Mark Sills, Editor
Fourth World Center for the Study of Indigenous Law and Politics
Department of Political Science
University of Colorado-Denver
Campus Box 90
P.O. Box 173364
Denver, CO 80217-3364
Phone: (303) 556-2850
Fax: (303) 556-6041

Gastón Institute Report, The
Lindo Kluz, Editor
Mauricio Gastón Institute
University of Massachusetts
100 Morrissey Boulevard
Boston, MA 02125-3395
Phone: (617) 287-3395
Fax: (617) 287-5788

HACU—The Voice of Hispanic Higher Education
Jorge A. Ramirez, Editor
Hispanic Association of Colleges and Universities
4204 Gardendale Street
Suite 216
San Antonio, TX 78229
Phone: (210) 692-3805
Fax: (210) 692-0823

Hispanic Newsletter
Cuban American Legal Defense and Education Fund
2119 Webster Street
Ft. Wayne, IN 46804
Phone: (219) 745-5421

Hispanoticias
Xavier E. Romano, Publications Coordinator
c/o Office of Student Activities
Santa Clara University
Santa Clara, CA 95053
Phone: (408) 554-4745
Fax: (408) 554-5544
E-mail: xromano@scuacc.scu.edu

Immigration History Newsletter
Joseph T. Makarewicz, Editor
Immigration History Society
Ethnic Studies Center
405 Bellefield Hall
University of Pittsburgh
Pittsburgh, PA 15260
Phone: (412) 648-7451
Fax: (412) 648-1148

Indian Affairs
The Association on American Indian Affairs, Inc.
245 Fifth Avenue
New York, NY 10016
Phone: (212) 689-8720

Indian Historian, The
American Indian Historical Society
1451 Masonic Avenue
San Francisco, CA 94117

Indian Voice
Donna Doss, Editor
Canadian Indian Voice Society
429 East 6th Street
Vancouver, British Columbia V7L 1P8
CANADA

Información Latina
Felix Masud-Piloto, Editor
Center for Latino Research
Department of History
2323 N. Seminary
Chicago, IL 60614
Phone: (312) 362-5607
Fax: (312) 362-5481

Institute of Indian Studies: The Bulletin
414 East Clark Street
Vermillion, SD 57069
Phone: (605) 677-5209

Intertribal News
Rick Wheelock
Native American Center
Fort Lewis College
Durango, CO 81301
Phone: (303) 247-7227
Fax: (303) 247-7108

IUP News Report, The
Maria Chacon, Editor
Inter-University Program for Latino Research
Centro de Estudios Puertorriqueños
Hunter College-CUNY
695 Park Avenue
New York, NY 10021
Phone: (212) 772-5674
Fax: (212) 772-4348

Kaleidoscope II
Judy Treskow, Editor
The University of Wisconsin System Institute on Race and Ethnicity
University of Wisconsin-Milwaukee
P.O. Box 413
Milwaukee, WI 53201
Phone: (414) 229-4804/6701
Fax: (414) 229-4481

La Nueva Vision
Luis R. Fraga, Director
Stanford Center for Chicano Research
Stanford University
Cypress Hall
E Wing
Stanford, CA 94305-4149
Phone: (415) 723-3914
Fax: (415) 725-0353
E-mail: ak.cla@forsythe.stanford.edu

La Paloma
Instituto Cultural Mexicano
600 Hemisfair Plaza
San Antonio, TX 78205

LATINO
Dromrac Wood, Communications Assistant
Latino Institute
228 South Wabash
6th Floor
Chicago, IL 60604
Phone: (312) 663-3603
Fax: (312) 663-4023

MANRRS Newsletter
Eunice F. Foster, Editor
Minorities in Agriculture, Natural Resources, and Related Sciences
Department of Crop and Soil Sciences
160 PSSB
Michigan State University
East Lansing, MI 48824
Phone: (517) 353-1784
Fax: (517) 353-5174
E-mail: fostere@msu.edu

MASRC Newsletter
Mexican American Studies & Research Center
Douglass Building
Room 315
University of Arizona
Tucson, AZ 85721
Phone: (602) 621-7551
Fax: (602) 621-7955

MCLR Quarterly Newsletter
Midwest Consortium for Latino Research
Michigan State University
216 Erickson Hall
East Lansing, MI 48823-1034
Phone: (517) 336-2220
Fax: (517) 336-2221
E-mail: mclr-l@msu.bitnet

Meeting Ground
Brenda Mannelito, Editor
D'Arcy McNickle Center for the History of the American Indian
The Newberry Library
60 West Walton Street
Chicago, IL 60610-3380
Phone: (312) 943-9090

Mexico Policy News
Institute for Regional Studies of the Californias
PROFMEX Mexico Policy News
San Diego State University
San Diego, CA 92182-0435

Migrant Health Newsline
C. Yvonne Dailey, Editor
National Migrant Resource Program, Inc.
1515 Capitol Highway South
Suite 220
Austin, TX 78746

Minority Notes
Wellard Administration Center
Room 203
University of Colorado
Boulder, CO 80309

Multicultural Messenger
International Multicultural Education Association
P.O. Box 70
Rochelle Park, NJ 07662
Phone: (201) 712-0090
Fax: (201) 712-0045

NACIE Newsletter
National Advisory Council on Indian Education
330 C Street, S.W.
Room 4072
Washington, DC 20202-7556
Phone: (202) 732-1353

NAES RULE
Robert V. Dumont, Jr., Vice President of Academic Affairs
NAES College
2838 Peterson Avenue
Chicago, IL 60659
Phone: (312) 761-5000
Fax: (312) 761-3808

NAPBC Newsletter
Stefanie Hare, Editor
Native American Public Broadcasting Consortium, Inc.
Box 83111
Lincoln, NE 68501
Phone: (402) 472-3522

NARF Legal Review
Ray Ramirez, Editor
Native American Rights Fund
1506 Broadway
Boulder, CO 80302
Phone: (303) 447-8760

NASP News
Earl Dean Sisto, Director
Native American Student Program
224 Costo
University of California
Riverside, CA 92521-0438
Phone: (909) 787-4143
Fax: (909) 787-2221

National Indian Social Workers Association Newsletter
National Indian Social Workers Association
1740 West 41st Street
Tulsa, OK 74107
Phone: (918) 446-8432

Native American Council News
204 Hagested Student Center
University of Wisconsin
River Falls, WI 54022

Native American Students of the Northwest Newsletter
University of Idaho
Moscow, ID 83843

Native Sun
Detroit American Indian Center
22720 Plymouth Rd.
Detroit, MI 48239
Phone: (313) 535-2966

NCBF Newsletter
Wornie L. Reed, Editor
National Congress of Black Faculty
P.O. Box 93457
Cleveland, OH 44101-5457
Phone: (216) 687-5490
Fax: (216) 687-5445

NCLR Agenda
Lisa Navarrete, Editor
National Council of La Raza
810 First Street, N.E.
Suite 300
Washington, DC 20002
Phone: (202) 289-1380

NCOBPS Newsletter
Nolan W. Zane, Editor
Kennesaw State College
P.O. Box 444
Marietta, GA 30061
Phone: (404) 423-6312

Negro History Bulletin
Karen Mcrae, Editor
ASALH
1407 Fourteenth Street, N.W.
Washington, DC 20005-3704
Phone: (202) 667-2822
Fax: (202) 387-9802

Network News
Arnoldo Garcia, Editor
National Network for Immigrant and Refugee Rights
310 8th Street
Suite 307
Oakland, CA 94607
Phone: (510) 465-1984
Fax: (510) 465-7548

New Americans
Martin Ford, Community Liaison Specialist
Maryland Office for New Americans
Department of Human Resources
Room 210
311 W. Saratoga Street
Baltimore, MD 21201
Phone: (410) 767-7514
Fax: (410) 333-0392

NEXO
Rosemary Aponte
The Julian Somora Research Institute
Michigan State University
216 Erickson Hall
East Lansing, MI 48824-1034
Phone: (517) 336-1317
Fax: (517) 336-2221

NHCOA NOTICIAS
Marta Sotomayor, President
The National Hispanic Council on Aging
2713 Ontario Road, N.W.
Washington, DC 20009
Phone: (202) 745-2521
Fax: (202) 745-2522

NHSF News
Ricardo D. Fouster, Editor
National Hispanic Scholarship Fund
1400 Grant Avenue
Novato, CA 94948

NIEA Newsletter
National Indian Education Association
1819 H Street, N.W.
Suite 800
Washington, DC 20006
Phone: (202) 835-3001

NOMMO: Power of the Word
Ciola Ross Baber, Editor
Afro-American Studies Center
Purdue University
110 Matthews Hall
West Lafayette, IN 47907
Phone: (317) 949-5680

Notas (formerly **Association for Latina/o Sociology Newsletter**)
P. Rafael Hernandez, Editor
Department of Sociology
Hunter College, CUNY
P.O. Box 6438, F.D.R. Station
New York, NY 10150
Phone: (212) 751-0019
E-mail: prhhc@cunyvm.cuny.edu

Noticias de NACS
Carlos S. Maldonado, Editor
National Association for Chicano Studies
Chicano Education Program
Eastern Washington University
MS170
Cheney, WA 99004
Phone: (509) 359-2404
Fax: (509) 359-6927

On the Way Up
American Indian Science and Engineering Society
1310 College Avenue
Suite 1220
Boulder, CO 80302
Phone: (303) 492-8658

Oyate-Anishanabe News
American Indian Student Cultural Center
104 Hones Hall
27 Pleasant SE
Minneapolis, MN 55404

Plural: The Interdisciplinary Chicana and Chicano Studies Newsletter
Cordelia Candelaria, Editor
Department of English
Box 870302
Tempe, AZ 85287-0302

Poverty and Race
Chester W. Hartman, President/Executive Director
Poverty and Race Research Action Council (PRRAC)
1711 Connecticut Avenue, N.W., Suite 207
Washington, DC 20009
Phone: (202) 387-9887
Fax: (202) 387-0764

PRSA News
Liza Fiol-Matta, Editor
Puerto Rican Studies Association
c/o Department of English
LaGuardia Community College
Long Island City, NY 11101
Phone: (718) 951-4872

Psych Discourse
Halford H. Fairchild, Editor
The Association of Black Psychologists
P.O. Box 55999
Washington, DC 20040-5999
Phone: (202) 722-0808
Fax: (202) 722-5941

Puerto Rican Research Exchange, The
Myra Y. Estapa, Editor
Institute for Puerto Rican Policy
286 Fifth Avenue
Room 301
New York, NY 10001-4512
Phone: (212) 564-1075
Fax: (212) 564-1014

SACNAS News
Society for Advancement of Chicanos and Native Americans in Science
Sinsheimer Laboratories
University of California
Santa Cruz, CA 95064
Phone: (408) 459-4272
Fax: (408) 459-3156
E-mail: gopher@papilo.ucsc.edu

SEM Newsletter
Ernest Douglas Brown, Editor
The Society for Ethnomusicology
Department of Music
Williams College
Williamstown, MA 01267
Phone: (413) 597-3266
E-mail: ebrown@williams.edu

Sinte Gleska College News
Library Media Center
Box 107
Rosebud Reservation
Mission, SD 57555

Smithsonian Runner
Dan Agent, Editor
Smithsonian Institution
Office of Public Affairs
A&I-2410 MRC 421
Washington, DC 20560
Phone: (202) 357-2627
Fax: (202) 786-2377

SOCI Newsletter
Sondra O'Neale, Chair
Sisters of Color International
Department of Women's Studies
University of Wisconsin-La Crosse
336 North Hall
La Crosse, WI 54601
Phone: (608) 785-8734
Fax: (608) 785-8909

Source, The
Office of Indian Affairs
224 E. Palace Avenue
Santa Fe, NM 87501

South Asia News
South Asia Regional Studies Department
University of Pennsylvania
820 WMSH/6305
Philadelphia, PA 19104-6305
Phone: (215) 898-7475
Fax: (215) 573-2138

Tapestry
Millie Riley, Editor
Division of Historical and Cultural Programs
Department of Housing and Community Development
100 Community Place
Crownsville, MD 21032
Phone: (410) 514-7624

Tomahawk
Oregon State University
P.O. Box 428
Warm Springs, OR 97761

TRC Report, The
Kimberly Mogavero, Director of Operations
The Tomas Rivera Center
Steele Hall, 3rd Floor
Claremont, CA 91711
Phone: (909) 625-6607
Fax: (909) 624-5954
E-mail: mogaverk@cgsuax.claremont.edu

UC Mexus News
Kathryn L. Roberts, Editor
UC Institute for Mexico and the U.S.
252 Highlander Hall
University of California
Riverside, CA 92521
Phone: (909) 787-3519
Fax: (909) 787-3856
E-mail: kroberts@ucrael.cur.edu

Unity/La Unidad
Jean Yonemura, Editor
P.O. Box 29293
Oakland, CA 94604
Phone: (510) 652-4327
Fax: (510) 652-4685

Voces Unidas
Roberto Contreras, Editor
Southwest Organizing Project
211 10th Street S.W.
Albuquerque, NM 87102
Phone: (505) 247-8832

Voice of Black Studies Newsletter, The
Jacqueline E. Wade, Editor
Ohio State University
208 Mount Hall
1050 Carmack Road
Columbus, OH 43210
Phone: (614) 292-1035
Fax: (614) 292-7363

WEB, The
Jennifer Bedell, Coordinator
American Indian Program
300 Caldwell Hall
Cornell University
Ithaca, NY 14853
Phone: (607) 255-4308
Fax: (607) 255-0185
E-mail: jennifer_bedell@qmcampl.mail.cornell.edu

Winds of Change
Norbert S. Hill, Jr., Publisher
American Indian Science and Engineering Society (AISES)
1630 30th Street
Suite 301
Boulder, CO 80301-1014
Phone: (303) 492-8658
Fax: (303) 492-3400
E-mail: aiseshq@spot.colorado.edu

WOC Newsletter
Sondra O'Neale, Co-Editor
Department of Women's Studies
336 North Hall
University of Wisconsin-La Crosse
La Crosse, WI 54601
Phone: (608) 785-8734
Fax: (608) 785-8909

Yoida Nava
Indian Club
Arizona Western College
Yuma, AZ 85364

ETHNIC STUDIES PUBLISHERS

Africa World Press, Inc.
Kassahun Checole, President/Publisher
P.O. Box 1892
Trenton, NJ 18607
Phone: (609) 844-9583
Fax: (609) 844-0198

Ahsahta Press
Department of English
Idaho State University
Boise, ID 83725

Akwe:kon Press
400 Caldwell Hall
Cornell University
Ithaca, NY 14853

Akwesasne Notes
Mohawk Nation
Rooseveltown, NY 13683

American Multi-Cultural Publications
1932 Chambers Street
Trenton, NJ 08610
Phone: (609) 777-5444
Fax: (609) 777-9500

Arte Público Press
Nicolás Kanellos, Publisher
University of Houston
4800 Calhoun
429 AH
Houston, TX 77004
Phone: (713) 743-2841
Fax: (713) 743-2847

Bilingual Education Press
Jeff Pinechet
2514 South Grand Avenue
Los Angeles, CA 90007-9979
Phone: (213) 749-6213

Bilingual Review/Press
Ann Waggoner Aken, Associate Editor
Hispanic Research Center
Arizona State University
Box 872702
Tempe, AZ 85287-2702
Phone: (602) 965-3867
Fax: (602) 965-8309

Blackberry Press
Gary Lawless, Editor/Publisher
Chimney Farm
RR #1
P.O. Box 228
Nobleboro, ME 04555
Phone: (207) 729-5083

Cinco Puntos Press
Bobby Byrd, Publisher
2709 Louisville
El Paso, TX 79930
Phone: (915) 566-9072
Fax: (915) 566-9072

Crossing Press
17 West Main Street
Trumansburg, NY 14886

Editorial Justa Publications
Herminio Rios
2831 7th Street
Berkeley, CA 94710
Phone: (415) 848-3628

Firebrand Books
Nancy K. Bereano, Publisher
141 The Commons
Ithaca, NY 14850
Phone: (607) 272-0000

Floricanto Press
16161 Ventura Boulevard
Encino, CA 91436
Phone: (818) 990-1885

Holy Cow! Press
P.O. Box 3170
Mount Royal Station
Duluth, MN 55803

Howard University Press
Dedra Owens, Publicity and Promotions
1240 Randolph Street, N.E.
Washington, DC 20017
Phone: (202) 806-4935
Fax: (202) 806-4946

Indian University Press
Bacone College
Muskogee, OK 74403

Intercultural Press
P.O. Box 768
Yarmouth, ME 04096

Kitchen Table Press
P.O. Box 908
Latham, NY 12110

Maize Press
961 Bakersfield
Pismo Beach, CA 93449
Phone: (805) 773-5977

Navajo Community College Press
Ed McCombs, Director
College Press
Navajo Community College
Tsaile, AZ 86556
Phone: (602) 724-3311 (ext. 322, 321)
Fax: (602) 724-3327

Northland Press
P.O. Box N
Flagstaff, AZ 86002

Oyate Press
2701 Matthews Street
Berkeley, CA 94707

Pemmican Publications
504 Main Street, Room 411
Winnipeg MBR3B 1B8
CANADA

Relampago Press
Juan Rodriguez
942 Reiley Road
Sequin, TX 78155
Phone: (210) 379-4126

Scarecrow Press
Amy R. Pratico, Advertising & Promotion Manager
52 Liberty Street
P.O. Box 4167
Metuchen, NJ 08840
Phone: (908) 548-8600
Fax: (908) 548-5767

Seven Buffaloes Press
Art Coelho, Editor and Publisher
Box 249
Big Timber, MT 59011

South End Press
Dionne Brooks, Editor/Publisher
116 Saint Botolph Street
Boston, MA 02115
Phone: (617) 266-0629
Fax: (617) 266-1595

Spinster's Ink
P.O. Box 410687
San Francisco, CA 94107

Sun Tracks Series, University of Arizona Press
Ofelia Zepeda, Series Editor
University of Arizona
American Indian Studies Program
Harvill Building
Tucson, AZ 85721
Phone: (602) 621-7108

Swift Kick Press
1711 Amherst Street
Buffalo, NY 14214

Texas Western Press
Marcia Daudistel, Assistant Director
University of Texas
Corner of Wiggins and Rim Roads
El Paso, TX 79968-0633
Phone: (915) 747-5688
Fax: (915) 747-5969

Theytus Book Ltd.
P.O. Box 218
Penticton, BC
V2A 6K3
CANADA

Third Woman Press
Ethnic Studies Department
Dwinelle Hall
University of California
Berkeley, CA 94720

Thunder's Mouth Press
93-099 Green Street
Suite 2A
New York, NY 10012

UCLA American Indian Studies Center
Duane Champagne, Editor
3220 Campbell Hall
405 Hilgard Avenue
University of California
Los Angeles, CA 90024-1548
Phone: (310) 825-7315
Fax: (310) 206-7060

University of Arizona Press
Stephen F. Cox, Director
1230 North Park Avenue
Suite 102
Tucson, AZ 85719-4140
Phone: (602) 621-1441
Fax: (602) 621-8899
E-mail: sfcox@ccit.arizona.edu

University of California Press
University of California
Berkeley, CA 94720
Phone: (800) 822-6657

University of Nebraska Press
University of Nebraska
312 North 14th Street
Lincoln, NE 68588-0484
Phone: (402) 472-3581
Fax: (402) 472-0308
E-mail: press@unlinfo.unl.edu

University of New Mexico Press
1720 Lomas Boulevard, N.E.
Albuquerque, NM 87131-1591
Phone: (505) 277-2346
Fax: (505) 277-9270
E-mail: unmpress@carina.unm.edu

University of Puerto Rico Press
Dalidia Colón Pieretti, Acting Director
23322
UPR Station
San Juan, PR 00931
Phone: (809) 250-0550
Fax: (809) 753-9116

University of Texas Press
Joanna Hitchcock
Box 7819
Austin, TX 78713-7233
Phone: (512) 471-7233

West End Press
P.O. Box 27334
Albuquerque, NM 87125

Bibliography

Resources on Ethnic Studies

Abrash, Barbara, and Catherine Egan, eds. *Mediating History: The MAP Guide to Independent Video by and about African American, Asian American, Latino, and Native American People*. New York: New York University Press, 1992. Brief essays and selected annotated bibliography of films appropriate for Ethnic Studies courses and programs.

Allen, James P., and Eugene J. Turner, eds. *We the People: An Atlas of America's Ethnic Diversity*. New York: Macmillan, 1987.

American Indian Studies Center. *American Indian Issues in Higher Education*. Los Angeles: American Indian Studies Center, UCLA, 1981. Essays on the purposes and history of American Indian studies in higher education as well as essays on Indian students and curriculum issues.

Asante, Molefi Kete. *The Afrocentric Idea*. Philadelphia: Temple University Press, 1987. Asante argues that Afrocentrism is the only response to Western cultural chauvinism.

———. *Afrocentricity*. Trenton: Africa World Press, 1988.

———. *The Historical and Cultural Atlas of African Americans*. New York: Macmillan, 1991.

Baker, Houston A., Jr. "Presidential Forum—Multiculturalism: The Task of Literary Representations in the Twenty-First Century." *Profession 93* (1993). Special issue. Houston Baker introduces three essays on the multicultural debate by Henry Louis Gates, Jr., Susan Stewart, and Sara Suleri.

Ballinger, Franchot. *A Guide to Native American Studies Programs in the United States*. Supplement to Vol. 5 *SAIL*. Published by the Association for the Study of American Literatures and supported by the University of Richmond, 1994. Descriptions of thirty Native American Studies programs including a listing of programs according to region and degrees offered.

Banks, James A. *Teaching Strategies for Ethnic Studies*. 5th ed. Boston: Allen and Bacon, 1991. In this updated study of ethnicity, Banks includes general information, specific strategies and bibliographies on ethnic groups, and a chronology of key events. Essays by experts in diverse areas are included.

Bengelsdorf, Winnie. *Ethnic Studies in Higher Education: State of the Art and Bibliography*. Washington, DC: American Association of State Colleges and Universities, 1972. Brief (13 pp.) early bibliography arranged by ethnic group.

Bernal, Martha E., and George P. Knight, eds. *Ethnic Identity: Formation and Transmission among Hispanics and other Minorities*. Albany: State University of New York Press, 1993. Collection of scholarly essays that focus on the development of ethnic identity from childhood through adolescence within families and across generations.

Bibliographic Guide to Black Studies. Boston: G. K. Hall, 1993. Lists publications catalogued yearly by the New York Public Library. It also serves as an annual
supplement to the *Dictionary Catalog of the Schoenburg Collections of Negro Literature and History* (G. K. Hall, 1962; *First Supplement, 1967; Sec-
ond Supplement, 1972.*)

Buenker, John D., and Lorman A. Ratner, eds. *Multiculturalism in the United States:
A Comparative Guide to Acculturation and Ethnicity*. New York: Greenwood
Press, 1992. Handbook on the history of ethnic cultures in America, focusing
on changes in cultures and changes in the overall American culture.

Burrola, Luis Ramón, and José A. Rivera. *Chicano Studies at the Crossroads: Alternative Futures for the 1980s*. Working Paper No. 103. Albuquerque: Southwest Hispanic Research Institute, University of New Mexico, 1983. Documents
issues and concerns facing Chicano Studies programs and makes recommen-
dations for future study.

Butler, Johnnella E., and John C. Walter. *Transforming the Curriculum: Ethnic and
Women's Studies*. Albany: State University of New York Press, 1991. Series
of essays on incorporating Ethnic and Women's Studies into the curriculum.

Castillo-Speed, Lillian, comp. and ed. *The Chicana Studies Index: Twenty Years of
Gender Research, 1971–1991*. Berkeley: Chicano Studies Library Publications
Unit, UC at Berkeley, 1992. A subject, author, and title index to approximately
1,150 journal articles, book articles, books, dissertations, and reports on all
aspects of the Chicana experience and the role that gender plays in Chicana
Studies.

Claerbaut, David, ed. *New Directions in Ethnic Studies: Minorities in America*.
Saratoga, CA: Century Twenty One, 1981. Series of essays focusing on minorities and race relations in the United States.

Cordova, Teresa, ed. *Chicano Studies: Critical Connection between Research and Community*. Albuquerque: NACS, 1992. This special volume of the NACS marks
its twentieth anniversary and contains essays from both NACS scholars and
community activists.

Davis, Lenwood G., and George Hill, comps. *A Bibliographical Guide to Black Studies Programs in the United States: A Bibliography*. Westport, CT: Greenwood
Press, 1985. Lists over 700 articles, books, and dissertations about Black Studies.

Duffy, David, and Mitsue M. Frey, comps. *Directory of African and Afro-American
Studies in the United States*. Waltham, MA: Crossroads Press, 1979. Complete
entries on 623 institutions with programs in African and African American
Studies and additional entries on institutions with courses in these areas.

Duran, Livie Isauro, and H. Russell Bernard, eds. *Introduction to Chicano Studies: A
Reader*. New York: Macmillan, 1973. Series of readings on aspects of Chicano
culture in the United States including an essay on the formation of Chicano
Studies programs.

Espiritu, Yen Le. *Asian American Panethnicity: Bridging Institutions and Identities*.
Philadelphia: Temple University Press, 1992. Discussion of the cooperation and
conflict that exist in Asian American attempts to come together as a panethnic
group.

Fowlie-Flores, Fay, comp. *Annotated Bibliography of Puerto Rican Bibliographies*. New
York: Greenwood Press, 1990. Bibliography arranged according to topic with
a focus on Puerto Rico with less emphasis on Puerto Ricans in the United
States. Includes Spanish text entries.

Fuchs, Lawrence H. *The American Kaleidoscope: Race, Ethnicity and the Civic Culture*. Hanover, NH: Wesleyan University Press, 1990. Historical study of
ethnicity in the United States with emphasis on political structures, education,
housing, and legal boundaries.

Furtaw, Julia C., ed. *Black Americans Information Directory*. Detroit: Gale Research,

1992. Guide to organizations, institutions, programs, and publications concerned with African American life and culture.

———. *Native Americans Information Directory*. Detroit: Gale Research, 1993. Guide to organizations, institutions, programs, and publications concerned with American Indians, Alaska Natives, Native Hawaiians, and aboriginal Canadians.

García, Eugene E., Francisco A. Lomelí, and Isidro D. Ortiz. *Chicano Studies: A Multidisciplinary Approach*. New York: Teachers College Press, 1984. Collection of essays on the development of Chicano Studies and specialized topics in Chicano Studies.

Gómez-Quiñones, Juan, and Albert Camarillo. *Selected Bibliography for Chicano Studies*. 3rd ed. Los Angeles: Chicano Studies Center, UCLA, 1975. Early bibliography arranged according to disciplinary areas.

Goniwiecha, Mark, Kyung-Hee Choi, and Francisco Garcia-Ayvens, eds. *Guide to Ethnic Sources at UC Berkeley*. Berkeley: Chicano Studies Library Publications, 1983. The directory was compiled by members of an Ethnic Studies class at UC Berkeley during the period 1973–83. It includes information on the ethnic centers at Berkeley.

Hammerback, John C., Richard J. Jensen, and José Angel Gutierrez. *A War of Words: Chicano Protest in the 1960s and 1970s*. Westport, CT: Greenwood Press, 1985. Essays focus on four principal leaders of the Chicano movement, Reies Tijerina, Cesar Chavez, Rodolfo "Corky" Gonzales, and José Angel Gutierrez, as well as five Chicanos in Congress with an emphasis on the rhetoric used to convey attitudes and persuade others of the need for action.

Harris, Robert L., Jr., Darlene Clark Hine, and Nellie McKay. *Three Essays on Black Studies in the United States*. New York: The Ford Foundation, 1990. Three essays that resulted from consultancies to evaluate Black and Africana Studies programs by prominent scholars in the field.

Hecker, Melvin. *Ethnic America 1970–1977: Updating the Ethnic Chronology Series— with Cumulative Index*. Dobbs Ferry, NY: Oceana, 1979. Updates a series of twenty-eight volumes, each of which focuses on a particular ethnic group in the United States up to the 1970s.

Heth, Charlotte, and Susan Guyette. *Issues for the Future of American Indian Studies*. Los Angeles: American Indian Studies Center, UCLA, 1984. Introduction on conducting a needs assessment for American Indian Studies with listing of ninety-four programs.

Hull, Gloria T., Patricia Bell Scott, and Barbara Smith. *All the Women Are White, All the Blacks are Men, but Some of Us Are Brave; Black Women's Studies*. New York: Feminist Press, 1982. Collection of essays on the past and future of black Women's Studies with seven specialized bibliographies and several sample syllabi.

Ireland, Sandra L. Jones. *Ethnic Periodicals in Contemporary America: An Annotated Bibliography*. New York: Greenwood Press, 1990. Source for newspapers, magazines, and newsletters published by and about American ethnic groups.

Johnson, Harry A., ed. and comp. *Ethnic American Minorities: A Guide to Media and Materials*. New York: R. R. Bowker, 1976. Films, filmstrips, video and audio cassettes, slides, transparencies, and prints are catalogued. Includes primarily African Americans, American Indians, and Hispanics.

Keller, Gary D., Rafael J. Magallán, and Alma M. García. *Curriculum Resources in Chicano Studies: Undergraduate and Graduate*. Tempe, AZ: Bilingual Review Press, 1989. Syllabi for courses in Chicano Studies at the undergraduate level and curricular resources for Chicano Studies at the graduate level. Includes a list of Chicano Studies programs and research centers.

Kim, Hyung-Chan, ed. *Dictionary of Asian American History*. Westport, CT: Greenwood Press, 1986. Contains essays, a selected bibliography, and a chronology of Asian American history, as well as a dictionary of important people and historical/cultural events in Asian American history.

———. *Asian American Studies: An Annotated Bibliography and Research Guide*. New York: Greenwood Press, 1989. Bibliography on history and social sciences that includes some entries on Asian Studies programs.

Kittelson, David J., comp. *The Hawaiians: An Annotated Bibliography*. Honolulu: Social Science Research Institute, University of Hawaii, 1985. Compiled particularly for those interested in Hawaiian Studies, this bibliography covers Hawaiian history and culture from 1778 to 1983. There are 2,712 entries, glossary, and index.

Klein, Barry T. *Reference Encyclopedia of the American Indian*. 5th ed. New York: Todd, 1990. Includes information on organizations, associations, government agencies, reservations, tribal councils, museum and library collections, schools, college and university courses, and other useful information on American Indian resources in the United States and Canada. A bibliography and biographical sketches are additional features.

Lopez, Ronald W., Arturo Madrid-Barela, and Reynaldo Flores Macias. *Chicanos in Higher Education: Status and Issues*. Monograph No. 7. Los Angeles: Chicano Studies Center Publications, UCLA, 1976. An edited and synthesized version of the May 10, 1975, Symposium on the Status of Chicanos in Higher Education designed as a resource document that provides information on the status of Chicanos in higher education.

McAdoo, Harriette Pipes, ed. *Family Ethnicity: Strength in Diversity*. 2nd ed. Newbury Park, CA: Sage, 1993. Collection of essays on African American, Hispanic American, Native American, Asian American, and Muslim American family issues.

McCarthy, Cameron, and Warren Crichlow, eds. *Race, Identity and Representation in Education*. New York: Routledge, 1993. Collection of essays focusing on issues of race and representation in education, Cultural Studies, Women's Studies, literature, sociology, and African American Studies.

Miller, Wayne C., ed. *Comprehensive Bibliography for the Study of American Minorities*. 2 vols. New York: New York University Press, 1976. Volume one includes Africa and the Middle East, Europe, Eastern Europe, and the Balkans. Volume two includes Asia, the Islands, Native Americans, and Mexican Americans. The bibliographies include general essays on the groups included.

Minority Organizations: A National Directory. 4th ed. Garrett Park, MD: Garrett Park Press, 1992. Contains a listing of minority groups and service agencies. The indexes also categorize types of racial/ethnic groups by geographical areas; programs, activities, and services; and types of membership. Nearly 10,000 organizations are listed.

Minority Student Enrollments in Higher Education: A Guide to Institutions with Highest Percent of Asian, Black, Hispanic and Native American Students. Garrett Park, MD: Garrett Park Press, 1993. List of 588 institutions where one minority group accounts for a minimum of twenty percent of the total student enrollment.

Montney, Charles B., ed. *Asian Americans Information Directory*. 2nd ed. Detroit: Gale Research, 1994. A comprehensive guide to resources for Asian and Pacific Islander Americans, this volume provides information on a wide range of organizations, government agencies, institutions, publications, broadcasts, and other resources for over twenty major nationalities and ethnic groups represented in the United States and Canada.

Moss, Joyce, and George Wilson. *Peoples of the World: North America*. Detroit: Gale Research, 1991. Includes culture, geographical setting, and historical backgrounds of thirty-seven North American groups. Maps, bibliographies, and photographs are included.

National Association for Chicano Studies. *History, Culture, and Society. Chicano Studies in the 1980s.* Ypsilanti, MI: Bilingual Press/Editorial Bilinque, 1983. Contains some of the papers presented at the conferences in 1980–82. The essays cover such disciplines as history, political science, sociology, and anthropology.

Nomura, Gail M., Russell Endo, Stephen H. Sumida, and Russell C. Leong, eds. *Frontiers of Asian American Studies: Writing, Research, and Commentary.* Pullman: Washington State University Press, 1989. Series of essays on Asian American history, social science, literature, and Asian American Studies. Includes bibliography.

Oaks, Priscilla. *Minority Studies: A Selective Annotated Bibliography.* Boston: G. K. Hall, 1975. Early bibliography of general works in Ethnic Studies as well as sections on Native Americans, Spanish Americans, Afro-Americans, and Asian Americans.

Okihiro, Gary Y., ed. *Ethnic Studies.* 2 vols. New York: Markus Wiener, 1989.Volume one includes Asian and African American Studies, and volume two includes Chicano and Native American Studies. Both volumes have syllabi and course outlines.

————. *Margins and Mainstreams: Asians in American History and Culture.* Seattle: University of Washington Press, 1994. Collection of lectures Okihiro presented during 1992 focusing on Asian Americans and the debate over the canon; Western civilization; and the influences of values and ideals of "marginal" groups such as people of color, women, gays, and lesbians.

O'Leary, Timothy J., and David Levinson, eds. *Encyclopedia of World Cultures.* 2 vols. Boston: G. K. Hall, 1990. Includes Canada, Greenland, and the United States. Socio-cultural information is provided for each group along with maps, a filmography, a name index, and a glossary.

Omi, Michael, and Howard Winant. *Racial Formation in the United States from the 1960s to the 1980s.* New York: Routledge, Kegan Paul, 1986.

Padilla, Raymond V. *Chicano Studies Revisited: Still in Search of the Campus and the Community.* El Paso: University of Texas at El Paso, 1987. An assessment of Chicano Studies in the 1980s in an Occasional Paper Series.

Ploski, Harry A., and James Williams, comp. and ed. *The Negro Almanac: A Reference Work on the African American.* 5th ed. Detroit: Gale Research, 1989. A combination of biographical sketches, historical narratives, and statistical graphs and tables, this work details nearly five hundred years of the African American experience. It also contains a selected bibliography.

Polenberg, Richard. *One Nation Divisible: Class, Race, and Ethnicity in the United States since 1938.* New York: Viking, 1990.

Rex, John, and David Mason, eds. *Theories of Race and Ethnic Relations.* New York: Cambridge University Press, 1986.

Rosaldo, Renato. *Chicano Studies, 1970–1984.* Stanford: Stanford Center for Chicano Research, Working Paper Series No. 10, July 1985. Review essay of the anthropological literature on Chicanos and Chicano Studies with an analysis for Chicana/o research in social science research. Bibliography of 228 sources.

Sanchez, Maria E., and Antonio M. Stevens-Arroyo, eds. *Toward a Renaissance of Puerto Rican Studies: Ethnic and Area Studies in University Education.* Atlantic Studies on Society in Change, No. 37. Highland Lakes, NJ: Atlantic Research and Publications, 1987. Eleven essays from a 1981 conference on the history and current status of Puerto Rican Studies programs in the United States with a specific example of curriculum from Brooklyn College.

San Juan, E., Jr. *Racial Formations/Critical Transformations: Articulations of Power in Ethnic and Racial Studies in the United States.* Atlantic Highlands, NJ: Humanities Press, 1992. San Juan uses Asian Studies to argue that it is race and not ethnicity that explains conflicting cultures in the United States and that it is race that serves as the determinant of exclusion and inclusion. Author argues that Ethnic Studies is a mechanism to revitalize scholarship by challenging existing paradigms.

Smith, Darren L., ed. *Hispanic Americans Information Directory, 1990–1991*. Detroit: Gale Research, 1990. Guide to nearly 5,000 organizations, agencies, institutions, programs, and publications focusing on Hispanic American issues.

Sollors, Werner. *Beyond Ethnicity: Consent and Descent in American Culture*. New York: Oxford University Press, 1986. Historical and critical study of ethnicity with attention to literary expressions of ethnic experiences and an examination of the tension between descent and consent as individuals and groups define their own ethnic consciousness.

———, ed. *The Invention of Ethnicity*. New York: Oxford University Press, 1989. Ten essays about ethnicity as "invention" with an introduction by Sollors in which he discusses new theoretical and critical approaches to Culture Studies and Ethnic Studies.

Sowell, Thomas. *Ethnic America: A History*. New York: Basic Books, 1981. Historical study of European Americans as well as Americans from Asia, Africa, and Latin America and their development within United States society.

Stein, Wayne J. *Tribally Controlled Colleges: Making Good Medicine*. New York: Peter Lang, 1992. Extensive discussion of history, curriculum, and governance of six tribally controlled colleges with brief comments about several other tribally controlled colleges.

Stevenson, Rosemary M. *Index to Afro-American Reference Resources*. Westport, CT: Greenwood Press, 1988.

Takaki, Ronald. *From Different Shores: Perspectives on Race and Ethnicity in America*. 2nd ed. New York: Oxford University Press, 1994. This update of Takaki's earlier book includes several additional essays on race and ethnicity and the relationship of culture to both. Includes a debate between Arthur Schlesinger, Jr., and Takaki on multicultural curriculum and other campus issues.

Tatum, Charles M. *A Selected and Annotated Bibliography of Chicano Studies*. Lincoln, NB: Society of Spanish and Spanish-American Studies, 1979. Bibliography with a focus on literature, language, and music.

Taylor, Charles A., comp. and ed. *Multiculturalism and "The Politics of Recognition."* Princeton: Princeton University Press, 1992. Includes an essay by Charles Taylor on the philosophical, theoretical, and historical concerns about multiculturalism with commentary by Amy Gutmann, Steven C. Rockefeller, Michael Walzer, and Susan Wolf.

———. *Guide to Multicultural Resources, 1993–94*. Madison: Praxis, 1993. Compilation of a variety of ethnic resources including education, community, libraries, publications, businesses, and organizations divided into five sections (African American, Asian American, Native American, Hispanic American, and Multicultural).

Thernstrom, Stephen, ed. *Harvard Encyclopedia of American Ethnic Groups*. Cambridge, MA: Belknap, Harvard University Press, 1980. Comprehensive compilation of specific ethnic groups along with essays dealing with such topics as politics, intermarriage, and language. Includes maps and statistics.

Trejo, Arnulfo D. *Bibliografia Chicana: A Guide to Information Sources*. Detroit: Gale Research, 1975. Bibliography divided into subject areas. Includes a directory of newspapers and periodicals.

Washburn, David E. *Ethnic Studies: Bilingual/Bicultural Education and Multicultural Teacher Education in the United States: A Directory of Higher Education Programs and Personnel*. Miami: Inquiry International, 1979. Results of a survey during 1977–78 of higher education programs in Ethnic Studies and teaching education that included European ethnic programs. Identified 526 Ethnic Studies programs, 241 bilingual/bicultural programs, and 135 multicultural teaching education programs.

Wasserman, Paul, ed. *Ethnic Information Sources of the United States*. 2 vols. 2nd ed. Detroit: Gale Research, 1983. This two-volume guide to organizations, institutions, media, libraries, and museums does not include American Indians, African Americans, or Eskimos.

Wei, William. *The Asian American Movement: A Social History*. Philadelphia: Temple University Press, 1993. Wei analyzes the growing movement of Asian American political consciousness and identity from the 1960s to 1991 within the variables of geography, class, and gender.

Weinberg, Meyer, comp. *Racism in the United States: A Comprehensive Classified Bibliography*. New York: Greenwood Press, 1990. Extensive bibliography arranged into eighty-seven sections; primary focus is on African American issues.

Wrobel, Alfred J., and Michael J. Eula, eds. *American Ethnics and Minorities: Readings in Ethnic History*. Dubuque: Kendall/Hunt, 1990. Collection of background essays on several ethnic groups, including European ethnic peoples, with varied political and theoretical approaches.

Zinn, Maxine Baca, and Bonnie Thornton Dill, eds. *Women of Color in U.S. Society*. Philadelphia: Temple University Press, 1994. Over a dozen essays examine race, class, and gender for women of color in the United States.

Please send information to:

NAES Directory Project   **Or FAX this form to:**
Department of English   (602) 951-8874
Arizona State University
Box 870302
Tempe, AZ 85287-0302

Name of Institution: _____

Name of Unit: _____

___ Program ___ Department ___ Institute ___ Center ___ Other (specify)

Type of Institution: ___ Public ___ Private ___ Center ___ Tribal
                   ___ 2 year ___ 4 year ___ 4 year + graduate

Contact Person: _____ Title: _____

Address: _____

_____

_____

Telephone: _____

FAX: _____

E-Mail: _____

Description of Program:

Major   ___ yes ___ no
Minor   ___ yes ___ no
Certificate ___ yes ___ no
Classes   ___ yes ___ no

Degrees offered (please specify areas): _____

_____

_____

Average number of majors per year:
Number of minors:
Current number of faculty teaching with program:
Year unit established:

Special Features (100 to 200 word description of special features):

List any other ethnic studies units and contact persons at your institution: